W9-BNN-405

The
NEW NEW HOME

The
NEW NEW HOME

Getting the house of your dreams
with your eyes wide open

BOYCE THOMPSON

The Taunton Press

Dedication

To my wife, Carol Anderson, and our children,
Christopher and Ethan Thompson, who don't seem
to mind detours to look at new homes

❖

The Taunton Press
Inspiration for hands-on living®

The Taunton Press, Inc., 63 South Main Street, PO Box 5506, Newtown, CT 06470-5506
e-mail: tp@taunton.com

Editor: Peter Chapman
Copy editor: Diane Sinitsky
Indexer: Jay Kreider
Jacket/Cover design: Rosalind Loeb Wanke
Interior design: carol singer | notice design
Layout: Amy Griffin
Cover photographer: Peter Aaron/OTTO

The following names/manufacturers appearing in *The New New Home* are trademarks: 2-10 Home Buyers Warranty®; All American Homes®; Andersen®; Apple®; Ashton Woods Homes®; Beaulieu®; Big Wheels®; Bluetooth®; Centex®; Clapper®; Craftmark Homes®; Crossville®; David Weekley Homes®; ECO by Consentino®; Energy Star®; General Electric®; Habitat for Humanity®; Harley-Davidson®; Home Depot℠; Hulu®; IKEA®; iPad®; iPod®; Irvine Company®; KB Home®; Kelly-Moore™; LivingSmart®; Lowe's®; Mannington®; Meritage Homes®; Microsoft®; Netflix®; Next Gen℠; Nexus EnergyHomes℠; Pardee Homes®; Partners in Building®; Pulte®; Radio Shack®; Room & Board®; Shaw®; Shea Homes®; Sherwin-Williams®; Spaces™; Verizon℠; Walmart®; WaterSense®; ZigBee® Alliance; Zillow®.

Library of Congress Cataloging-in-Publication Data in progress

ISBN: 978-1-62710-385-5

Printed in the United States of America
10 9 8 7 6 5 4 3 2 1

Acknowledgments

I ACKNOWLEDGE THE MANY BUILDERS and architects who shared their hard-earned trade secrets and enriched me with their ideas through the years. The list starts with people who designed and built my show homes, especially the late Barry Berkus and Tim Eller, who designed and built the first one, shaping the program in the process. I'm grateful to several builders who took big chances on these "concept" homes, particularly Ian McCarthy, David Weekley, and Craig Perry, who hold the distinction of each building a series of three; Chris Stuhmer, Charles Clayton, and Mike McGee for each building one that sold for the price of three; and Steve Glenn, who took on the highest-risk project, a modular home that had to be put together on a show floor in three and a half days.

Every journalist has a network of friends who become his or her most important sources of information and inspiration. A short list of mine would have to include Mike Woodley, Carson Looney, Larry Webb, Geoffrey Moeun, Peter Simons, Bill Kreager, Andres Duany, Wayne Speight, Steve Alloy, Joyce Mason, Tony Green, Dave Steinke, Barb Nagle, David Pace, Glenn Cardoso, Tom McCormick, Eric Brown, John Wieland, Tom Wade, CR Herro, Don Jacobs, Gonzalo Romero, Pete Osterman, Debra Falese, Don Anderson, Marianne Cusato, Bill Devereaux, Ken Neumann, and Sandra Kulli. They were all there when I needed them, especially when I was working on this book. I also thank the talented group of writers and editors I've worked with through the years, many of whom brought the projects in this book to life through print, especially Denise Dersin, Jenny Sullivan, Carolyn Weber, James Wilson, Rich Binsacca, Rich Schwolsky, Nigel Maynard, Debby Leopold, Matt Power, and Cati O'Keefe.

Finally, I thank my wife, Carol Anderson, who read every word of this book, offering critical suggestions to improve its tone and content; Peter Chapman, who took a chance on a first-time book author and guided me expertly through the process; Warren Nesbitt, the publisher of *Builder* magazine and my show-home partner for 15 years; and my two sons, Christopher and Ethan, who when they were young, after listening to my stories about the show homes I was building, thought I was a builder, not a journalist.

Contents

INTRODUCTION

2

CHAPTER ONE

A NEW BEGINNING 4

CHAPTER TWO

LESSONS FROM THE FALL 18

CHAPTER THREE

HOME BUILDING'S MIXED RECORD ON INNOVATION 34

CHAPTER FOUR

SPACE PLANNING COMES OF AGE 47

CHAPTER FIVE

GREEN GOES MAINSTREAM 68

CHAPTER SIX

PERFORMANCE TAKES CENTER STAGE 102

CHAPTER SEVEN

THE QUEST FOR NET ZERO 114

CHAPTER EIGHT

UNIVERSAL DESIGN MAKES A LOT OF SENSE 130

CHAPTER NINE

GENERATIONS JOIN UNDER ONE ROOF   143

CHAPTER TEN

NEW HOMES GET MORE AFFORDABLE   153

CHAPTER ELEVEN

BUYERS BETTER BEWARE   162

CHAPTER TWELVE

CONTEMPORARY DESIGN LEAVES ITS MARK   178

CHAPTER THIRTEEN

THE RISE OF IN-TOWN LIVING   185

CHAPTER FOURTEEN

MODULAR MANIA TAKES HOLD   200

CHAPTER FIFTEEN

SMALL WILL REMAIN BEAUTIFUL   211

CHAPTER SIXTEEN

WHAT TO ASK FOR IN A NEW HOME   223

CHAPTER SEVENTEEN

FUTURE-PROOFING YOUR HOME   234

INDEX
248

CREDITS
250

Introduction

FOR DECADES, HOMES PROVIDED a financial bedrock for American families. They functioned like an annuity, steadily rising in value even as they provided creature comforts and a place to raise a family. Tax and financial systems encouraged the American dream of homeownership, even the dream of steadily trading up to better and bigger homes and one day harvesting all that equity for retirement. By 2006, at the height of the housing boom, households had about $22.6 trillion in equity in real estate, slightly more than half of their wealth. With values steadily rising and seemingly no threat they would ever fall, new homes could be bought and sold based on diversions such as whether dining room windows afforded a nice view of woods in the backyard or the dream of spending cool winter nights luxuriating in a hot tub. No one, not even Alan Greenspan, the chairman of the Federal Reserve Board, thought the party would end, that home values in this country would ever decline.

The housing boom brought on legendary excesses. Brokers made second mortgages (home-equity loans) to homeowners even as they wrote them first mortgages. The rise of "no doc" and "liar" loans meant that buyers didn't even have to prove income levels or job status. As television shows like *Flip This House* proliferated, Americans thought of their homes as investments rather than places to live. "Animal spirits," a term popularized by Yale economist Robert Shiller, took hold as people, fearing they might miss out on the next great investment, like the dot.com stocks of 2000 to 2001, rushed in to get their piece of the action, bidding up prices. Builders encouraged investor behavior by building ever-bigger, overfeatured homes, sometimes in suspect locations that didn't matter much to investors. As demand for housing outstripped supply and prices in some areas rose 20 percent a year, buyers neglected the basics of housing investments, such as where the home was located, how well it was built, and what their utility payments would be.

Then, starting in 2007, what no one thought would happen actually did—home values started a long, 33-percent decline that lasted through 2011. Prices fell steeply in most cities throughout the country, especially in places like Phoenix, Las Vegas, and southern Florida, where many new homes had been built during the previous decade. The collapse in housing values wiped out 18 years of gains for family wealth, and it eventually led to the decline of the entire American economy. Roughly 5 million borrowers lost their homes in foreclosure and another 2 million walked away from them in short sales. The housing bust proved conclusively that there is a downside risk to housing investments, the biggest purchase that most people ever make. By 2012 household equity had only recovered to $17.3 trillion, according to Fed statistics.

The five-year housing downturn produced dramatic changes in the design and construction of new homes. The few people with the guts to buy during that period demanded homes that were more space efficient. They refused to pay for a bedroom that wouldn't be used. They questioned whether they wanted to pay for utilities to heat and cool a volume-ceilinged great room. They looked for hard evidence that builders would provide quality construction. Builders who managed to survive the housing recession had no choice but to comply. The most progressive of them designed and built better, greener, and more space-efficient homes, finally incorporating long-proven methods to optimize construction. I like to think that they created a new generation of homes—what I've called *The New, New Home*—that may hold their value even if property values fall again.

This book is dedicated to the idea that lessons learned during the housing recession should not be forgotten. Many of them need to inform buying decisions under all economic conditions. Buyers need to focus on what used to be secondary considerations—things like how well a home is built, how much water it consumes, and whether its energy consumption can be monitored. As you go into the search process, keep one eye peeled on the future. Think about how a home will work for you as your needs change—where an elderly parent or jobless college graduate could live, whether the home accommodates advancing age—and how the home may be perceived by future owners. With some careful planning, a new home should be flexible and durable enough to support your family's needs throughout your lifetime and retain its value should you need to sell it. Let's hope that as the real estate market improves, American homebuyers and builders don't repeat the mistakes of the recent past.

CHAPTER ONE

A New Beginning

FOR 15 YEARS I HIRED the best architects and builders in the country to develop concept homes. The experience was not unlike building concept cars, except we explored ideas that could be put to work immediately, ideas like building homes that produce as much power as they consume, reimagining conventionally sized production homes, assembling super-green modular homes in factories, and dropping live-work lofts into urban frinsge neighborhoods. Our emphasis was on exploring innovations that could immediately improve the mass market for housing, ideas that could result in better, more affordable, greener, and cooler new homes for as many people as possible, *if* the industry paid attention. The demonstrations worked most of the time— we would tour thousands of people through the homes during builder shows, generate reviews in major newspapers, and maybe move the industry's needle, if only a little. Many of the forward-looking concepts we explored caught on in subsequent years. This was especially true during the recent housing recession when builders searched for anything they could do to help their homes stand out from a glut of cheaper foreclosures and resales. Innovation became a tool for survival. Many of the concepts that had been kicked about in research labs and tested in demonstration homes were put to work.

Our first project, appropriately but perilously named the Home of the Future, built in a Dallas subdivision in 1997, was an attempt to shock an industry traditionally slow to change. As editorial director of *Builder* magazine, I worked with futurists and consultants to peer 10 years into the future, trying to anticipate likely changes and incorporate features that might be common in the new century. Our architect, the late Barry Berkus, decided that the futuristic home should have a familiar look. He designed three-story old-world turrets on the front facade that purposely belied the home's futuristic focus. (One architectural critic, asking why we hadn't included a moat, said he half-expected to be showered with hot oil when he walked toward the

front door.) The towers housed his-and-her home offices, an uncommon feature at a time when most new homes weren't even wired for broadband access. Upstairs, one of the turrets contained a sleeping bunk decorated to look like a space capsule. Berkus, widely considered the father of production housing architecture, visited a nearby space center to collect an old space suit to "merchandise" the room. We put it in a corner and asked the interior designer to paint a night sky on the ceiling. It was the ultimate sleepover suite. At least that's what my young sons thought when they toured the home months later.

Three-story turrets greeted visitors to the Home of the Future, a 1997 attempt to look 10 years into the future of home building. Located in an otherwise sleepy suburban Dallas subdivision, the home was powered by photovoltaic panels, heated and cooled by a geothermal heat pump, and run with an early-generation home-automation system.

The house employed a host of energy features that were futuristic then but commonplace today. For example, photovoltaic panels on the roof converted sunlight to electricity. Back then, solar panels were usually found only on custom homes built in rural areas, often by builders and architects pursuing an energy agenda (the wonderful wing of the industry always experimenting with the next big thing). The panels, designed to blend with the roof's shingles—though you could still spot them from a block away—supplied enough electricity to power the main systems in the home should the power go out in the booming Dallas suburb of Coppell, Texas. Which of course it did, at seemingly the worst time: during a press conference. Thankfully, the home's back-up system didn't miss a beat. Lights remained on in the kitchen and under the stairs, where we had put them to protect against falls. Computers stationed in the home offices continued running, as did the jerry-rigged computer system that operated the house.

Because we tried to incorporate features with a realistic chance of going mainstream, we didn't include some out-there ideas futurists were talking about at the time—fuel cells to power the home and in-home medical diagnostics are two that come to mind, though if I were planning a home of the future today I'd be tempted to include them. We did decide to take a chance on geothermal energy—technology that taps the relatively constant temperature of the earth to heat and cool the house. In geothermal systems, fluid piped through underground wells is cooled to the earth's temperature, which is pretty constant below 6 feet. The liquid travels through a heat pump that conditions the air. Though our system was very good for the time, even better geothermal heat pumps have hit the market in recent years. Adoption of geothermal technology reached a flash point during the green building movement of the last decade; it started showing up in many of the coolest projects, the ones that architectural magazines fight to publish. Geothermal systems may not pay for themselves in utility savings for several years. But some builders and buyers no longer care; they've got to have the technology. That's the way it works sometimes.

Most of the major systems in the Home of the Future—at least the ones for security, energy, and communication—were linked via a prototype smart-home system that operated from strategically located touch panels. We preprogrammed the home for modes such as "Time for Bed," so that parents from their bedroom on the second floor could conveniently close the windows and lock the doors on the floor below. Though many new homes are operated in this fashion today, production homes weren't that smart at the time. About the best that you could do was control the pool from a panel by the back door or maybe see who was at the front door from a television screen in the kitchen. With some trepidation, we linked the home's systems through a central processing unit bolted to a closet wall, knowing it had the potential to freeze up, just like any PC at the time. The systems were linked to each other and the Internet through so-called structured wiring, an unusual upgrade then but a standard spec in new homes today. Worried that more bandwidth might be required later on, we "future-proofed" the home by pulling the wire through plastic tubes, or conduit, in the walls so that it would be easy to fish out and replace. That precaution makes sense if you are building a new home today.

Our builder, Randy Luther, decided it would be worth the expense also to run fiber-optic cable to the curb to ensure that the home would "always" have enough bandwidth. We were concerned about predictions that computers might one day replace televisions. In that case, futurists warned, the homes would need enough bandwidth to download and watch streaming video on the computer. I laughed when a Verizon^SM rep showed up at our front door a couple of years ago to interest me in bringing fiber-optic cable from the curb to my home. That had seemed pretty far out when we built the Home of the Future back in the days of painfully slow dial-up modems. The future inevitably arrives.

TRYING TO PREDICT THE FUTURE is a daunting and exciting task. We didn't get it all right in our project, nor did we expect to. The home's movable walls—basically big custom-built cabinets on lockable

Moving walls (left), an expandable table, and translucent shoji screens provided the flexibility to configure the Home of the Future's great room for a variety of uses. Guests at one industry party were invited to first view space as a conventional family room, then invited to see it set up for a holiday dinner. Movable walls never really caught on, but sliding translucent doors have become a common way to separate and combine spaces.

wheels—seemed like a good idea at the time; architects and futurists are still trying to find ways to make that concept work. The portable walls gave us the flexibility to easily rearrange the great room to accommodate different happenings at home. To demonstrate this during one industry event, we invited people to see what the space looked like for everyday use—we left it wide open with ottomans and armchairs clustered around a television set and nothing separating living space from the kitchen. Then we reconfigured the space for a big holiday meal by moving the walls to separate the television viewing area from the dining room where the table had been expanded to seat 12 people. We even closed off the kitchen to hide the caterer's mess, using shoji screens that slid into fixed walls. Though I'm sad to say that movable walls haven't really caught on in new homes, designing great rooms flexible enough to accommodate dramatically different furniture arrangements certainly has. We made some other interesting bets that didn't pan out. For example, European plastic mortar used between the bricks, designed to stop wind-driven rain, never became a common spec, though it mitigates an important problem. In addition, we tried to run all the home's appliances through one remote but couldn't get the manufacturers to cooperate.

Nonetheless, my experience demonstrates that the home-building industry does embrace change, albeit slowly, and typically only after a strong kick in the behind from a recession. For instance, you'd be hard-pressed to find a new home today without structured wiring for fast Internet and entertainment services, even as wireless systems infiltrate the house; it provides more reliability and speed at a small expense. Some large production builders now build homes with photovoltaic systems that can supply *all* the electricity a home needs at a manageable up-front cost—thanks to dramatic decreases in costs, improvements in conversion efficiency, and new leasing options. And geothermal energy has become much more commonplace due to lower installation costs coupled with the development of a new generation of more efficient systems. It's amazing what people who really want a geothermal system will do to get it. I recently walked a townhome project in downtown Washington, D.C., where the builder had found a way to drill wells in a backyard that was little more than a grassy patch. Miss Utility had to be called in to make sure contractors didn't pierce the walls of the subway system below.

INNOVATION TOOK OFF DURING THE home-building recession when builders searched for ways to stand out in a market glutted with homes for sale. Builders and their staff designers, sometimes with the help of outside architects, rethought floor plans to make them as flex-ible as possible, cutting out wasted, showy space in favor of square footage that gets used the most. They eighty-sixed living rooms and sitting rooms even in habitually conservative markets, such as St. Louis and Washington, D.C., in favor of more flexible great rooms with lower ceilings. Some finally embraced contemporary aesthetics—simple, unadorned lines—to stand out from the surfeit of traditional homes built during the last boom. Meanwhile, a cadre of nimble modular home companies burst on the scene, some fueled by venture capital, all of them motivated by a desire to provide cutting-edge, green architecture to mainstream buyers.

Development patterns changed dramatically, too, providing new-home shoppers with a tempting array of much-improved close-in locations that didn't seem as likely to lose their value. The lack of funding for new master-planned communities on the outskirts of town, coupled with competition from close-in homes for sale, all but forced builders to investigate suburban and urban infill locations. As a result of this work, many downtown and close-in suburbs—even in cities such as Kansas City; Columbus, Ohio; and Tucson, Ariz.—now lay claim to exciting housing markets that didn't exist even a decade ago. They have taken on a life of their own, presenting a tantalizing lifestyle option to buyers of all stripes, especially baby boomers with no kids in school to worry about.

Builders during the recession became much more responsive to market research, buyer wishes, and available technology for fear that other builders might beat them to the punch. They dusted off long-ignored textbooks on building technology to produce better-performing homes that cost much less to operate. They introduced a new generation of homes that are greener, more flexible, and more efficient than ever before. At the same time, they found ways to cut expenses and maintain some high-end features that became standard during the housing boom—granite countertops, stainless-steel appliances, and lavish showers come to mind. If history is a guide, builders aren't likely to abandon the tactics that got them through the hardest of times, even as market conditions improve. Once companies invest the sweat equity to incorporate a better building system, it becomes a core competency—one that they market with gusto.

All these choices, coupled with the new knowledge that rising real estate values are no longer a slam dunk (they fell 33 percent nationally during the housing bust), create a challenge for people willing to wade into the new-home market. You may be able to buy or build the new home of your dreams, given that new homes are much more affordable today than they were during the unprecedented housing boom. What's more, production builders are much more willing to customize their homes to meet your lifestyle needs and desires, and many of them now know how to build better homes that will cost considerably less to operate. But that means you need to go into the home-buying process with a much clearer idea of what you want, because your builder isn't always going to take the time to find out. And that's no easy chore, given that buying a new home presents a seemingly endless and complicated set of design, financial, and product choices. A home is easily the most complicated product most people ever buy. It can also be the most satisfying. But you better keep your eyes wide open.

Today's buyers need to be extremely smart shoppers if they want to obtain a home that will gain in value and work for them while they live in it. Future appreciation probably won't be as strong as it was during the last housing upturn, especially as mortgage rates inevitably rise, making homes less affordable and depressing prices. This much is certain: Lenders won't be handing out mortgages like Halloween candy again. Unless you can qualify for low–down-payment, government-insured mortgages, larger down-payment requirements in the 10 to 20 percent range are likely to remain in force for the foreseeable future. The huge percentage of the population that remains underwater on their home investment, roughly 25 percent by the end of 2013, will continue to limit the pool of people who can afford to move. Against that backdrop, it pays to shop wisely and get the most for your money, just as the institutional buyer of a commercial building would.

These dangers aside, the rise of innovation will come as refreshing news to new-home aficionados, the roughly one third of the American population that our surveys over 15 years showed would prefer a new home, if they could get one. Even more people would buy a new home if the value compares favorably to an existing home. Maybe you are among the people who love to cruise builder model centers on week-ends, gathering design ideas. Perhaps you are a devotee who notices when builders start new developments and signs the prospect list to get an early glimpse of what the builder has planned. Maybe you are one of those people who collect home plans from magazines and books, always noodling an ideal floor plan and front facade in your head. Perhaps you are drawn to a new home by the prospect of ridding yourself of an annoying fixer-upper that stands between you and a lower golf handicap. Surveys show that what people like most about new homes is that "everything is new"—not just the floor plan, but the carpeting, the hot water heater, and the paint, too. One builder went way over the top marketing new homes during the housing recession. In a desperate attempt to stand out, she asked potential buyers whether they really wanted a disgusting "used" home with mold in the air handler and toenail clippings in the carpet.

The downside of the recent groundswell of innovation is that buyers today confront a confusing and potentially paralyzing mix of choices. Builders who traditionally shied away from new energy technology—items like on-demand hot water heaters or heat-recovery ventilators—now commonly offer them. You need to figure out what these energy features entail—part of the mission of this book—and whether you really want or need them. Builder salespeople typically aren't much good when it comes to helping buyers understand high-tech features; they know that things like schools, community features, and design are bigger motivators. However, even builders who don't list, say, super-efficient, low-emissivity windows as a standard specification will probably install them if you ask. And, to get the sale in a competitive market, many builders will move walls in their standard plans, change elevations, bump out the back wall to create a bigger family room, and even add whole rooms. They may not advertise it, but they often still do it. As long as you ask for these changes before construction begins, so that the builder can alter computer-aided design (CAD) drawings and alert subcontractors, extra charges are likely to be minimal.

The reality is that today, on the heels of an unprecedented collapse of real estate values, it makes no sense to buy more house than you need. It's no wonder that many of the oversize entries and great rooms with 16- and 20-foot ceilings that were commonplace during the last housing boom are gone. Needless hall space, walls to separate formal rooms, and oversize foyers have been dropped from production plans in favor of tighter, more flexible room arrangements that can make life at home more convenient and enriching. You still see vaulted space in new homes today because it can be exciting, and it's something hard to find in an older home. But it's used much more judiciously, typically for visual impact in higher-end homes.

DEMOGRAPHIC FORCES MAY CONSPIRE to keep a lid on new home sizes and real estate prices for many years to come. The biggest growth market of the next 10 years will be aging baby boomers looking to trade down to smaller homes now that their children are gone. They won't need as many bedrooms or a big yard for their children to play in. The second biggest demographic driver will be young buyers looking for their first home. Saddled with large college debt and cursed with low-paying jobs, Generation Y buyers, born between 1985 and 2004, according to the Harvard Joint Center for Housing Studies, may have to settle for smaller homes than they would like. The softest sector of the housing market during the next decade will be the cohort who often wants the biggest homes: family buyers. Most family buyers will be drawn from the ranks of Generation X, born between 1965 and about 1984. Not only is this group comparatively small, but it will also have a plethora of big existing homes from which to choose—thanks to overbuilding during the 2000s. Against this backdrop of weak demand for large homes, it doesn't make a lot of economic sense to buy a bigger house than you need.

For these reasons, we are likely to see more inspired small-home designs in the future. While no one home style will characterize future housing design, homes like the one shown below, designed by Union

Studio, point in a likely direction. There's nothing ostentatious about this cottage home located near the shore in Washington State. Its simple, elegant form relates to its function. There's just enough trim to make the cottage feel authentic, and the attractive wraparound porch is deep enough (8 feet is a minimum) that it can be comfortably used to sip morning espresso or evening cosmos. Inside, the architect and builder made every inch of space count, creating sitting spaces in window alcoves and squeezing closets out of extra room under the stairs. The home is a model of energy efficiency, too, despite its many windows.

This unpretentious seaside cottage in Washington State typifies the best work done during the downturn. Designed by Union Studio, the home's simple footprint makes it inexpensive to build, and close attention to energy details make it inexpensive to heat and cool. Inside, every square inch of living space was maximized.

Homes like this one stand in sharp contrast to new homes designed during the housing boom. Then, builders and architects often added as many elements as possible to the home facade to justify higher prices. So we saw designers apply confusing lick-and-stick siding elements, mixing two, three, and even four types of siding to bizarre effect. The rise of easy-to-apply synthetic stone and brick meant that those materials could go anywhere—even though an informed observer would expect the hardest elements to go along the foundation where they would appear to support the home. Builders installed false dormers to make single-story homes look like they had a second floor, even if it was an unfinished attic. They appended unusable porches and balconies to make homes look like big money. The number of hips and gables on some luxury production homes put Nathaniel Hawthorne's House of Seven Gables to shame.

During the boom, it was perfectly fine for front facades to advertise Mediterranean or Craftsman looks that interior spaces didn't give a thought to delivering. Interior "merchandising" was too often motivated by the desire to create memory points, even if the only thing memorable was the decorator's fondness for jaguar throw rugs. You saw French country kitchens in homes of every style, sometimes with enough fake roosters to start a small farm. Interior trim, which builders during previous cost-cutting periods were reluctant to spec, now often got out of hand. A judge in one of our design competitions, forced to confront a particularly overwrought three-tiered tray ceiling with built-in fiber-optic lighting, commented, "Is this your first visit to the star chamber?" Gazing at a gaudy rec room, another juror observed that the interior design was "one step above dogs playing pool," a reference to the ubiquitous C. M. Coolidge painting used in many man caves.

Less is refreshingly more on new-home exteriors and interiors today, sometimes by necessity but often by design. Simple boxes have always been the most cost-effective to build. The effect of deleting needless ornamentation is often to let the home's pleasing bones shine through. Too little attention was paid during the boom to principles that produce homes of classic proportions, like the way arches, windows, and doors work together to pleasing effect. You may not even realize initially that there's a hierarchy to the arches in a Spanish-style home, with bigger ones below and smaller ones above—the home just registers as more pleasing. Embellishments like wrought iron on the front door or a bracket above the garage work best when they complement the architecture, rather than create a distraction.

THE WONDERFUL THING ABOUT HOUSING DESIGN is that everyone's opinion, no matter how uneducated, counts. I learned this lesson when, as a young editor covering the home-building industry, I went on a bus tour of new-home communities in Southern California. Legendary architect Walt Richardson, who pioneered many of the attached housing concepts that people take for granted today, was on the tour. He kept asking me what I thought of the houses I had seen, no doubt testing my still-infant design acumen. I valiantly tried to critique the homes but often resorted to subjectivity. The showy windows on the front elevation of one home didn't make up for a flat and boring rear facade. The bathroom windows in another home looked right into a neighbor's bedroom, I noted. The heavy gables on a third home made it look like it might tip over. He nodded. "That's the thing about good design," Walt said sagely. "It doesn't have to cost extra. It's largely a matter of getting proportions right."

Unfortunately, most builders of production housing will tell you that few Americans can distinguish between good and bad design. Their primary interest is getting as much space for their money as possible. They are more interested in living in a neighborhood with a good school district than a home that could make the pages of *Architectural Digest*. Inattention to good design came back to haunt many builders during the recession; too many continued building characterless new homes at a time when buyers had unprecedented choice in new and existing houses. Buyers who dared to buy homes while prices were dropping—often because they had to due to job relocation or divorce—

sought out the best-looking ones with the lowest operating costs. They went for a new generation of better-looking, better-built homes, and they left builders who didn't adjust in the dust, sometimes filing for bankruptcy protection.

Management guru Tom Peters, speaking to chief executives of the nation's largest home-building companies at the nadir of the recession in 2011, reminded them that all transformative ideas take root during the worst of times. He challenged the builders to look for concepts that would alter the way they did business in the future, suggesting that green building, female-centric floor plans, and urban housing would gain in popularity. He urged the audience to adopt the latest thinking in construction, technology, and design as a way to stand out from the sea of existing home resales that flooded the market—many of them homes the builders had built themselves only a few years before. Little did Peters know that many of the CEOs were already betting on these transformative concepts. ❖

CHAPTER TWO

Lessons from the Fall

TENS OF THOUSANDS OF HOMEBUILDERS in this country went out of business during the housing recession, as new home starts contracted by 75 percent. One of the biggest sectors of the American economy was decimated. The smartest of the bunch had sold their companies before the housing bust arrived in 2007–08, realizing that they worked in a fundamentally cyclical industry and the good times wouldn't last forever. When the contraction began, the first to go out of business were builders that had purchased these other companies or bought a lot of land during the boom, assuming debt that pulled them under once their income dissipated. Next to go were big private companies that built high-end homes no one wanted anymore. Most public companies survived the onslaught, since they could more easily write off bad debt to balance their books. Public builders tracked by Zelman & Associates generated $39.8 billion in pretax income during the building boom from 2004 to 2006. During the bust, from 2006 to 2011, they wrote off a nearly equal amount ($38.9 BILLION) in impairments from bad land, joint venture, acquisitions, and other investments.

Against this backdrop of corporate carnage and financial distress, builders searched desperately for a market niche—a new type of home, a better location, or a new mode of operation—that might ensure their survival. New homes got smaller, and they also got greener and more energy efficient. Builders went beyond the superficial "greenscaping" of the previous decade, when about the most they would do is install compact fluorescent light fixtures or carpets made with recycled soda bottles. In many cases, they reassessed *all* the products they were using to build houses, deleting ones that weren't absolutely necessary and adding substitutes that performed better and lasted longer. Most important, some builders finally reexamined the engineering and systems they used to build homes. They completely overhauled the home's inner workings and, in a huge break from tradition actually called attention to the way the home was built, instead of focusing on antiqued cabinets or built-in wine chillers.

One of the most exciting examples is the deconstructed model home done by Meritage Homes®, the ninth largest homebuilder in America. Meritage, which builds throughout the West and Southwest, began inviting potential buyers to look under the hood, so to speak, or in this case into the floor, ceiling, and walls. While half of their displays may be tricked out like the typical model home, with stainless-steel appliances, draperies, and

Deconstructed model homes by Meritage invite homebuyers to look behind the walls and learn from technology displays. During the downturn, progressive builders called attention to how they built homes, highlighting high-performance features such as heat-recovery ventilators, spray foam insulation, and post-tension slabs rarely found in less-efficient resale homes.

tile floors, the other half is more like a building-science museum. The idea is not only to lay bare superior construction practices but also to get people to linger and explore. The more time shoppers spend immersed in this experience, the builder reasons, the more likely they are to buy a home. Competing builders also flocked to the homes, but for a different reason. They used the models as an educational tool, since they displayed many best practices in an easy-to-learn, interactive setting.

A Meritage deconstructed model in Phoenix, for instance, illustrates (with the help of drywall cutaways and videos) the airtight seal polyurethane insulation makes when it's blown into the ceiling and walls and around pipes and electrical wire. Placards in a skeletal living room point toward a heat-recovery ventilator nestled above the joists that, as its name implies, recovers heat from stale air before it's exhausted outside, reducing new energy needs. A roped-off floor section demonstrates proper pouring of a post-tension slab, a foundation suspended by rebar that allows a house to adjust to shifting, sandy soil—an important precaution in some Southwest regions. (We employed one in our Home of the Future project in Texas.) To cap the memorable experience, a sign by the door proudly displays the home's home energy rating systems (HERS) score of 40, well below any other new house in the neighborhood. The lower a home's HERS rating, the better its energy performance. A typical existing home has a HERS rating of about 130, while most new homes, since they are built to stricter building codes, rate about 100.

ANOTHER MAJOR DEVELOPMENT of the housing bust was the rise of net-zero homes that produce as much energy as they consume. In 2010, Meritage was selling about $35,000 in options to the Phoenix homes (a photovoltaic system and some energy upgrades) that would produce a net-zero home that frees buyers from electric bills. Net-zero homes can have strong subliminal appeal. Consider the aging baby boomer that I met in the Meritage model. His Harley-Davidson® parked outside, he wanted to pay cash and take the net-zero option. He imagined a retirement utopia in which he would have no housing expenses besides property taxes now or in the future. This was the latest variation on a long-standing American dream to cash out of expensive housing markets in California, the Midwest, and the East Coast and buy less expensive homes in the Sun Belt, where property, income, and estate taxes are also lower. Del Webb, the baseball player turned homebuilder, created an entire business model, Sun City, on this widespread desire for a retirement with financial independence.

Unfortunately, for anyone pursuing this new dream, the definition of a net-zero home is somewhat confusing. Technically, a HERS rating of 0, meaning the home produces as much energy as it consumes, produces a net-zero home. But the Department of Energy proscribes that homes be net-zero only on a theoretical basis. That's because the net-zero calculation may depend on utilities buying excess power produced during the day, and utility policies vary. It also hinges on the type and number of appliances run in a home. Another big variable is how diligent homeowners are about home energy consumption. If you monitor energy consumption closely, you may be able to go the final quarter mile—to go in effect from a HERS rating of roughly 25 down to zero—yourself, though it's not easy because of the energy consumed by appliances. Most builders still charge a premium of from $25,000 to as much as $50,000 for a net-zero home, an added cost that forces you to consider how diligent you are at closing blinds on hot days and turning off lights when you leave rooms.

There are pleasant paybacks to investing in a home with a HERS rating of zero. If you are conscientious about your energy consumption, for instance, you may wind up in the enviable position of producing more energy than you need. Then you could turn your home into a cash machine, selling excess power to the utility, an opportunity that consumers who aren't big fans of utilities may find particularly gratifying. You can also protect yourself against utility rate hikes in the future.

HERS ratings have become the single best way to judge the energy efficiency of the best-built homes. During the housing bust, they superseded the Environmental Protection Agency's (EPA) Energy

Star® for Homes standard because so many high-performing homes easily exceeded those guidelines. Even so, the Energy Star standard remains an important benchmark, a *de minimis* standard if you will. Fully one-quarter of homes built in 2010 carried an Energy Star label, and the EPA upgraded its standard to Version 3 in 2012, requiring that new homes achieve a HERS rating in the low 70s or better.

The Energy Star standard provides important assurances. Builders must inspect their homes for moisture problems and hire certified HVAC contractors. Homes must resist thermal transfer through walls; builders need to install a continuous layer of rigid foam insulation of at least R-3 in warmer climates and R-5 in colder ones, or use one of several "alternative" wall systems discussed later in the book. The standard also prohibits builders from using any material, including framing lumber, with "visible mold," a stipulation that will be difficult to enforce. All this costs money, but it's cash that some builders now spend willingly to get a competitive edge and a government seal of approval.

One weakness of energy ratings is that they often don't fully consider other green issues, such as how much recycled content is used in drywall or flooring, whether paints and furniture emit noxious or even toxic fumes, or how big a carbon footprint a home leaves on the planet—a seemingly cosmic notion that, nonetheless, can be measured. When it comes to greenness, the LEED (Leadership in Energy and Environmental Design) standard promulgated by the U.S. Green Building Council may be a better indicator. It creates a system of points—two points for enhanced control of refrigerants and two to four points for water-efficient landscaping—that can be accumulated to achieve a series of rankings, LEED Platinum being the highest. (The standard isn't perfect. Critics like to point out that you can score enough points to get a low-level LEED certificate without doing an exceptional job on energy conservation.) The home-building industry publishes the National Green Building Standard that considers six major green categories, including indoor air quality and homeowner education, to produce ratings. And many cities now have their own green building code. Austin, Texas, was the first in 1991. Usually, it costs extra to build to a green building standard, but it's often money well spent, especially if you can get a certificate to pass on to the next owner.

IS THE GREEN MOVEMENT A PASSING FAD or here to stay? There's little doubt that it will grow in force. Already, many jurisdictions take provisions from voluntary green standards and drop them into mandatory building codes. Manufacturers of building products often at great expense have adjusted their production processes, using recycled carpet fibers and even scraps swept off the factory floor to create greener products. And builders who took the time to investigate green building techniques during the housing apocalypse aren't turning back. If new homes are a pale green now, they will ripen into a dark shade in years ahead due to this confluence of forces. As a result, the new home you buy or build today will have to compete with even greener homes when you sell it. That's one reason why investors in commercial buildings want to buy the greenest building possible. They want to protect their investment down the road.

Another striking development during the housing bust was the long-awaited rise of contemporary-style production homes, which often went hand-in-hand with a deepening green building movement. Previously, buyers who wanted a more modern-looking home—characterized by strong geometric forms and the use of basic materials such as glass, concrete, and steel—were compelled to hire a custom builder and architect. That often meant having your own lot, an expensive and sometimes risky proposition. Until the housing downturn, off-the-shelf contemporary homes were only available in a few places such as Palm Springs, Calif., or Miami, Fla., where builders felt the pool of potential buyers was big enough to offset the risk. But now, devotees of this style, popularized by architectural magazines, may be able to find them in neighborhoods of production homes built in Salt Lake City, Phoenix, Denver, Austin, and several other Western markets.

The distinctive wing over the entry to the Lime series of contemporary homes is a nod to Denver's Stapleton Airport, which used to be on this site. Designed by architect Michael Woodley for Imagine Homes, the homes feature a creative palette of exterior materials, including limestone and black concrete. Standardizing on window sizes and building a rectangular form made the home relatively inexpensive to produce, despite its fresh appearance.

Some builders are drawn to modern design because it can be cheaper to build. Others want to stand out from the glut of traditionally styled homes constructed during the boom. Still others have always had a hankering to build in this vein and believe that demographic — young buyers seem drawn to the style — and economic moons have aligned. In any case, the results have been striking. Shea Homes®, one of the largest private builders in the United States, has had so much success with its Spaces™ series of space-efficient, contemporary homes that it tries to include them in its new master-planned communities. The homes, which start at about $250,000 in California, Arizona, and Colorado, sold during the downturn at a rate of three or four a month per community, compared with the usual one to two. Until recently, it was virtually impossible to find a contemporary design at this price in a new or existing home. While Shea initially aimed the small, hip homes at young buyers, it quickly discovered that baby boomers were drawn to the mostly single-story homes as well.

Interestingly, Spaces started off as an exercise in value engineering—finding the most economical way to build a structure. As part of this process, Shea, with the help of marketing consultants, also tried to figure out what people probably wouldn't pay for in a down market. Deciding what to leave out is the hardest part of any design process, and it's one that every homebuyer should go through. One of the first deletions was the rarely used oversize, jetted tub in the master bath—a symbol of excess from the housing boom. Colossal tubs, typically set on a podium to look like a Roman bath in front of big windows, may have enticed a few well-heeled exhibitionists into buying new homes. But market research shows that after the initial excitement wears off, they don't get used much. Many people, particularly time-pressed couples trying to raise kids and juggle jobs, would prefer a bigger walk-in shower that gets used everyday. It can have sex appeal, too, especially if there is room for two. The Spaces homes still have a tub, but it tends to be in a hall bath near the children's bedrooms, since kids tend to take more baths.

Formal living rooms, dining rooms, and parlors, which also don't get used that often, are also deleted from the informal Shea plans. Instead, the builder found that its target buyers would prefer a highly customizable great room, albeit one with a low ceiling that's less expensive to heat and cool. Taking a page from the apartment industry, brochures and Internet tools—you can drag and drop furniture into online floor plans—show how furniture can be arranged differently in open spaces. Here's how to furnish the great room for an overgrown child of a husband who likes to play interactive video games on a big-screen television. Here's how the home might look as a bachelor pad with a pool table in the living room and bulky loudspeakers in the corners. And this is what you could do to compartmentalize the room, throwing down rugs to establish boundaries for a reading nook in the corner, cordoning off space to build a small dining area to one side of the room, or dropping the ceiling in one spot to create what feels like a conversation pit.

The next order of business was standardizing a few sizes of big-ticket items such as windows, doors, and cabinets. Too often during the housing boom builders went overboard with fanciful exterior touches—gables, dormers, and bump-outs—that required different, often expensive millwork treatments. They wound up having to buy windows, doors, and trim in many sizes, sacrificing economies of scale. The recession forced them to simplify housing forms, settle on a few millwork sizes, and buy in greater bulk to obtain better prices. The thinking isn't much different than what Levitt and Sons went through when the company designed some of the earliest production neighborhoods. Some architects of low-income housing are real masters at this; they know how to create distinctive designs with a limited palette of inexpensive materials, often using color to intriguing effect. (One analogy: Nobody seems to mind that most Apple® products all come with the same sleek anodized aluminum frame; it's a point of pride to own one. You can always customize the product with your own case. And besides, you are the master of the personalized content inside.)

Shea played the energy card here as well, knowing it could draw younger, environmentally conscious buyers. Insulation was blown into the walls and ceilings. Blown-in insulation, though more expensive to install than batts, provides much better coverage of the wall cavity and higher energy performance. To reduce the need for artificial lighting, Shea installed solar tubes—basically metallic cylinders that cut through the roof and reflect sunlight into living spaces—in dimly lit areas. (The idea isn't new; Jefferson did it at Monticello. And I recently visited a 150-year-old, five-story home in Natchez, Miss., that had light-wells cut into the floors.) The garage even has a place to charge an electric car, a conscientious and increasingly commonplace touch, even if few potential buyers have one.

ONE UPSIDE TO THE HOUSING BUST—if you could possibly overlook the incredible pain that it brought many families—is that it left builders with time on their hands, time they could spend constructing

The Sage, a 1,400-square-foot demonstration home built in Eugene, Ore., riffs on the neighborhood's material palette—clapboard siding and asphalt roofing—to make its own, more contemporary statement. Built with a double-wall system to thwart thermal transfer, redwood reclaimed from benches at a local amphitheater, and a small photovoltaic system, the home was one of the first to achieve LEED Platinum status west of the Rockies.

demonstration homes. It's amazing how many built prototypes for local events or just to have something to talk about. One of my favorites is the small (1,400-square-foot) super-sustainable infill home shown above, built in 2009 for a local home show in a suburb of Eugene, Ore. The Sage, designed by the local firm Arbor South to educate its architects as well as the public, manages to embody nearly all the trends manifested during the downturn. The design sympathetically picks up on material—clapboard siding and asphalt roofing—used in the surrounding neighborhood. But its building form, especially the roofline and structural massing, are much more contemporary. The house meets the delicate challenge of constructing infill housing— how do you create something innovative and fresh that still makes a good neighbor?

The home is built with a full complement of energy-efficient materials and methods, including double walls—essentially exterior and interior wall systems separated by insulation. Formerly considered heretical, double-wall systems caught on during the recession as builders, especially in cold climates, looked for the next big thing in energy performance. Building separate wall systems for the inside and outside portions of the house might seem redundant, but the incremental cost pays back over the long term from the efficiency gained from reducing air-conditioning and heating needs. When interior and exterior elements touch, it creates a thermal bridge that makes it easier for exterior heat to transfer into cooled interior space in the summer and for interior heat to move into cool exterior air in the winter. Several alternative building systems, including structural insulated panels (SIPs), insulated concrete blocks, and adobe construction, are designed to overcome this problem.

The Sage not only minimized material waste on the job but also used reclaimed siding and flooring, an increasingly common green practice enabled by the rise of local salvage firms in many cities. The redwood siding was milled from benches reclaimed from a local amphitheater. In addition, the architects employed a host of sustainable building materials such as cork, recycled paper, fly ash concrete, and wood grown with sustainable forestry practices. Strategically oriented to gain maximum natural light, the home included a full complement of renewable systems, including solar hot water, a 2.1-kilowatt photovoltaic system, passive ventilation (allowing hot air to rise through a vertical space and venting it), rainwater collection, low-flow faucets, and dual-flush toilets. The architects estimated that it cost an additional $35,000 to build the $450,000, two-bedroom, two-bath home to such a high environmental level. When completed, the Sage was the highest-scoring LEED project west of the Rockies, earning Platinum status.

One of the most striking aspects of the home may be its "soft-loft" interior architecture, borrowed from the urban loft movement of the last 20 years. The vent hood and island, two items often overlooked by

Structural elements—exposed ducts and a range hood—complement stainless-steel appliances to produce a loftlike ambiance inside the Sage. Though the home is small, Arbor South generously allocated space to a kitchen anchored by a functional island with built-in seating.

designers, appear as almost structural elements. The stainless-steel finish to the ducts and range hood is picked up in the appliances. Together they form a uniform palette that mutes the intense grain patterns in the floor and backsplash. The home may be small, but the designer left plenty of room for the all-important kitchen where so much family and party activity takes place these days. As space is taken from needless hallways, over-wrought master bathrooms, and infrequently used formal rooms, some of it is going into kitchens, great rooms, and porches that get more use. In this fashion, it's possible to design a home that actually feels bigger and lives better than the McMansions built during the decade of the 2000s.

That was the thinking behind one of the early success stories of the housing recession. The Irvine Ranch of Southern California has long been a breeding ground for innovation in production housing. With 798 acres in holdings, the Irvine Company® is the biggest source of raw land for new housing in Southern California. Many of the best production-housing architects have offices nearby, and they are often tasked to develop novel design concepts for new neighborhoods. Several prototypes for high-density design got their start there—homes that share easements and cluster communities with combined driveways and parking come immediately to mind. But during the housing boom, much of the development at the Ranch was of the super-high-end production variety—semicustom homes, some with Pacific Ocean views, with striking architecture that could sell for $3 million after buyers were done selecting from a rich palette of design options and product upgrades. The market for these homes, fueled by cheap mortgage money and relaxed underwriting, came to a screeching halt at the onset of the housing downturn.

As the housing recession dragged on, it created worry within the Irvine Company that lot sales would suffer for a long, long time. So Donald Bren, the billionaire owner of the Ranch, took matters into his own hands. At a time when new housing developments had come to a virtual standstill, he dispatched market researchers to ask people what it would take to get them to buy. The answer: more storage space, great rooms as opposed to formal living spaces, and functional porches that work with indoor spaces. And, oh, a great price, too.

The findings were anathema to what most of the region's designers and builders had practiced for the previous 10 years. New homes in Southern California had gotten steadily more elaborate during the housing boom. Trying to slake a thirst for traditional designs, the region's many prominent architects hauled out increasingly sophisticated variations on old styles that hadn't been seen in years, starting with Old California designs then moving into historical Mediterranean styles. The addition of numerous formal spaces often made some homes feel like mazes, albeit delightful ones. You were never quite sure where you were when you walked through a "front door"; it was often a false front door that led to a courtyard. At the height of the boom, builders were putting courtyards everywhere—off the kitchen, bedrooms, and dining rooms—making indoor and outdoor spaces unrecognizable to capitalize on the moderate, year-round climate. The closets in some master bedrooms, big enough to sleep two children, were sometimes appointed with exotic hardwood, precious hardware, and velvet linings reminiscent of five-star hotels.

Bren knew he had to break with the past, if only to send a message that his homes were more economical. He dialed back interior and exterior specs, working with architects to develop a series of simpler homes that emphasized practical living. The new plans were long on storage space, often the first thing left on the cutting room floor when builders try to produce smaller homes. They typically came with a mudroom by the garage to store school backpacks and dirty soccer shoes (what family with young children doesn't value that?), large functional closets with inexpensive metal and pressed wood organizers, and a second-floor laundry room with large linen closets. Instead of sitting rooms, libraries, dining rooms, music rooms, or other stuffy spaces, Bren had homes designed with great rooms flowing into large kitchens with eating nooks, ideal for everyday living. Most designs also included a celebrated "California room," an under-roof patio space big enough for a table, lawn furniture, and even a built-in grill.

"Defeaturing" homes, along with a reappraisal of lot prices, meant that Bren could market homes at 35 to 40 percent below peak housing boom prices, a magic threshold that seemed to stimulate sales during the housing bust. He was so confident the plan would work that he took nearly all the risk, enlisting a group of companies to build the homes for a fixed price. The experiment more than worked: Homes in some sections of the Irvine Ranch sold at a rate of 20 a month, right in the teeth of the housing recession. As it turned out, the attraction wasn't just design and price. The Irvine Ranch is home to some of the best schools in California, a fact known to many Asian-American buyers who jumped at the opportunity to live there. At some of these new communities, two of every three sales were going to people of Asian heritage. People were coming from overseas to buy the homes.

Because they emphasized space used most frequently, the homes felt larger than their square footage indicated. David Kosco, the director

California rooms, such as this one from Woodbridge Pacific Group, were popularized by the Irvine Company during the downturn. Designed by Hannouche & Kang Architects, the room without walls is less expensive to produce than interior space yet provides an ideal setting for entertaining or relaxation. Fold-away walls connect it to the interior.

of design at Bassenian Lagoni Architects, who worked closely with Bren to design most of the homes, took me on a tour of the prototypes. As we sat in the great room of one 2,400-square-foot home looking out on the backyard, the big comfortable space felt more like what buyers used to get in a 3,200-square-foot production home, partly because of the long diagonal view across the living areas in the back of the house. Kosco hadn't sacrificed space or amenities where families spend the most time. The house still featured a large kitchen with an island, granite countertops, and adjacent dining nook. French doors connected the great room and kitchen to a covered outdoor dining area, magnifying the living large impression.

Kosco had taken space out of rooms used less frequently, like secondary bedrooms, which now often shared baths. The master bath, sometimes missing a soaking tub, was smaller than the faux spas found during the boom. Fewer separate formal areas meant fewer walls to take up space in the plan, producing construction savings. Livability got a big assist from the location of the garage in the front of the home, even if it didn't make for the most attractive facade. "Front-loading" the garage meant that the entire rear of the home could be used for living space, and you could create a bigger backyard, too. Sitting in the great room, it was easy to imagine kids playing two-on-two soccer while you watched the evening news and dinner was cooking. "It feels pretty good, doesn't it?" asked Kosco.

Executives at the Irvine Ranch asked the architects and builders of these homes not to disclose the research findings that went into the designs or the intimate details of the home designs. They were asked to speak only in the most general terms about the project. But as word spread within the industry that the "recession busters" were selling so quickly in a moribund market, builders throughout the country flocked to see the models. The astute ones could see immediately how value had been maximized and take home lessons worthy of imitation. The Irvine Ranch had renewed its reputation as a center of innovation within the home-building industry. ❖

CHAPTER THREE

Home Building's Mixed Record on Innovation

BUILDERS BELIEVE THEY HAVE a public relations problem when it comes to innovation. The best production builders develop whole new home designs incorporating the latest technical and floor plan innovations each time they open a new community. They bring in key consultants, suppliers, tradesmen, and designers to gather the latest thinking, and they almost always wind up offering something new in their base house. Then they create a fresh set of options, often grouping them into packages of, say, kitchen, bathroom, flooring, or energy upgrades—not unlike what carmakers do with wheels, seats, and communication technology. Packages, which can get down into color choices, make life easier for people who don't have a strong design sensibility, since a designer who lives and breathes this stuff has already selected complementary finishes.

Each year, custom builders produce an amazing body of work, building homes underground, on the edge of cliffs, and into the sides of mountains. Virtually anything is possible for a custom-home client with deep enough pockets. A cursory Internet search reveals homes that are upside down, shaped like toilets, look like monsters, or appear to have been dropped from outer space. Many of the most innovative, coolest custom homes are never publicized; they are often built for secretive, wealthy Americans. The big exception is the 66,000-square-foot behemoth built for Bill Gates in Median, Wash. Guests at the Microsoft® founder's home receive pins with microchips that, based on their personal preferences, automatically change a room's temperature, music, and lighting. Family members and security staff can tell by the weight of footsteps who is in the home at any time. Those fortunate enough to swim in the Gates pool are treated to underwater music and a floor painted in a fossil motif.

Even factory-built housing is shedding its image as a creative backwater. A new generation of more imaginative modular and manufactured housing looks more like the site-built variety. Some companies even provide the option of mixing and matching factory-built boxes on your lot with site-built decks and breezeways. Most manufactured homes, built to a federal building code to withstand highway transportation, can't be customized much. But you may be able to alter the design of modular homes—built to local building codes—before they go into the factory. Customization of factory-built housing nearly always involves a price, though, since it interferes with the builder's ability to mass-produce. The beauty of building a home in a factory, of course, is that construction quality can be much better controlled.

But the industry's reputation for innovation doesn't rest on ingenious custom homes or factory innovations. It rises from featureless, mass-produced homes in far-flung tracts. Maybe that should be the case, given that low-end production housing accounts for the majority of new homes built each year.

The home-building industry certainly leaves a lot of creativity on the table. Builders, architects, and tradespeople have an uncanny ability to see things in three dimensions, things that just look like lines on paper to most people. After studying a set of one-dimensional drawings, everyone involved in the project seems to share a common vision that they can noodle in their heads. I sat in my share of design meetings where conversation took this common vision to surprising places. One year we built the Destinations Home with a serpentine floor plan that included courtyards off multiple rooms. It was difficult to remember which spaces were indoors or outdoors, much less where the back door was located. Then in a meeting the floor plan got flipped to accommodate a sloping lot, which raised a new set of problems. Everyone in the room just turned the floor plan in their head. Conversation ensued about how to make the garage and back door work at different slopes. I was hopelessly lost. That's why you hire professionals.

One of the industry's greatest challenges is that when innovation does occur it often goes unnoticed by the public. The car industry has been generating publicity at its annual auto show in recent years for its ingenuity at putting screens in cars—first television screens for movie viewing in the backseat of family vans, then dashboard screens for viewing the gas and electrical consumption of hybrid vehicles, and now screens tied to cameras that help you back into a parking space. Yet, builders have been installing similar displays in homes for at least a decade, with much less fanfare. Security screens that allow you to see who is at the front door from your bedroom, or even from your computer at work, go back even further. Eight years ago, we installed a television monitor in a show home behind a bathroom mirror—it was visible only when it was on—so that you could watch the news while shaving in the morning. More recently we placed a movie screen at the far end of a swimming pool so that bathers could comfortably watch the show from a raft. And a demonstration home we built with Martha Stewart and KB Home® came with a program for viewing the energy production and consumption of the home on a computer, tablet, or smartphone.

But that's just one advanced home in one location. Breakthroughs take time to work their way through the decentralized home-building industry. Innovation within the consolidated computer industry, by comparison, often quickly lifts the entire industry's boat as competitors scramble to catch up, then be first with the next big thing. Each new generation of computer processing units (CPUs) famously provides twice the processing power for half the price. When 4G smartphones arrive, 3G models become functionally obsolete. When Apple or Microsoft introduces new tablets, smartphones, or PCs at big computer shows, it creates instant buzz that drives early adopters to queue up at stores. It's hard for most consumers to keep up with the latest computer software and hardware.

Prototype homes, by contrast, may be offered within only one subdivision at a single location in the country. The inspired accessory apartment designed for an aging parent, or the student who needs a rental, may only be available from one builder in Phoenix. Or the cute little contemporary home with the frosted-glass bathroom doors and big-screen television in the living room for less than $250,000 may only be found in one Denver community. Another obstacle to the spread of innovation: Suburban neighborhood covenants may prevent you from duplicating the idyllic Montana cabin design that you saw in *Fine Homebuilding* magazine. High costs for new design ideas or technology can be another stumbling block. It may be expensive to imitate the folding glass exterior wall that you saw in *Elle Decor*, though you could probably find a builder willing to do it. But that builder may say nothing about this option to his next customer, especially if he fails to make any money on the job.

The small size of most custom builders—most build only a few homes a year—limits the spread of innovation. Plus, these firms may closely guard a design, construction, or material innovation as a trade secret. That said, new design and construction concepts tested in the custom market often trickle down to production housing. Features common in mass-market homes today, like large built-in kitchen islands, oversize master suites with sitting rooms, big-volume spaces, whole-house home automation systems, and interior courtyards, all began as custom-home specs. The dynamic is not unlike what happens in the automotive industry. Electronic ignition, automatic windshield wipers, power steering, air bags, and cruise control all began as prototypes that eventually found their way into nearly every new car.

Some luxury production homes in warm climates now feature fold-away patio doors that blend indoor and outdoor living, a feature that began in the custom home market and migrated into production housing. The story is similar for kitchen islands, large master baths, and granite countertops. As use grows and prices fall, features common to custom homes find their way into production neighborhoods.

A WIDE VARIETY OF FORCES conspires to prevent the spread of transformative ideas within the home-building industry. Restrictive neighborhood design covenants may make it impossible for builders to construct anything but traditional homes on big lots with big setbacks, much to the chagrin of progressive urban planners who prefer to see more affordable homes built. Local zoning ordinances may prohibit builders from offering accessory apartments with full kitchens and baths—officially they may be labeled a fire hazard, but the real opposition comes from neighborhoods that worry about having renters on the block. Decentralization also hampers the spread of innovation. The 20 biggest home-building companies, which account for nearly one in three new homes built in the United States, are so decentralized (with such headstrong, highly paid division presidents) that they even have trouble achieving company-wide rollouts. One example: After we built the Home of the Future with corporate executives at Centex®, the Dallas division, which built homes in the same subdivision, was reluctant to incorporate most of the new concepts into its next series of homes. Most buyers, division officials reasoned, wouldn't pay for photovoltaic or geothermal power, and incorporating those features into base models would raise prices and scare away buyers.

In a seeming paradox, the home-building industry has been best known for innovation that limits consumer choice. The best examples of this are the Levittown suburbs of New Jersey, New York, and Pennsylvania, developed in the late 1940s and early 1950s. William Levitt found a way to build affordable homes for returning veterans by offering only three choices—exterior color, rooflines, and window placements. The homes were built on slabs, without basements or garages, with radiant heating coils in the floor. Levitt offered five alternative house facades, but all the interiors were the same. That way, subcontractors could move easily down the assembly line, a block of houses

Local code restrictions nearly prevented us from including this accessory apartment in a 2012 show home project in Orlando. A work-around was devised—we built a breezeway to attach the apartment to the home. Even so, the city wouldn't allow an oven or a stove in the room. Whoever lives here, whether it's an elderly parent, an out-of-work brother, or a boomerang child, will have to settle for a coffee maker and a microwave.

in this case, performing the same work over and over. Later, as demand dissipated and competition increased, Levitt deviated from its original formula. The company began to offer more choices and features—including carports, built-in television sets, and partially finished attics. That's almost the more interesting part of the story because it demonstrates the need to increase value in the face of slackened demand.

The biggest builders often have superstar divisions operating in one metro area that regularly innovate, but other divisions within the company may not follow their lead for one reason or another. The Las Vegas division of Pulte®, for instance, may figure out how to build with 2x6 wood studs, instead of 2x4s, and pack more insulation into the walls—and do so at no additional cost by reducing the amount of lumber it uses. But the South Carolina division may be reluctant to change the way it has always built homes, especially if its framing subcontractors are comfortable using traditional 2x4s and they can procure labor cheaply. Division presidents may also point to regional preferences as the reason they do or don't implement a best practice. Take hurricane-prone Florida. When we built our first show homes in Orlando, we learned that, following Hurricane Andrew, buyers expected the first floor to be built with concrete block so that it stood a better chance against high winds. When we returned to Orlando a few years later, after another large storm had blown through the city, many builders were doing the second story with block as well, especially on high-end homes.

A landmark 2004 report, published before the building bust, pinpointed causes for the slow pace of innovation within the home-building industry. Compiled by the National Association of Home Builders (NAHB) Research Center in conjunction with Virginia Tech University, the report concluded that it often takes up to 25 years for a new product or idea to go mainstream. Researchers attributed the slow uptake to the dominance of small firms in home building, poor information flow among industry players (something our show homes were designed to overcome), and diverse local building codes. The downturn, which wiped out thousands of home-building firms, changed this dynamic somewhat. The biggest firms now control a bigger share of the market and in recent years—thanks to a push from the housing bust— have shown greater willingness to experiment. Plus, every builder that survived was forced to find some edge to differentiate their homes. Companies that build high-performance, green homes now monitor each other's prototypes, regularly attending meetings where successful innovations are discussed.

MUCH OF THE INDUSTRY'S TRADITIONAL reluctance to innovate dissipated during the recession in the face of a dire need to do something different. During the hard times, builders found that even if only a small segment of the buying public craves a passive solar, contemporary, or green home, it may make sense to offer one just because they are hard to find in the resale market. Case studies abound of builders who outperformed their peers because they built homes, especially high-performance green homes, that buyers couldn't find elsewhere.

The new-home market became a buyer's market, to be sure, as the few buyers willing to stick their neck out looked for homes that might not drop in value overnight, like shiny new cars driven from a new-car lot. In demanding homes that were built better and better suited their needs, they shook a balance of power that had previously belonged to builders. One reason for the rise of McMansions is that during the housing boom builders made most of the decisions. They kept pushing square footage at the expense of style and function because customers perceived that they were buying a short-term investment as much as a house. It didn't matter if ceilings were so high you felt like you lived in a handball court, or if cooking a meal in the kitchen was like running a track meet. You were going to flip the home for a profit in a few years anyway, probably to another poor sucker who would have to take what he or she was given. The frenzy resulted in all sorts of design abominations that made life interesting for headline writers—snout homes with multiple garage doors protruding into the street, faux chateaus, and "big hair" houses with fake third stories. It was another story for buyers who had to pay to heat, cool, and clean these showy homes once their value plummeted.

When I first started writing about home building in the 1980s, home designs varied little within production neighborhoods. That started to improve with the adoption of computer-aided design (CAD) in the 1990s and a push from some local governments that required less monotony before they would grant building permits. During the 2000s, builders increased the number of exterior styles they provided, allowing buyers to mix and match facades with a limited number of pre-planned floor plans that were economical to build. In a neighborhood with three or four floor plans, they would create incentives for buyers to step up from three- to four-bedroom plans and beyond. Sometimes they would stagger the number of "Plan 3s" or Craftsman-style homes available on the block. That way, if you were particularly fond of that plan or style, you would have a limited number of lots from which to choose. Later, during the building boom of the mid-2000s, good design took a backseat to large volume as buyers looked for the biggest home they could afford, and builders obliged by constructing the gauche boxes characterized as McMansions.

TO DEMONSTRATE THE OPPORTUNITY that builders were missing, we challenged three talented production architects for our 2005 show homes to design the coolest homes possible within the footprint of the typical new home—2,300 square feet at the time. In our first meeting on the New Urban Challenge project in Orlando, Fla., the architects elected to draw for different customer segments— a family of four, a working husband and wife with no kids, and an older empty-nester couple. They also decided to work within different architectural styles—Dutch Colonial, Spanish, and Classical— to provide the pleasing design diversity that you sometimes see in older neighborhoods. Then they put their creativity to work, drawing floor plans that weren't even remotely similar but that worked perfectly for their target buyer. Sitting side-by-side-by-side in an Orlando suburb, the homes looked anything but cookie-cutter. In fact, it was hard to imagine that were built by the same builder, David Weekley Homes®.

The empty-nester plan, created by Seattle architect Bill Kreager, borrowed from Dutch Colonial architecture, with its gambrel roof and dormers. The story-and-a-half plan featured a brightly lit formal dining room with bay windows looking out on a public green space, a so-called mews, where an older couple could watch kids play (if they wanted to). The master bedroom was conveniently located on the first floor toward the back of the house. There were two

Our New Urban Challenge project, built at the height of the housing boom, challenged architects to do more with less in a production neighborhood setting. One of three homes built for the project, this Dutch Colonial-style home was designed by Bill Kreager for an empty-nester couple. Critical elements included a first-floor master bedroom, formal dining space (behind those front box windows), and a side porch.

additional bedrooms on the second floor—one decorated for visiting grandchildren, the other as a hobby room. A large living area that combined a comfortable family room and gourmet kitchen served as the guts of the house. A curved kitchen island with four seats opposite the sink allowed cooks to interact with diners. A kitchen nook, located around the corner from the great room, provided an ideal setting for breakfast with a crossword puzzle. The space was bathed in light, thanks to French doors that opened onto a spacious, private side porch.

The second home, designed by New York architect Donald Rattner, had a much different target buyer—a dual-income couple without kids. The home's Spanish-inspired architecture was so true to historic precedent—it featured massive stucco walls, a limited number of inset windows, and inviting arches—that it nearly didn't receive approval from the board governing design in the traditional neighborhood, which initially objected to the lack of fenestration. The arches graced a super-comfortable front loggia furnished with an outdoor couch

and armchair in the tradition of older Orlando neighborhoods, where people sit on their porches in near living room settings on cool summer evenings. The Spanish look continued inside with traditional touches like molding with dark stains, a stairwell done with a traditional groin vault (two barrel vaults that intersect at right angles), and large-tile floors. The two-story living room, separated from the foyer by little more than a standing screen, felt like the lobby of a small, boutique hotel. A large fireplace surrounded by armchairs and couches invited leisurely reading or intimate conversation with guests. You could imagine how, during a party, activity would flow from the living room to a large dining room table that could easily be served from the U-shaped gour-

Donald Rattner's design for a dual-income couple without children featured an elegant, comfortable great room, the perfect setting for reading a book or quiet conversation. Detailing such as dark-stained millwork and large-tiled floors spoke to the home's Spanish bearing. The first floor included a library that could be used as a guest suite and a large dining room for entertaining, with French doors that opened to a covered patio.

met kitchen. A downstairs office included a full bathroom so that it could double as a guest room, if need be. The master bedroom and a true guest bedroom were located upstairs.

Architect Geoffrey Mouen's family-oriented home couldn't have been more different. Designed as a classic cottage, it featured a huge front porch, 15 feet by 14 feet—big enough for two conversation pits—where parents could sip lemonade (or something stronger) with neighbors and watch their children play on the shared lawn. From the entryway, visitors could see through the home to a covered back porch with a grill and a rectangular pool. The immediate sensation was that the home couldn't possibly be only 2,300 square feet. Ground zero for family life would be along the back of the home, where a kitchen, eating nook, and family room combined to create a large informal living space, similar to the ones found on the Irvine Ranch several years later. It was connected with French doors to a family study room where parents and children could work together on their computers.

The centerpiece of Geoffrey Mouen's classic cottage design was a big family room/eating nook/kitchen combination along the back of the home that looked out on a covered porch and pool. Mouen also managed to fit a small dining room, three bedrooms, two master baths, and a large office into the compact 2,300-square-foot plan.

The space could also have been set up as a studio or music room. Three functional bedrooms upstairs were in close proximity so that parents could easily look in on young children. Mouen found a way to squeeze his-and-her bathrooms into the master suite of the very tight plan, though only one had a bath and shower.

This may have been the most rewarding of all the concept homes we built because of the premise—trying to demonstrate all that the typical production home could be. When I returned to see the homes recently, it was gratifying to find a thriving garden alongside the empty-nester home, a well-used front porch outside the dual-income home, and bicycles parked in front of the family home. David Weekley, who took a chance building small, heavily featured homes, was rewarded when they sold for even more than he expected, evidence, at the time at least, that people will pay for quality even in smaller homes. I wish I could say that the project changed the way builders thought about production housing. Building more production homes in this style would not have prevented the building bust, to be sure, but the discipline of trying to build better small homes may have insulated some companies from its ruinous impact. ❖

CHAPTER FOUR

Space Planning Comes of Age

THE IRONY IS THAT ROUGHLY a decade after our demonstration project in space-efficient design, most builders, architects, and homebuyers today are trying hard to do more with less. With future appreciation no longer a slam-dunk, despite recent increases, no one wants to waste space in a home design anymore. But the challenge is to economize without gutting the home of character. Most people still want some architectural drama in a new home, like an open front staircase, a master bedroom with killer views, or a back porch connected to interior spaces, elements that are hard to find in older homes. Against this backdrop, it's helpful to enter the new-home–buying process with the answers to some baseline questions.

For starters, how big does your master bathroom really need to be? It's nice to have enough separation that two people can comfortably use the master bath. But during the boom, many master baths got so palatial that even a long, hot shower couldn't heat the space on a cold winter morning. Here's another question for people living in markets dominated by traditional housing styles: Do you really need both a dining room and a living room? Most new-home buyers find that one formal room, typically for dining, will suffice. Not too surprisingly, the NAHB in a 2011 survey of builders concluded that by 2015 the living room was likely to vanish or merge with other spaces in the home. The same survey showed that the great room, a less formal living space that doesn't necessarily have a vaulted ceiling, is the likeliest room to be included in the average new home.

During the housing recession, builders and architects found that they could design smaller production homes that lived much larger than the previous generation of McMansions. As we did in our New Urban Challenge project, they connected great rooms and kitchens to large back porches that, viewed through French or folding doors, looked like an extension of interior spaces. They oriented important rooms like kitchens and family rooms to face windows so that homes felt larger. As they deleted formal rooms, they took out walls, creating greater openness and improved sight lines. And they improved the practicality of plans by taking pains to include important utility spaces like mudrooms, pantries, linen closets, and second-floor laundries that sometimes got overlooked during the go-go years.

After years of browbeating from small-home advocates who argued that human scale had been lost in production housing, many builders joined the space-saving movement during the housing recession. One hundred sixty-eight square feet, about the equivalent of one large room, was deleted from the median size of new homes started between 2007 and 2010, and that doesn't count the "cubic feet" that came out of new homes as ceilings came down to size. Although by 2013 new-home sizes had returned to 2007 levels, builders and designers were still using the space-saving tactics they discovered during the downturn to give buyers more for their money. Industry surveys showed that about half of homebuilders changed their design strategy during the recession to build smaller homes. Some did it the wrong way; they took old house plans to the copy machine and pushed "reduce 20 percent," an approach that just perpetuated outsized design on a smaller scale. Others dusted off small-home plans from more than a decade before and started to build them again, ignoring changes in consumer tastes.

IN 2009, WE ATTEMPTED TO show the right way to design a smaller home. We designed a virtual show home—there was no stomach to build a real spec at that time—that demonstrated how big a small home could live. We also created a floor plan flexible enough to change over 40 years as family circumstances shift. It's never made sense that families must uproot themselves because their home can't accommodate a new circumstance—when they have another child, an in-law comes to live with them, or they lose a job and can't afford mortgage payments. The home-building industry partly depends on design obsolescence; it wants buyers to outgrow a home just as they would a car. More than one leader of a production home-building company has stated as a goal having loyal customers buy from him a series of homes as their needs

Though conceived as a virtual show home, as shown here, the Home for the New Economy wound up being built in several communities throughout the country. Builders and buyers were drawn to the home's simple, symmetrical design, which featured a deep front porch, a detached garage, and a side entry to an adaptable suite.

evolve, starting with a townhome, moving to an entry-level detached home, and eventually purchasing a retirement villa, perhaps even with additional steps along the way. Yet a carefully designed new home should be able to make all these lifestyle transitions with the owner. In fact, that may be the ultimate statement of sustainability, because it obviates the need to build more homes. It's too bad that more builders don't give buyers plans to evolve their home, whether it entails converting a first-floor studio into a master bedroom or putting an addition on the back. That could be an ace in the hole for a builder who wants to stand out from the pack.

Working with Marianne Cusato, who designed the Katrina Cottage, a series of affordable homes for Gulf residents displaced by the hurricane, we devised a way to comfortably fit four bedrooms and three-and-a-half baths into a 1,770-square-foot footprint and give people all the flexibility they would need to live there for a lifetime. Many builders would have trouble finding space for three bedrooms and two bathrooms in a floor plan this size. The key starting point for the Home for the New Economy was to dispense with formal living spaces. Instead, Cusato drew a practical great room with ample 9-foot ceilings along one side of the house that served as informal dining and living space. To make the space seem even more realistic, we furnished it with virtual furniture samples from Room & Board®. You can still take the virtual tour online at builderconcepthome2010.com.

Along the rear of the house, in a bow to the realities of the economic recession, Cusato designed an "adaptable suite"—a 13-foot by 11½-foot room with a full bath and its own side entrance. Plumbing was roughed into the closet so that a small kitchenette could be easily added later on. Think about all the possible uses of this space. During hard times, the suite could be rented out as an accessory apartment to produce income, a feature that probably would have kept legions of out-of-work homeowners in their homes during the bust. Renters could come and go through the side entrance without disturbing anyone. If someone lost a job and needed to work from home, the suite could also comfortably house a small in-home start-up business. It was big enough to hold a large desk and a small meeting. Customers and messengers could enter through the dedicated entry.

But that's only the beginning of possible uses for this space. A first-floor bedroom suite, especially one with a porch, is the ideal location to house a parent who comes to live with you. The suite would also work well, perhaps too well, for a young adult who has returned from college to find work and repay debt. The space could easily function as a guest suite. A family with very young children might want to use it as a playroom to keep toys and clutter out of the family room, which could then work as a sanity-preserving getaway. It could become your primary bedroom if you decide that you don't want to climb stairs anymore. Or you could just live there temporarily while your knee or hip heals. And, though you'd never see it marketed this way, the adaptable suite would be ideal for a divorcing couple who can't afford to have two independent households.

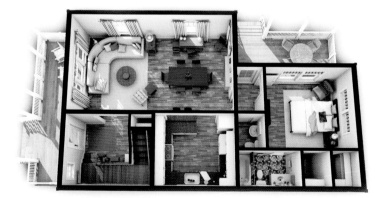

The adaptable suite (shown to the right) in the Home for the New Economy could function as an office, guest suite, or second family room. During hard times, it could even be rented as an accessory apartment, since a closet with roughed-in plumbing could be inexpensively converted to a kitchenette. The great room, shown with distinct living and dining areas, could be used in a variety of fashions as well.

We designed a similar amount of flexibility into the second-floor living area. A swing space off the master bedroom could begin life as an unfinished storage area (not finishing off the space may enable you to buy the house at a lower price). Then, after some income growth and the arrival of a first child, it could be finished as a nursery. After the child moves into her own room, the sky's the limit for this space. It could morph into a toddler playroom, a sitting room to escape the children, an office, or even a home theater. In any event, a room that provides double-, triple-, or even quadruple-duty provides a ton of value—and not just while you are living there but also when you sell it.

Cusato, who wrote the book *Get Your House Right* (Sterling, 2008), took pains to design a very comfortable home that you wouldn't want to leave. Where possible, she drew rooms with windows on two sides to allow for cross ventilation, a consideration that makes rooms feel more comfortable. The windows are modestly sized so they won't create unwanted glare and heat that strains the air-conditioning system. Nine-foot ceilings on the second floor allowed Cusato to specify tran-

Most second-floor rooms include windows on two sides to promote cross breezes. Transoms over the interior doors and ceiling fans help ventilate the second floor as well. A swing room (to the right) could be used as attic storage at first, converted to a nursery later, and ultimately become a home office or home theater.

soms over doors to bedrooms to improve light and airflow into hallways. Many new-home plans address the issue of parent privacy by isolating the master bedroom in a separate wing, but you don't have that luxury in a compact plan. So, instead, Cusato specified extra insulation in the bedroom wall and closet to cut down on noise transfer. The attention to sound reduction means that one day a second-story room could be used for quiet work—as a library, studio, project room, or home office—without a big added expense.

In a smallish home, having enough storage becomes very important. Unfortunately, many builders, when they shrink floor plans, cut storage space in favor of living areas because they don't want to interfere with the marketability of the house. They flirt with danger because surveys of new-home shoppers have shown for decades that storage space is the biggest homebuyer hot button. Storage space is one area where the automotive industry seemingly has a leg up over home building. Carmakers have ingeniously found places to store coffee cups, CDs, sunglasses, maps, manuals, and nearly anything else you would want to carry in an automobile. For many builders, however, providing storage is an afterthought, even though people have far more things to store in a home.

Cusato considered storage and clutter at every turn. For starters, the swing room upstairs could function as attic storage for holiday decorations, among other things. The adaptable suite features two large closets, which would come in handy if you ran a business from there or if an in-law came to live with you. In the living/dining area, she made room for a closet deep enough to hold coats but also games, a vacuum cleaner, hats, umbrellas, and boots. The kitchen is a relatively tight 11 feet by 12 feet, but every square inch has been accounted for. The cabinets make use of deep storage areas with long drawers and wide pantry shelves. Stacked upper cabinets rise nearly to the ceiling, providing spots for items that aren't needed every day. The two-level island is a perfect place for casual eating. When unexpected guests arrive, the higher counter level hides dirty dishes and clutter from the great room, a feature we included in several show homes.

THE HOME FOR THE NEW ECONOMY ended up getting built after all. A few builders thought so highly of the concept that they bought the plan and built variations in traditional neighborhood developments from Warwick, N.Y., to Norfolk, Va., to North Augusta, Ga. In some cases, prices started as low as the mid-$200,000s.

We weren't the only ones at the time to promote home designs that could provide protection from the recession. Bigelow Homes made national headlines in 2009 with a "Recession-Proof" home. The Chicago builder, to allay buyer concern that they may buy a home that would immediately depreciate in value, not only offered to refund the difference if home values did decline, buying insurance to cover the risk, but it went two steps further and offered to pay your mortgage if you lost your job. It also provided homes with an accessory apartment, much like the one Cusato had designed, with a separate entrance and space for cooking. Such "apartments" are common in many urban areas, where townhomes have basement flats that you can rent out. One caveat: Not all communities allow these arrangements. The best place to ask is the local zoning department. Where accessory units are permitted, you can typically rent either the main house or the accessory unit, but usually not both. It's a shame more communities don't encourage accessory apartments because they can help people stay in their homes in the event of a job loss.

House-plan designers got into the space-conserving act as well, taking wasted, showy space out of their best-selling designs without hurting their livability or looks. One of the top-selling plans drawn by Donald A. Gardner Architects, which in many years sells more house plans to builders than any other firm, provides a wonderful illustration. Designers took a 3,000-square-foot plan down to 2,500 square feet without sacrificing the facade or livability. They started by taking out an oversize breakfast nook in favor of a large dining space, 14 feet by 11 feet, that could be used for both formal and informal meals. Then they brought the master bedroom down to earth by removing a separate sitting room and, instead, creating sitting space within a still-generous bedroom

FLOOR PLAN
PLAN NO. 1299

Donald A. Gardner Architects reconfigured one of its best-selling plans during the downturn to make it more space efficient without sacrificing its basic appeal. The firm took 500 square feet out of the house plan by deleting one formal room, reducing the size of the master bedroom even while leaving a sitting area, and shrinking what was an oversized master bath. It kept a study that one day could be converted to a second master suite by moving walls to encompass a hall bath.

area. Children received slightly smaller bedrooms and were asked to share a hall bath. Volume ceilings came down throughout the house. A 15-foot ceiling in the great room became a lower "coffered" ceiling with sunken rectangular trim. A vaulted ceiling in the master bath became a barrel vault. Twelve-foot ceilings came out of the foyer. Wall bump-outs were deleted in favor of straight exterior walls. While designers largely preserved the home's appearance—including window styles, trim, and flower boxes—they made the home much less expensive to build.

The designers retained the home's key interior features, even as they brought it down to size. The house still provides ample, comfortable space for informal living with a combined kitchen and great room looking out on a rear porch. The new plan keeps a study off the downsized foyer, a swing space that could also be used as a small living area or music room. The powder room remains a full bath, and, because of its close proximity to the study, it could become part of a second master suite, with a reconfiguration of interior walls. Or it could be built as a fourth bedroom to begin with, providing a pretty high bedroom count for 2,500 square feet. The master bathroom may be smaller, but it retains his-and-her lavatories and closets, along with a private commode. The master bedroom still serves as a sanctuary for parents, with a separate bedroom wing for their children.

It was interesting to examine best-selling house plans during the recession for clues about the market. A surprising number of them provided "bonus" space over the garage that could be left unfinished and used for storage or finished to create a bedroom or family room. The majority of these house plans were great-room plans with combined kitchen and family room spaces along the back, often looking out to covered and in some cases enclosed porches. The typical plan had only a single formal space that could be reconfigured as a bedroom. A large kitchen, typically with space for an island, usually figured prominently in the plan. And many of the best-selling plans included pass-through "Jack-and-Jill" bathrooms that could be shared by kids, sometimes with separate lavatories.

HOMEBUYERS WHO WANT TO OPTIMIZE their home's floor plan and buy a home with maximum flexibility should start by asking themselves questions about how they might use the home. Most people begin the shopping process by thinking about how many bedrooms, bathrooms, and garage bays they need—the basic program for a home. That's not a bad tactic because it dictates much else about the home. Another basic question is whether you prefer formal or informal living spaces. Some people settle on a living room or parlor before they even walk into a model home or talk with an architect or builder. Others are drawn to informal living spaces. Still others may be focused on obtaining a kitchen, big enough for entertaining, because they've visited friends who have a similar setup. Here are a few critical questions that anyone shopping for a new home needs to answer, regardless of their means:

How long do you plan on living in your home? A recent survey found the average buyer of a single-family home now expects to stay in that home for 13 years. For that reason, it makes sense to think about how you will live in the home down the road, after your children—if you have any to begin with—leave the nest. Having a first-floor bedroom, or at least space that could eventually become one, is a key concern. That's not going to be a problem in a market dominated by single-floor living; roughly half of new homes have only one story. But whenever land is expensive, builders will naturally compensate by building homes of two or more stories. That second-story space is often the least expensive way to add square footage. Then the question is whether you could carve out a first-floor master suite, if you needed one. A first-floor guest suite could easily be converted to a master bedroom. But, as the Donald Gardner plan illustrates, so could a large first-floor room adjacent to a full bath.

What kind of lifestyle do you live at home? Some people, though they appear to be in the minority today, still value formal rooms where they can visit with friends and relatives. My grandmother entertained that way. If I can't imagine her living without such a space, I can't imagine having one myself. How does your family entertain? In small or large groups? Inside or outside? Where does your family typically eat—at the table, in front of the television, in the backyard, all of the above? The answers to these questions could determine whether you need formal or informal dining areas.

How big do your children's bedrooms need to be? I'm always amazed to visit new-home models in Southern California and see kid bedrooms that are so small they can't hold a desk in addition to a bed and dressers. Don't the kids need private, quiet space to do their homework? Some do, some don't. One of our children preferred to do his work at the kitchen table, where he felt like he was part of the action. The other, who was better at math, needed a desk in his room to concentrate.

How close do your children's bedrooms need to be to your bedroom? This was a question we confronted each time we built a show home, which had to be sold by the builder once the event was over. Most young parents want to be on the same floor as and close to their children. Once the kids become teenagers, however, both parties would prefer more privacy. Yes, you can use monitors to hear whether a sick child is having trouble sleeping. But for worried parents there's no substitute to close proximity. We used to leave bedroom doors open when our child was really sick just so we could hear him.

Do any of your children really need their own bathroom? If you are like me, you grew up sharing a hall bath with your siblings and turned out just fine. Builders who cater to second-time move-up and luxury buyers typically give at least one child her own bathroom; at the highest end of the market everyone gets their own bathroom. Most buyers, though, must make trade-offs. One great space-saving option for parents with two kids is to have them share a Jack-and-Jill bathroom. Each kid gets his or her own entry. Some may get their own lav. But the rest of the fixtures are typically shared.

How often do you bathe rather than shower? What would you rather have in your master bathroom, a jetted tub or an ample walk-in shower that gets used everyday? The pendulum seems to have shifted to a nice shower. In one recent show home, we designed a "dry off" space with a drain and towel bars at the entrance to a large shower that got great reviews—what better way to leave the stall and dry off before you walk across an otherwise dry floor? It makes sense to have at least one bathtub in the house, but the better location may be in a hall bath where the kids can share it. We built three show homes in 2012 for target buyers of different ages, and none of them had a bathtub in the master bath.

Does anyone work from home? These days, with wireless Internet connections, you can work from a computer anywhere in the house. That's great for responding to email or reading the news. But if you really need to concentrate—maybe you are an engineer and need to create diagrams—or you need privacy—say you are a tax attorney who does confidential work—you probably need a dedicated room. In that case, you may want to locate the home office away from the main rooms of the house. Then you need to decide whether you need a separate entrance for business visitors and whether you need space for a table for meetings. Also, if you are running a full-fledged home business, you probably need ample space for document storage and a copier.

What kind of outdoor space do you desire? Many people swear by a wood deck and couldn't imagine life without one. But others would just as soon have a cozy stone terrace that puts them closer to gardens and shrubbery. In some hot, buggy climates, a screened porch may be a necessity to enjoy the outdoors. In others, a big grassy backyard to kick around a soccer ball may be ideal. It all depends.

How many garage bays do you need? Builders try to maximize the number of garage bays they offer, particularly in markets where it's difficult to build a basement or an attic. In that case, part of the garage almost always winds up getting used for storage. The answer to the question of how many you "need" gets complicated once your kids start to drive or if someone in the household is fond of collecting automobiles. It's also influenced by how many family members commute by car to work. Nearly 20 percent of new homes now have garages that will fit three cars, though the vast majority, 68 percent, have a two-car garage.

Does anyone play the piano or another musical instrument? This is a huge concern in my home, where two out of four people practice musical instruments daily. We're lucky to have a living room big enough to accommodate a baby grand, though that's not the ideal spot—when it's played it can be heard everywhere in the house. Having a parlor to house the piano would be ideal. With the doors closed, that would also be a good place to practice the trombone or clarinet. If you have room for a basement, that might be an even better fit. A related question is whether you need space for someone to work out at home. During the housing boom, many high-end builders offered exercise rooms large enough for a couple pieces of equipment, some free weights, and a mat off the master bedroom. The location never made sense to me, given that teenage children are just as likely to use the equipment, and to do so they would have to traipse through their parents' bedroom.

Answers to many other personal questions may affect the design of your home. Do you have a large family heirloom—a painting or a credenza, perhaps—that could influence the size of a room? One architect likes to ask his clients where they put their shoes on in the morning, because if it's in the bathroom, they may need room for a chair. Another wants to know whether couples share time together in the bathroom in the morning getting ready for work. Many couples these days watch television in the bedroom, but some also want space there to read or relax. Others believe that bedrooms are for sleeping and don't want to waste precious square footage there. Whether you have kids also can influence whether you want a generously featured bedroom to which you can escape.

Ask kids these kinds of questions and you may get completely different responses, as we discovered when we convened a focus group with children before building the Ultimate Family Home. First, we asked a cross section of kids to draw their favorite room in the house. Surprisingly, a couple of kids drew the garage. One of them, the child of divorced parents, spent weekends working on projects with his father in a garage equipped with a television set and a refrigerator. One of the young girls in the focus group, whose parents were separated, drew a big, comfortable couch in front of a television set. That was her favorite spot because it was where she spent quality downtime with her mother, watching their favorite television shows. If your family watches a lot of TV, as many do—the typical American household watches an amazing four hours of television a day—it's important to create a comfortable setting where family members can gather and interact as well as watch TV.

The fun part came when we asked the kids to draw a room that they would really like to have in their house. Several children immediately imagined the home as a castle, complete with a moat and turrets. One said he wanted a big fire pole that he could use to slide down from his room on the second floor to a secret escape tunnel in the basement, where a boat would await him. Several drew outdoor space—elaborate forts and pools in the backyard being a favorite. From this exercise and conversation with the kids afterward, we learned that outdoor space was, in some cases, more important to the kids than indoor space. Something else came through loud and clear—teenagers wanted private space where they could escape with friends and wouldn't be bugged by their parents. Some wanted to be able to make noise with a guitar or drums.

Armed with this intelligence, we designed some killer spaces in our Ultimate Family Home. The backyard featured a large faux-rock, climbing structure—you could slide from it into a pool. There was a fire pit for grown-ups to gather around and maybe talk about all the photovoltaic panels in the trellises. (The Ultimate Family Home was one of the first large-scale zero-energy homes built.) We designed the ultimate backyard teen hangout, complete with an outdoor television, stove, and refrigerator, for concerned parents who wanted to make sure that if their kids went to parties, the parties were at their house. Inside, we designed a third-story loft as the ultimate gaming retreat. It was set up not only for online gaming with a large plasma television but for old-fashioned board games like Risk and Life as well. Much of this may seem over the top because it is. The house, after all, was the *Ultimate* Family Home. The idea was to show builders and homebuyers all the possibilities so they could pick and choose individual features that they wanted. While we didn't build a two-story fire pole in the middle of the house, we did create a secret dance practice room, complete with glass walls and a video monitor.

Custom builders and architects will tell you that it's helpful to collect pictures of design features that you like, whether they are torn from magazines or reside on the Internet in a place like Houzz.com. Most people who aren't professional designers may not know the exact terminology for the look or feature they desire. You may think that what you like is Tuscan, when it's really Spanish. What you call a "distressed" look in cabinetry may really be something else. But when you show a designer or builder the image, they often know immediately what you are talking about. They may also know a more cost-effective way to achieve the same result. That's the case, for example, with the cool, elaborate folding patio door systems that you see in many new homes today. Several manufacturers in recent years have come out with less expensive sliding doors that may roll back into walls. They can do the trick at a fraction of the cost.

Writing to your builder or architect, describing in as much detail as possible what you want, can be an effective way to communicate and crystallize your desires and needs. Architect Barry Berkus asked me to do that before he would design our Home of the Future. I wrote him that I wanted a home that wouldn't require a costly remodel with each new wave of technology that influenced the home. (His response was to specify plastic tubes behind the walls that could accommodate technological changes.) I told him I wanted a home that would look as much in place a century from now as it would today (I got turrets on the exterior), a home that was technically advanced but intuitive to operate (result: touch screens to power the home automation system), and a home that would work for a family now and in the future, no matter how family circumstances may change (result: movable walls).

A decade later we conducted professionally moderated focus groups with homeowners to ask about their use of technology in the home. At the time, email and computers were taking over people's lives. Sociologists worried that families were spending so much time in isolation on computers that they weren't talking to each other as they should. What our market researcher found was that homeowners didn't covet the next new gadget as much as added time that the convenience promised. One self-described early adopter of technology wished that he had more time—in fact, any time at all—to enjoy the home theater he had just installed. An aerospace engineer raising kids coveted more tools for automating housework, not for automating office work, so that she could spend more time with her children or do volunteer work. The group felt let down by the promise of new technology. They were annoyed at how hard it was to program the thermostat, DVD player, and alarm clock. Everyone, it seemed, wished that technology, instead of dominating their lives, would give them more time to enjoy it.

Our response to these findings was the 2007 InSync Home, an attempt to design a home that would work for its occupants, not the other way around. We put simple-to-use LCD screens all over the house to control all the home's major systems—audio, security, climate, and lighting. Broadband and wireless Internet was served to nearly every room to facilitate mobile computing so that family members wouldn't be isolated in a few rooms with Internet access. Some home systems, like landscape fountains and window blinds, worked automatically, controlled by an astronomical time clock. Motion detectors turned on lights as you entered the master closet and the pantry, a great convenience when your arms are full of dry cleaning or groceries. You didn't have to get up to operate the shades—they could be controlled with a remote control from your armchair. When you were going on vacation or having a party, you could push a button to change the lighting, which was preprogrammed for different modes.

The "distributed audio system" was to die for. New music sources had burst on the scene—the iPod®, computers, the Internet, and satellite radio—and no one was quite sure how to integrate these sources with the CDs, tapes, and records being played on home stereo systems. The solution was a multiple-room home audio system that made music from any source available in any room through the home control touch screens. You could even adjust the bass or treble based on the size of a room or whether it had hardwood floors or carpeting. Music played over a new generation of built-in speakers that install flush in ceilings and walls. Outdoor speakers sounded great, too—on the night of our grand opening party, faux rocks were alive with the sound of music! The price of multiple-room audio systems, which typically run over structured wiring behind the walls, has come down to where you can buy a four-room system with good built-in speakers for less than $1,000. Most builders offer one as an option. That's something to think about because it's easier and cheaper to install one while building a home than as a retrofit later on.

DURING THE HOUSING BOOM, I confess that we built a few lavish show homes that are outside the focus of this book. But it's worth writing about some of the research for those projects that delved into the psyche of homebuyers. Before we built the Destinations House in Las Vegas, we invited a dozen wealthy Las Vegans to a catered lunch and asked them what it would take to get them to trade up to the home of their dreams. Talk turned to what constituted an "authentic" home, one that looked as though it had been there for generations rather than thrown together in a hurry with cheap materials. The women told us it would be important that their next home be built with stone because that denoted lasting value and quality. They preferred a home designed with classic European architecture. Their dream home would be like an oasis in the desert landscape, with the sound of running water everywhere. An outside fountain would be a refreshing welcome home from work; a beautiful pool in the backyard was an important creature comfort. The women expected some high-end conveniences—a wine chiller in the kitchen, a place at home to have their nails done or get a massage. If these buyers wanted the easy life, they wanted a charmed life as well. And they desired a home with the amenities of the upscale resorts and clubs that they frequent.

After that flight of fantasy, it was time to get down to reality for our 2006 show home, the Reality House. This time we sent a flight of researchers into the modest homes of recent new-home buyers to see how they actually lived in them. Our researchers found that in many of these homes builders and architects hadn't left enough room for storage. They found homes with so much stuff piled up in the garages that cars were parked on the street (less than half of new homes come with a full or partial basement). Without a convenient place to leave newspapers, mail, and homework, they were strewn all over the house. Kitchen counters cluttered with juice makers, cappuccino machines, and toaster ovens sometimes looked like "appliances on parade" with nowhere to hide. But here's the kicker: Some owners of big homes were still paying $300 a month to keep stuff in off-site storage facilities because they didn't have enough storage room at home. This was particularly true of multigenerational households with older parents who had accumulated a lifetime of belongings with which they just couldn't part.

Working with architect Carson Looney, we sweated the small details of home design that can make a big difference in how people live on a daily basis. Looney was one of the first production architects (he has a custom practice, too) to bring back the mudroom, a utility space by the back door that he likes to call the "liver," a place where messy stuff gets filtered before it enters the house. The Reality House, ironically built in Walt Disney's Celebration neighborhood in Orlando, Fla., had a side entrance that was designed to be a main route into and out of the house. By that door Looney designed in pegs for hanging backpacks, a bench where you could sit and take off and store muddy boots and soccer cleats, and cubbies for leaving homework. Kids could take a back

Ethnographic research that revealed how multigenerational families really live in new homes guided the design of the Reality House in Orlando's famed Celebration neighborhood, done by Walt Disney Company. Designed in 1920s Arts and Crafts style with cross-gable roofs, ornamental rafter tails, and distinctive millwork trim details, the home included space for very modern activities—storing bulk purchases, washing the dog, and running a business.

staircase from this door right to their rooms on the second floor. Utility spaces of this kind gained in popularity during the housing bust. So did second-floor laundry rooms, which make a lot of sense since dirty clothes are left in bedrooms. If you'd rather the laundry room be on the first floor, close to the kitchen perhaps, a laundry chute can make a world of difference.

Most new homes today feature a family office space, typically in the kitchen, for paying bills, making phone calls, surfing the Internet, and other day-to-day tasks. More often than not, though, the space is out in the open, which can sometimes make it difficult to get real work done when everyone is at home. Looney instead put the family office in a quiet alcove, not far from the kitchen, in a semiprivate space where chores like talking with a teacher about your child's performance in school, getting bids from a HVAC service company, or doing some part-time fundraising could get done. Built-in cabinetry provided convenient spots for storing bills, mail, and stationery. A cell-phone charging station also came in handy. There was even counter space to work on a project or help kids with homework.

The home had a second, more formal home office on the other, quiet side of the house. Many home offices designed during the housing boom were shown with built-in bookcases, shelving, and woodwork, maybe a bar, and a to-die-for mahogany worktable in the middle of the room. The idea was to impress potential buyers with a baronial space that said, "I've made it." But when buyers moved in, the room quickly became dysfunctional. First, they had to hang unsightly wires from the computer and printer that didn't exactly contribute to the overall ambiance. The shelves worked great for showing off thick hardbacks, but there was no place to store real business records. Where was the copy machine to go? God forbid you needed to store real product inventory in this space. We left room in our office for all these business necessities. There was even space by the window to sit in chairs with a client and talk. And the office had a dedicated door to the back terrace so that you could slip outside to make a call or read the paper.

We left room for bulk storage in the utility room after research showed that people were buying in bulk from warehouse stores and then had nowhere to put 20 rolls of paper towels or a year's worth of cleaning supplies. The utility room was also home to a washer and dryer, of course. A pet shower made this an ideal place to also wash the dog, which could come and go to an enclosed pet yard through a small door. Considering that nearly half of American households own a dog, it's surprising more new homes don't accommodate them. The room featured a Dutch door so that the dog could be quarantined should allergic visitors arrive but still see out to the hallway and feel part of the action. In case that wasn't enough storage space, Looney designed a 640-square-foot bonus room over the garage that could be used like an attic to store holiday decorations, family heirlooms, business records, and anything else you need to keep but don't need to use everyday. After much debate, we showed it as a playroom.

The most ingenious feature of the plan, though, may have been the second entrance to the master suite. Several of Looney's clients had asked for this in custom homes. Here's the idea. You work late and come home after your spouse has gone to bed. Or you are a businessperson who travels a lot. So, instead of going right into the master bedroom and waking your spouse as you empty your pockets and traipse into the bathroom, you could enter the bathroom directly from the hall. We left space in the bathroom for a dresser, where you could drop your wallet, keys, and change. Then you could go to bed, presumably without waking your spouse. A marriage saver for the sleep deprived. ❖

CHAPTER FIVE

Green Goes Mainstream

HOMEBUYER PRIORITIES SHIFTED DRAMATICALLY during the housing downturn. Nowhere was this more evident than in the growing demand for green homes. Most industry surveys show that new-home buyers now want more than just a recycling center in the kitchen or engineered lumber in the rafters. They want their home to consume the least possible amount of energy and water. They want a clean indoor air environment. They know that natural resources are in short supply, and, as world population grows, the situation isn't going to get better. They understand that new development consumes open space that the rest of the population would otherwise enjoy. For that reason, many buyers are intrigued by the prospect of buying a home that treads as lightly as possible on the planet, one with the smallest carbon footprint. There's only one problem: They don't want to pay extra for it.

Most potential homebuyers believe it's the builder's responsibility, not theirs, to build the greenest home possible. That makes perfect sense, in more than one respect. The builder, presumably an expert consumer who buys the material to build homes over and over again, is in the best position to decide whether, say, cotton insulation made from recycled denim is a viable alternative to insulation made from paper or fiberglass. Complicating matters, many green features—gray-water systems that reuse bath water for toilets come to mind—need to function alongside and be integrated with other systems in the house. That puts the builder in the best position to decide whether any one system is a good idea. Unfortunately, cost is always part of that calculation, and many green building products and systems are more expensive than traditional ones.

Many builders decided during the downturn to bite the bullet and build green homes. (In the last J.D. Power survey, conducted in 2010, 52 percent of new-home buyers said they bought what their builder marketed as a green home, though purists would say many were a very light shade of green.) Building green was not only the single best way to stand out from the glut of existing homes for sale, but case studies abound of builders who outperformed the industry by virtue of taking the sustainable-building path. The most demonstrable evidence that green is growing, though, may be that several of the ten largest production builders in America, companies that have historically restrained from adding any incremental expense, now aggressively market green homes. Green has gone mainstream.

IT MAKES EMINENT SENSE for buyers to insist on the greenest home possible. That's what is happening in the nonresidential real estate market. Institutional investors such as pension funds and life insurance companies wouldn't dream of financing a new commercial building that wasn't super-green. Investors want to ensure that when they sell the building it will fetch the highest price possible. The advantage for commercial-building owners is that the value of the building is often calculated from its net operating income—rental income minus the cost of operation. So when a building incorporates a high-efficiency boiler that takes less energy to operate, the savings and the value go right to the bottom line.

Buyers of new homes need to think the same way. Some already do. They envision a day when their home sells for a premium because it costs so little to operate. Mortgage lenders may even buy into this dream by providing underwriting leeway on a green home, as long as an energy inspector certifies it. The most difficult aspect of buying a green home today may be weighing competing marketing claims, which requires some technical knowledge. The definition of a green home is unclear. Most green homes marketed today are resource, energy, and water efficient. Some may have healthier indoor air, too. It's advisable to think of each category separately because each offers different benefits and poses different challenges. Here's a rundown:

Resource efficiency refers to the sustainability of the raw materials used to produce building products. The calculation includes much more than the forestry practices for the lumber used to build the home—that is, whether the lumber was harvested from a sustainable forest. It considers everything from the recycled gypsum often used to make new drywall to industrial scrap metal used in some funky countertops. Increasingly, resource efficiency even reaches into the practices used by building-products companies—whether they recycle wood shavings from the factory floor or capture waste to power boilers.

Energy efficiency is all about reducing the amount of natural gas and electricity that your home consumes. Most people are keenly interested in this aspect of green building since the results translate into lower monthly bills, or even no electrical bill in the case of net-zero homes. A new generation of monitors—we've gone way beyond the controllable thermostats of the 1980s—enables you to track your electricity and gas consumption in real time and even turn off appliances from a smartphone or tablet. Several builders now give buyers a "free" tablet loaded with energy-management software for this express purpose.

Reducing water consumption is the toughest nut to crack. Water remains cheap in most cities—the average American household still pays only $335 a year for water—so the monetary savings may not be great. And the trade-offs for using less water may affect your lifestyle—you may not get the glossy green lawn you desire, or your shower on a cold winter morning may not be as satisfying. But many new-home buyers have no choice but to reduce their water consumption; it's being driven by government regulation in many arid metro areas.

Finally, **indoor air quality** involves reducing emissions from the building products in your home, properly venting combustion by-products, and introducing a continuous supply of fresh air, an especially important precaution in a tightly constructed energy-efficient home. You will probably need an energy-recovery ventilator, though you may be able to get by with a carefully designed ventilation system that includes super exhaust fans in the bathroom, a range hood in the kitchen, and a fireplace vent.

WHETHER YOU ARE BUILDING a green custom home or buying the production variety, the best place to start is with an analysis of its design. Choices you make in the beginning can dramatically influence the home's energy consumption later on. The first consideration is the home's relationship to the environment, especially its orientation to the sun. The sun is a free source of energy to heat the home during winter months, but you'll need to strategically employ roof overhangs, awnings, and trees to block its rays during summer months. The next consideration is the layout of the home. Basic decisions—like whether you want a one- or two-story house, whether the garage will be attached, the height of ceilings, or whether you use dark or light colors on exterior or interior surfaces—profoundly impact energy consumption. Building the home with an airtight frame is important as well, although optimal airtightness varies by climate.

Peter Pfeiffer, an architect from Austin, Texas, who is one of the leading lights of the green building movement, told builders at their annual convention in 2013 that initial design choices can take you 90 percent of the way to a green home. A two-story house, for instance, is inherently more energy efficient than a single-story home, square footage being equal, because it creates a bigger barrier between a hot roof and primary living spaces that must be cooled. Plus, if all your bedrooms are upstairs, the second floor must only be conditioned at night. Similarly, lower ceiling heights translate into fewer cubic feet of air to heat and cool. Detaching the garage from the home eliminates the major source of indoor air pollution, but it's not the most desirable option if you don't like carrying groceries or dry cleaning in the rain or snow. Using light colors on the roof and exterior of the home reflects heat, reducing cooling requirements indoors. Light colors on exterior walls may even throw more light inside the home, reducing the amount of electrical lighting required.

One of the major tenets of green building is that, before you buy something to solve a problem, you are better off trying to solve the problem. In other words, instead of deciding on an energy-saving tankless hot water heater that you must flush every year, reduce your hot water needs up front by purchasing a more efficient washing machine and installing low-flow showerheads and faucets. Similarly, cutting water consumption through the use of low-flow toilets, faucets, and fixtures may be a better investment than buying a rainwater-collection system. And before you generate power with photovoltaic panels, which need to be cleaned regularly to maintain their efficiency, think about all the ways you could reduce your need for electricity, like using light-emitting diode (LED) lightbulbs or painting the walls a light color to reflect sunlight through the house. Only after designing a home that requires as little energy as possible to cool and heat does it make sense to add equipment that needs to be maintained and may break down. As Peter Pfeiffer has said, "A lousy house with solar panels is a lousy house," adding that shading windows may save more energy than photovoltaic panels will produce. "It's like smoking vitamin-enriched cigarettes."

Best green building practices vary by climate, to be sure. In Austin, where winters are milder than Minneapolis, it doesn't make sense to overdo insulation. It's more important, as anyone who has snow-skied knows, that insulation is everywhere. For that reason, most green-home designers advocate using spray insulation, whether foam or cellulose. Pfeiffer likes spray foam insulation because it can stop humidity from infiltrating the house, reducing the chance of condensation building up in walls during the winter. He typically specs a reflective barrier in the roof to inhibit heat transfer via thermal radiation. Adding an extra

Concord Riverwalk, a project of 10 "net-zero-possible" homes, relies on tight, highly insulated construction and solar thermal panels to get the job done. Designed by Union Studio, the homes, which range in size from 1,200 to 1,500 square feet, employ a variety of small-home principles—diagonal views, varied ceiling heights, and activity zones—to create the impression of larger living space.

layer of wall insulation in Austin probably doesn't cut operating costs by a lot, Pfeiffer pointed out, but tightening up on air infiltration may save as much as $600 a year in utility bills.

PARDEE HOMES®, WHICH BUILDS IN THE WEST, was early to the green building party. Pardee has steadily added more green products and features through the years. The company went all in on green building during the housing recession, introducing a new series of LivingSmart® homes that not only included a full complement of energy- and water-saving features but also touted a green lifestyle. In one Los Angeles suburb, Pardee went so far as to put composting bins in the backyard of a model. Three bins, situated where a disappearing-edge swimming pool or a big fire pit would have gone during the housing boom, were showcased through big rear windows. The front yard was equally interesting; it was mostly rocks interspersed with a few indigenous and drought-tolerant plants, so-called xeriscaping. Photovoltaic panels greeted visitors at the front door of the first model. "It's a badge of honor," said Joyce Mason, vice president of marketing for Pardee, which used to try to hide the panels in back.

Pardee conveniently divides its green program into four components that are similar to the categories outlined above—health smart, energy smart, earth smart, and water smart. The base house includes low-e windows, radiant barrier roof sheathing, and high-efficiency air conditioners, but buyers must pay extra for a photovoltaic system, Energy Star appliances, tankless hot water heaters, and an expanded package of fluorescent fixtures and lights. The earth-smart features, typically included in the price, include engineered wood, carpets made from recycled fibers, fiberglass entry doors, and a recycling center in the kitchen.

Pardee Homes, one of the earliest production builders to build green homes, doesn't try to hide the photovoltaic panels that power its green homes, built to tight energy specification. Some Pardee models further advertise a green lifestyle with composting pits in the backyard and landscaping done with native plants and rocks.

Pardee has pushed harder than most production builders to incorporate water-saving technology. It's one of the few builders to actively market xeriscaping. Drought-tolerant plants are highlighted in an almost arboretum-type setting in the front yard, with small placards identifying the species. Homes with grass yards come with irrigation systems that tie into communication satellites; they won't water the lawn if rain is on the way. Pardee employs the latest water-saving toilets and faucets as well.

Water may be cheap now, but that could change soon. Many experts believe the 20 percent nationwide increase in water prices from 2010 to 2012, brought on by droughts and short supply, portends greater increases in the future. In high-growth cities such as Phoenix and Las Vegas, dwindling supply of city-provided potable water has become a full-blown crisis. Part of the problem, according to the EPA, is that residential water use grew during the housing boom as homes got bigger and required more dishwashers, and lawns got bigger and required more irrigation. (Lawns and gardens account for at least 15 percent of the water used each year by the typical household.)

Even places where you'd think water is abundant, Georgia, for instance, are concerned about keeping up with demand. After Georgia's Environmental Protection Division imposed water restrictions in 2010—you can only water the yard in the evening—a large local builder, Ashton Woods Homes®, put together a five-acre community, Riverwalk, that included a rainwater-catchment system to irrigate lawns and water drought-resistant plants. The system, which added $1,500 to the price of each home, collects rainwater that runs off the back roofs of houses, through downspouts, and into a 6-inch collector pipe that connects underground to three 2,500-gallon cisterns. With 1 inch of rain, the system collects 7,500 gallons, enough to irrigate the community two or three times.

Custom homebuilders are way ahead in the green game, since sustainable construction is much easier to accomplish on a bigger budget, especially when it's part of the homeowner's mission.

Shown below, the beautiful, three-level Michigan home, which has won several awards for its sustainability, was built in part with trees felled on the site, just as in pioneer days. The home was oriented on its remote 20-acre site to absorb as much sunlight as possible during cold winter months, and overhangs prevent sunlight from penetrating and heating the home during warm summer months. The house was built with structural insulated panels (SIPs) and even has a geothermal heating and cooling system, like the one we put in the Home of the Future many years before. The bottom line: It averages less than $50 a month in utility costs.

Trees cut down to make way for this super-green custom home in rural Michigan were used to build the structure. Oriented to soak up winter sun, with overhangs to keep out summer sun, the home costs less than $50 a month to heat during the winter, thanks to SIP construction and a geothermal heat pump.

PASSIVE SOLAR TECHNIQUES, which were thoroughly explored by research organizations and builders in the 1970s and '80s, are receiving renewed attention during this green building era. Part of the motivation is that they provide a free source of energy. The basic idea, as simple as it sounds, is to install glass on the south side of the home to maximize solar gain in the winter, when you need heat the most, then situate overhangs so that when the sun is high in the sky in the summer not as much direct sunlight enters the house. Orienting the home toward the sun is often easier to do on a custom home, especially one built in a remote location, than on a production home in a neighborhood that's already been platted. Most developers lay out subdivisions to maximize sales, orienting homes to capture views that can bring a premium and leaving space for as many homes as possible. You want a home on an east-west street, which will provide more south-facing opportunity.

I visited my first passive solar house as a cub reporter almost 35 years ago, during the housing recession of 1980–81. Located in a Maryland suburb, the show home was one of 20 orchestrated by the NAHB Research Center to demonstrate a path toward energy self-sufficiency (the Mideast oil boycott was still fresh on people's minds, guiding public-policy decisions by the Carter Administration) and perhaps show builders a way out of the recession. Back in the day, passive solar homes could be pretty strange looking. The home I visited had a large, sun-facing interior "trombe" wall (pioneered by French engineer Felix Trombe in the 1960s) in the living room. It was made with concrete to absorb heat through the windows during the day and transmit it into the house at night. Concrete floors between the windows and the awkward trombe wall also served as a heat sink. Airflow through the home was carefully choreographed. Fresh air entered through low windows on one side and vented through higher windows on the opposite side. This isn't new; builders 100 years ago achieved roughly the same effect by putting double-hung windows on opposite sides of a room, and strategically placing transom windows above doors so that air could flow from one room to the next.

Twenty-eight years later, I got to explore passive-cooling techniques in the luxurious Tradewinds House built for the 2008 International Builders Show in Orlando. The home's lakeside location allowed us to harness prevailing winds off the water to power a passive ventilation system that reduced the need for standard air conditioning. The design process began with a wind analysis by a local research group that showed how prevailing winds would blow on the home's lot, data that's widely and inexpensively available. The findings were confirmed by the orientation of runways at a nearby airport; they were parallel with the prevailing winds coming off the lake. The research group also provided diagrams that illustrated how sunlight would strike the home throughout the year. Several off-the-shelf software programs allow anyone to perform a similar analysis today.

Using the data, our architect, Geoffrey Mouen, designed a home with high cathedral ceilings and operable clerestory windows that allowed heat to vent naturally, with lakeside breezes ensuring constant air circulation. The form of the building, two long wings, each less than 25 feet wide, lent itself to passive ventilation. Long interior walls and windows could be opened to an interior courtyard for ventilation. The shell was constructed of concrete and stucco with deep overhangs to prevent unwanted solar heat gain, big shutters to keep out rain and sun, porches sheltered from the sun, and a reflective metal roof. This was island architecture, albeit with a strong traditional bearing.

The big green idea in Mouen's mind was that you could simply turn everything off to save energy and let nature do its work. Instead of building a closed-up envelope that requires forced ventilation—the typical response to energy-efficient construction—the guiding principle was that you could switch off the air conditioning, open the doors and windows, and enjoy a native climate that is pleasant in all but the hottest summer months. As an added benefit, indoor air quality becomes less of an issue with fresh air circulating through the house. On days when it had to be used, the air-conditioning system was designed for maximum efficiency, with ducts radiating from the garage, a central location that allowed for shorter runs. One downside was that the house needed a special heavy-duty dehumidifier that could work with either the passive ventilation system or a traditional air-conditioning system.

Mouen considered the home's solar orientation when designing the floor plan. He put the sleeping wing on the east side of the house so you could wake to the morning sun and connected the master wing to a Zen garden with a small pond. He located the living area on the west side of the house to take full advantage of sunlight in the late afternoon and early evening, when its occupants would be home. He designed large overhangs that provided much-needed shade in warmer months but permitted sun to shine into rooms in the winter, when the sun is lower. A front porch along the south side of the house, made from termite- and rot-resistant cypress, provided privacy from a bike trail and shaded an outdoor dining and grill area. Louvered doors and Bahaman shutters could be opened and closed, depending on the preferred temperature and time of year. A three-story cupola served not only as a nature observatory but also as a cooling tower. Opening a single window in the cupola, along with folding doors along the inner courtyard, drew cool air across the pool area into the living spaces, an ancient passive cooling technique. The constant, gentle breeze promotes evaporation on the skin that can make the spaces feel 10 degrees cooler.

Maximizing passive solar potential requires a delicate balance between the orientation of the building, window placement, building

The big idea in our Tradewinds show home was that you could open interior window walls, turn off the forced-air system, and enjoy cool breezes. The observation tower functioned as a passive ventilation system, venting hot air during summer months. The home design revolved around an interior courtyard with a pool that helped cool temperatures.

mass, and insulation. A higher concentration of windows should be on the south side of the house so that they draw inside as much sunlight as possible during the winter. The wider the window array, the more light penetrates interior spaces, obviating the need for artificial lighting. Experts say that in North America you want to orient the house to within 30 degrees of due south. A house that faces due south achieves the equivalent of 100 percent potential solar heat gain through windows. But rotating the house to within 30 degrees of due south still provides about 90 percent of the potential solar gain. Beyond 30 degrees, however, architectural shading gets difficult, which can lead to overheating.

South-facing glass needs horizontal shades to protect against solar radiation on midsummer days. It also helps if overhangs extend out on both sides of the windows to protect from late morning and early afternoon sun. A host of factors determine the optimal size of the south-facing glass, including its location on the side of the house, the amount of sunshine it will receive, and the heat loss of the house. Thankfully, you can plug the key variables into one of several commonly available software tools to guide the design of your home. One of the leading programs is Energy-10, developed by Dr. Doug Balcomb at National Renewable Energy Laboratory. The latest version even assists in sizing solar hot water and photovoltaic systems.

If you are interested in going the passive solar route, operable clerestory windows, like the ones we put in the Tradewinds house, are important to ventilate spaces during summer nights. In most climates, though, the windows also need to be insulated so that they retain heat during the winter. When it comes to a heat sink, there are a lot of alternatives today to trombe walls. These days you'll find everything from concrete to brick, stone, and tile used to capture heat during the day and radiate it inside the building at night. The size and placement of heat sinks are careful calculations, too. The amount of glazing and insulation used determines how much mass you need to keep the house from overheating during the day and help keep it warm at night. Also, thermal mass that absorbs direct sunlight is much more effective than mass that receives only reflected light, which means you need to be careful where you put the mass.

Window placement on the three other walls is tricky, too. Windows are important for cross ventilation, of course, and they influence the overall look and personality of the house. But you need to guard against getting too much solar gain in the summer, heat that will tax the air-conditioning system. Windows on the east and west sides of a house pose a special challenge in regions with hot summers because they face low solar angles in the mornings and afternoons. The best spec in those cases is glass that reduces solar heat gain, but you'll probably want to investigate shading devices, too.

The strategic planting of choice trees, something our ancestors probably understood intuitively, can be an effective tool for limiting summer heat gain as well. Not just any tree will do. In the best of all worlds, you want trees and bushes that leaf out in summer to shade the window when it's hottest outside and drop their leaves in the fall to provide for light and ventilation. You also need to be careful not to select a species that grows too tall and loses its lower branches, reducing its shading potential. Planting trees on the east side of the home to prevent unwanted heat gain in the morning may make sense. And since the west side of the home gets the most intense afternoon and evening solar sun, you may want to put rooms that aren't used much on that side—the garage, the utility room, and the laundry room, for example.

THE PASSIVE-HOUSE MOVEMENT HAS GATHERED serious steam in recent years thanks to an international organization, the German Passivhaus Institut, that has popularized passive concepts throughout the world, including, most recently, the United States. Dennis Wedlick, a prominent New England architect, studied at the Institut in 2008, then put what he learned to work designing the beautiful, 1,650-square-foot home in Upstate New York pictured on the next page (and on this book's cover). What's perhaps most interesting about the home is that it doesn't have the active systems typically found in super-energy-efficient homes. There are no photovoltaic arrays, no geothermal heat pumps, no wind turbines. Instead, the home works like an immaculately insulated thermos, retaining the heat it naturally collects from the sun and its human occupants and shielding the home from the sun when solar gain is not wanted. It uses about 78 percent less energy, most of it to power appliances and heat water for showers and washing dishes, than the typical home. Inside temperatures remain at about 70 degrees year-round, remarkably without any on-site heat source.

Unlike most green homes, which tend to be contemporary in design, Wedlick's house has the easy appearance of a barn, albeit one where spiritual meetings might take place. The home was quick to construct, an important consideration in Northern climates with short building seasons. A series of graceful bow-arch beams, 25 feet at their apex, frame an open loftlike floor plan. Skylights funnel daylight into back rooms of the house that don't benefit from the large south-facing

This passive house in Upstate New York works like a thermos bottle, trapping heat within its walls and shielding interiors from the sun during the summer. The home is built so tightly and insulated so heavily that it gets most of its heat from the sun and its occupants. One-foot-thick structural insulated panels join to create an open barn form.

expanse of glass. The home's high performance stems mostly from its architecture and construction. To achieve passive-house certification, homes must be virtually airtight. Once again, the design process starts with proper siting of the home on the lot. A 23-foot-wide window on the south side welcomes light and heat to enter in the winter when the sun is low in the sky. An overhang blocks sunlight during summer months when the sun is higher. There are no windows on the east side of the house and just a single door and window along the west wall. The super-low-emissivity R-6 windows are made with double panes and a layer of transparent vinyl in between. They are complemented by thermal window shades on the south and north sides.

The home's architecture, a rectangle with a high ceiling, inspired by Iroquois long houses that used to populate the Hudson Valley, helps retain heat. Cathedral ceilings preserve heat from the sun during the winter months, so much so that, when construction crews were finishing the house on frigid winter mornings, inside temperatures were still in the 50s and 60s. During the summer, those same high ceilings, coupled with operable windows, help create airflow that vents hot air. To further save energy, the kitchen and bathroom were designed back to back, shortening mechanical runs and reducing heat loss during transmission.

Wedlick compares the frame of the home to a thermos. Twelve-inch-thick SIPs join to create a frame that was carefully sealed, especially at critical intersections between the walls, the roof, and the foundation. The walls have a super-high R-value of 50, two or three times higher than Energy Star requires. The roof, built with 12¼-inch-thick SIPs, scored even higher with an R-value of 53. Other than the windows and doors, nothing penetrates the walls. Utilities enter the house through the ground, and the foundation is super-insulated. The foundation consists of a concrete slab that sits on layers of gravel, expanded polystyrene foam, and extruded polystyrene. The combination results in an extraordinary R-value of 60, way above what's usually achieved on a conventional home.

The major takeaway of Wedlick's passive-house experience is the importance of airtightness. The house set a local record. "Most people don't realize that the number one cause of energy loss is air infiltration," he said. "If you feel a draft at home, that has a major impact on the home's energy load. Most new-home builders aren't achieving anywhere near airtightness. That's the new world that the passive house opened up." Homes this airtight, of course, need a source of fresh-air intake. Wedlick used a heat-recovery ventilator that collects heat from the house—steam from parboiled vegetables and hot showers, breath from humans and pets—cleans it, and uses the heat to warm cool air coming back in the house. The ventilator creates a constant, regulated pull of fresh air that results in cleaner indoor air than a leaky conventional home.

CLEAN INDOOR AIR is the part of green building that most excites many people. Besides energy efficiency, it is one attribute of a green home that, surveys show, homebuyers will pay a little extra for. One of the reasons is that many people in this country have breathing problems. Government data estimate that 26 million Americans have asthma, including 7 million children. Moreover, roughly 20 percent of asthma cases are linked to mold and moisture problems in the home. The majority of them occur in older homes, of course, because existing homes vastly outnumber new ones. If a family member suffers from eye irritation, allergies, headaches, or asthma, you may want to focus on creating the healthiest possible indoor air environment. That means paying particularly close attention to design and construction details that keep water out of the house, properly venting the house to prevent moisture buildup, and eliminating as many sources of in-home contaminants as possible.

The EPA heightened concern about indoor air quality several years ago with a report concluding that pollution in some indoor air environments can be twice as bad as it is outdoors. This was after some builders in the late 1990s started building airtight shells to improve energy performance without adequately ventilating them or providing a dedicated source of fresh-air intake. As a result, some new homes developed widely reported problems with mold and foul indoor air. To demonstrate better design and building techniques, the U.S. Department of Housing and Urban Development in 2007 built what was described as a "mold-free" home. Located in Chesterfield, N.H., the home was designed with large eaves to direct water farther from the foundation and a wall system that would drain moisture. The whole idea was to keep water away from the house and, therefore, remove mold's potential food sources.

The key architectural elements of the home included a roof with large overhangs—$2\frac{1}{2}$ feet as opposed to the typical 1 foot—that directed rain farther from the foundation. The high-pitch slate roof was designed so that water would roll off freely and so that ice dams— which sometimes form at the edge of a roof, preventing melting snow from draining off the roof—wouldn't occur at roof edges and in the gutters. Water that backs up behind an ice dam can leak into a home, causing damage to walls, ceilings, and insulation. Large overhangs and high-pitched roofs are both added expenses that most production builders would just as soon avoid. But they can contribute significantly to the architectural character of a house in addition to improving its performance.

The wooden house frame was built with two layers of drains, one at the footings and another halfway up the foundation wall. First, the frame was covered with housewrap, a lightweight synthetic sheathing that prevents rain from getting into the wall cavity while simultane-ously allowing water vapor to pass to the exterior. The vapor barrier was in turn covered with a ventilating, self-draining rainscreen; it allowed for about $\frac{3}{8}$ inch of airflow and permitted water to easily drain down the side of the house. Inside, the home used paperless drywall in the walls to allow moisture to escape. This was after forensic engineers found that traditional drywall covered with paper trapped moisture behind the wall under certain conditions in some climates.

Specialized insulation, covered with a permeable vapor barrier that allowed for air exchange in cold, dry weather, was used in the walls and ceilings. It served double duty, preventing humid air exchange on hot, muggy days. The wooden components of the house were coated in a permanent antimicrobial spray. The home was built with permeable wood siding, which seems counterintuitive. However, it isn't a problem as long as moisture can drain inside the wall, which it could in this case. After it was complete, the home was inspected to make sure water wasn't unintentionally introduced into the home. It wasn't.

Most builders would tell you that building a home to these specifications is overkill. They prefer to focus on less expensive solutions that can still make a big difference, especially at move-in when chemical fumes from paints, carpets, and even furniture can be in the air. They will use paints, solvents, and adhesives that emit as few volatile organic compounds as possible. Cabinets and other woodwork made without urea-formaldehyde glues is another common specification. As a matter of course, conscientious builders will vent all household appliances and install carbon monoxide detectors. Most also offer the option of a central vacuum system, which can really help if you have pets—dander from pets is a leading cause of allergies. And builders who market super-energy-efficient homes are probably installing heat-recovery ventilators that clean the air. But that may be the extent of their indoor air-quality efforts. Many builders perceive the issue as a can of worms that they would rather not open, unless asked, because they don't want to be responsible for guaranteeing indoor air quality, especially since homeowners may unknowingly introduce air-quality problems into their home.

Some leading causes of indoor air pollution are preventable. It makes sense, for instance, to air out new carpet and padding for a few days prior to installation. Because many pollutants, including carbon monoxide, enter the home from an attached garage, it's important not to break the seal between the garage and the living areas of the house by, say, allowing an electrician to install a panel on an inside wall that air could seep behind. Air wants to travel from hot to cold, so in the summer it will be pulled into conditioned space from the garage. You also don't want to create negative air pressure in the house, which will pull in outside air. So, that fan over the cooktop should only be as powerful as necessary. Indoor humidity needs to be controlled as well; keep it below 50 percent to prevent bacteria and viruses from gaining a foothold. Showers, of course, are a major source of indoor humidity. It makes sense to put a timer switch on the bathroom fan so that it stays on for another five minutes after you shower.

Several voluntary government and industry programs would take indoor air-quality specs to a much higher level. They are worth checking out, especially if someone in the family has asthma or allergies. The EPA's new voluntary program, Indoor airPLUS, builds off the results of the Chesterfield mold-free house. Very few homes have been built to these standards, which require new homes to direct water at least 5 feet from the foundation, or—in the case of roofs without gutters—into a grade-level rock bed with a waterproof liner and drainpipe that deposits water onto a sloping finish grade. Homes also must have continuous drainage planes behind the exterior wall cladding, with a drainage system at the bottom of exterior walls to direct water away. Window and door openings must be fully flashed so that water doesn't get inside. You need to ask about this last precaution no matter what type of new home you build, since anecdotal evidence indicates that poor flashing techniques may be the single biggest source of water leakage into new homes. Concrete walls that go beneath the foundation must be finished with a damp-proof coating. In addition, all likely entry points for pests must be fully sealed, caulked, or screened.

It would be easier to find builders willing to ascribe to the program's ventilation requirements, which start with designing HVAC systems along Energy Star guidelines, with ducts and equipment designed to minimize condensation problems. They go on to require both whole-house ventilation and spot ventilation for oil- and gas-fired equipment and fireplaces. Bedrooms must have carbon monoxide alarms. Building materials should be selected that reduce exposure to chemical content and the risk of moisture damage. And homes should be ventilated prior to occupancy.

The hurdle that few builders are willing to jump over voluntarily is the requirement that the garage be fully sealed from living spaces. To make sure the seal is done right and carbon monoxide fumes won't be sucked into the house from idling cars, the EPA requires a visual inspection by a trained third party. Before insulation is installed, the inspector must examine the common walls and ceilings between attached garages and living spaces to ensure they are air-sealed. Also, all connecting doors between living spaces and attached garages need to include an automatic closer. And, those doors must be installed with gasket material or be made "substantially airtight" with weather-stripping. Plus, the builder needs to vent the garage with an exhaust fan vented directly outdoors with a minimum installed capacity of 70 cubic feet per minute (cfm). And the fan must be rated for continuous operation. If the system includes automatic fan controls, they must activate the fan whenever someone is in the garage and for at least an hour afterward.

If you live in certain areas of the country, you should also be concerned about radon gas seeping into your home. Radon, an odorless gas that is produced by decaying uranium, can enter a home through cracks in walls, basement floors, and the foundation. It is the leading cause of lung cancer among nonsmokers. The good news is that after years of research and public awareness campaigns, it's pretty clear which regions of the country are most likely to have a radon problem. It is easy to determine whether your home might be a candidate by doing an Internet search or by contacting your local building department. Best practices for mitigating radon haven't changed in years. You need to put in gravel and plastic sheeting below the slab, fully seal and caulk foundation cracks, and run plastic vent pipe from below the slab through the roof. It's a good idea to install an attic receptacle so you could easily add an electric fan to the vent pipe if needed.

DESPITE ALL THE GOOD SCIENCE, green homes suffer from a fundamental problem: They aren't sexy candidates for advertising campaigns. That's because builders, by and large, do a miserable job marketing the positive lifestyle attributes of living in a green home. We decided to tackle this problem three years ago by designing a super-green show home with partners KB Home and Martha Stewart, the lifestyle maven who was deep into green living at the time; deeper, it turned out, than anyone expected. The home incorporated all the green products and features that you would expect. All the products were selected with the goal of limiting off-gassing, maximizing recycled content, and reducing waste.

What made the home markedly different was our attempt to portray a sustainable lifestyle. That started by making sure the main living areas of the house were suffused with healthy, inviting natural light. To provide plenty of fresh air, we used retractable sliding glass doors to connect an immaculate, beautifully organized kitchen—what else

This show home built with Martha Stewart and KB Home was designed to demonstrate the benefits of a green lifestyle. Those benefits start with abundant sunlight and fresh air. But they also include motion detectors to turn off the lights or send hot water, and a bin under the kitchen counter for recycling vegetable scraps.

would you expect from Martha Stewart?—to a generously sized back porch that was ideal for entertaining. The home was equipped with a variety of hidden features that automatically reduced energy consumption, like motion detectors that turned off lights when you left a room. It included all the accoutrements needed to grow your own vegetables, such as a stainless-steel bucket under the kitchen counter to catch vegetable scraps, animal fat, and other organic waste, and a compost pit and garden in the backyard. Martha surprised reporters at our press conference when she announced that none of her homes, not even her New York City apartment, had a garbage disposal.

Our demonstration home included a simple program on a home computer that showed owners how much power their home produced and used each day, as opposed to waiting until utility bills arrive at the end of the month. The idea was to reinforce positive behavior so that homeowners would think twice before leaving the doors open on a hot day or failing to turn off lights as they left a room. The system was connected to the Internet so that you could check on things—turn down the air conditioning, for instance—from a smartphone or computer while you were away. We proudly displayed the monitor in a kitchen alcove where visitors would notice and ask about it. It could become a point of pride at cocktail parties. (Two years later, KB Home includes in all its homes a cloud-based energy-management system that tracks energy usage by dollars and kilowatts down to the hour. The system can be upgraded with smart plugs to monitor individual appliances.)

Speaking of cool stories to tell at parties, the show home included motion detectors in the bathroom that triggered a message to send hot water to faucets and showers when someone entered the room. A button in the kitchen served the same purpose. The beauty of the system is that hot water doesn't sit cooling in pipes. The typical hot water distribution system wastes 10 to 15 percent of the energy it consumes, according to government data. Shorter plumbing runs increased the home's efficiency, as well. Water was heated on a rooftop panel, stored in an 80-gallon tank in the garage, then routed through a compact distribution system. Each plumbing route off the main loop was less than 10 feet long.

A big part of any green building project, one measured by most green building programs, is not wasting material to build the house. KB Home is particularly fanatical about this; the builder kept its construction waste to an absolute minimum, which isn't always easy to do on a show-home project where you may use unfamiliar vendors. The builder made sure not to order too much material by carefully calculating from the architect's blueprints exactly how much it would need. Some builders rely on their supplier to do their so-called blueprint takeoffs. That can result in overestimating materials and purchasing unneeded lumber and panels. Some suppliers overestimate in good faith. They want to make sure running out of materials doesn't slow the project. Losing time on a project to order more material may cost a builder more in the long run than paying for too much material. Other suppliers overestimate to pad their profits. Compounding the problem, builders may not carefully monitor their subcontractors to determine whether they are wasting material in construction. KB deals with this by providing its subcontractors with detailed drawings for cuts and installation. The end result is that KB filled up less than two dumpsters with waste on this project, far less than is typical.

Builders have plenty of incentive to reduce construction waste. Financial motivation comes from escalating fees, so-called tipping fees, to haul the trash away, not to mention the transportation costs to get the unnecessary material to the job site in the first place. The National Association of Home Builders found in a 2009 study that the typical new 2,000-square-foot home generates 8,000 pounds of waste, most of it in wood, cardboard, and drywall—though metal, vinyl, and masonry waste is produced as well. Roughly 80 percent of the waste, it found, is recyclable. Estimates are that construction waste accounts for between 25 percent and 40 percent of the solid waste that winds up in the nation's landfills. That's a huge number and a major cause for concern.

There are several things you can do to cut down on waste in building your new home. The first is to use a builder with a track record of building efficiently. Another is to substitute salvaged material for new material when appropriate. A whole new industry of localized building-material salvage haulers and dealers has developed in the last 15 to 20 years. We made use of such a network in 2003 when we built a duplex with Habitat for Humanity® in Annapolis, Md. The first order of business was to tear down a derelict building located only blocks from the state capitol. We found condom wrappers and syringes inside the dilapidated structure, which had become a hangout for drug dealers. But we also found some beautiful old beams that could be salvaged, along with lattice in a historic pattern. Instead of throwing it away, we called a firm that took it to a nonprofit company with a warehouse in Baltimore that would reuse the material mostly on inner-city projects. Had our work been for an individual rather than a nonprofit, the owner would have qualified for a tax credit for the donation. We went back to the warehouse later to find a few things that we needed for the building exterior to help the new structure fit in the historic neighborhood.

Our architect on this project, Wayne Speight, made heavy use of a salvaged material network. Several years ago, when a client wanted to build a Mediterranean-style house, unusual for Annapolis, that would require a tile roof and exposed timber, he charged his salvage dealer with finding the material. Sure enough, the dealer called one day to say he was demolishing a home with a clay-tile roof. The client and his son rented a truck to collect the 5,000 square feet of tile, paying only $500. The client, who wanted a mix-and-match look in the roof, wound up having to pay market rates—about 100 times more—for the second color of tile. The dealer managed to find the timbers, too, which the client and his son also fetched. "The owner used his Harley to drag chains over them to give them a distressed look," Speight recalled.

If you do wind up with leftover material—and it seems inevitable considering how difficult it is to order the exact amount of material for a new home—you may be able to recycle it rather than clog the landfill. If the material is in good shape, you also may be able to donate it to a local Habitat for Humanity affiliate for use on one of the organization's next homes. Nonprofits have sprung up in major metro areas that specialize in salvaging reusable material. They can help you find a second use for the material. Wood can be recycled into reclaimed or composite-wood products such as furniture and plastic/wood-composite decks as well as mulch. (You don't want to reuse treated wood, though.) Asphalt, concrete, and rubble can be recycled into aggregate or new asphalt and concrete products. Metals, including steel, copper, and brass, are a valuable commodity to recycle. Waste not, want not.

GREEN BUYERS AND BUILDERS have been aided in their quest by significant advances in the quality of green building material and improved transparency among building-product companies. Early-generation green products, which first hit the market 20 years ago, often left much to be desired. Builders complained that the first low-volatile-organic-compound (VOC) paints, for instance, didn't cover surfaces that well. Today you can find low- and no-VOC paints that are every bit as good as mineral-based ones. There was also negative feedback to the first low-flow (1.8 gallons per flush) toilets. Builders and their customers beefed that they had to be flushed twice. That led to the creation of a black market for the older, more reliable ones that used 3.6 gallons per flush. In recent years, a new generation of highly efficient toilets that use only slightly more than 1 gallon to flush has arrived on the scene. People marvel at their efficiency, though builders say that not all brands are equal.

Twenty years ago, when I was editing a building-material retailing magazine, you had to search long and hard to find retailers with the guts to carry "environmentally friendly" products. Our search then for green retailers took us to the Soho district of New York City, where an environmental lumberyard sold a quirky collection of products that included insulation made from blue jeans and floor tile composed of golf tees, broken glass, and plastic scrap. The store displayed small samples of early low-VOC paints and steel-framing systems. (Whether steel framing is greener than wood framing is still the subject of intense debate, since steel takes a lot of energy to produce.) Many of these early green products had to be special ordered, which always involves a cost and potential delays. The stuff wasn't cheap.

Mainstream retailers reasoned that few people wanted to buy green goods because of higher prices and reliability fears. And they weren't getting much help from their vendors. At the time, some manufacturers almost covertly were using synthetic gypsum taken from scrubbers at coal-fired utilities to make drywall. Vinyl siding companies employed resin from recycled soda bottles to produce their product. But the companies didn't market these advances for fear that competitors would argue that they produced inferior products. Green wasn't gold then, as it is today. Now, you can walk down the aisles of a Lowe's® or Home Depot℠ and buy fluorescent lightbulbs and fixtures that cost a fraction of what they sold for 20 years ago. Most paints sold today are made with solutions that include far fewer VOCs, if any at all. Virtually every faucet in the plumbing aisle economizes on water flow, thanks largely to government regulation. You can buy green cleaning materials for the home and even organic fertilizer for the yard. It's a whole new, greener world.

FIFTEEN YEARS AGO, IT WAS A THANKLESS TASK to report on green building products. Most manufacturers didn't want to talk about where they sourced their raw material or where the waste from their factory processes went; they didn't want to give competitors a marketing edge. Even in 2008, when we tried to gather information to build a super-green modular show home with LivingHomes (based in Santa Monica, Calif.) for the International Builders Show, it was a bear finding manufacturers who could give us the information that we needed to work toward our goal: LEED Platinum. Part of the problem was that manufacturers in their marketing materials would trumpet one product attribute—that it contributed to cleaner indoor air, for instance—then upon further digging you'd find it was made from virgin materials, recalled Amy Sims, the design director for LivingHomes, who worked closely with us on the project. "Just because the product comes from the earth doesn't make it sustainable," she said, noting the environmental havoc that cutting down trees in any forest can have.

After extensive research, Sims settled on an unusual exterior cladding for the home—bio-composite panels made with resin, sawdust, and laminate that were more often used on commercial buildings. The 4-by-8-foot panels were shipped flat on trucks, then reassembled on the show floor in a staggered pattern to hide the telltale horizontal seams of a modular structure. The deck on the front of the home was built from composite decking largely made from recycled plastic bags and wood waste. The composite Andersen® windows were manufactured from 43 percent preconsumer recycled content, a combination of sawdust and polymer largely reclaimed from the manufacturing plant.

Our interior designers led by Don Anderson had a field day selecting the interiors, many of which were sourced locally to reduce shipping costs. They found side tables made from old railroad ties; modular coffee tables, bureaus, and bookshelves manufactured with reclaimed wood from old buildings; a dining room table built with glued-together scrap furniture remnants; a handwoven bamboo floor lamp; and a table and chairs made of recyclable polypropylene (see the photo on p. 96). Picture frames, built with wood from reforested trees, displayed art printed on cotton canvases with low-VOC inks. Recycled glass was used to make the countertops and tiles. The showstopper on tours, though, was the desk chairs made from vintage advertising rulers. Dozens of people wanted the source for those.

Two years after we built the show home and the LEED standard had permeated the industry, it was easier to find green products and compare competing claims. When I strolled the floor of a trade show for floor and wall covering companies in 2010, for instance, most major manufacturers—not just the boutique vendors—had a clearer story

The interiors for the LivingHomes show home featured a wide variety of finish and furnishings with recycled content, including countertops made with recycled glass and coffee tables built from reclaimed wood. Thanks to a strong energy and conservation program, the modular home achieved a LEED Platinum designation.

to tell. The biggest change was that companies were talking openly about how much post- and preconsumer waste was used in everything from floor tile to tin ceilings. Stuff that would have otherwise clogged landfills was being used to create some pretty funky products. Sometimes that meant investing in new equipment and processes that could work with lower-grade raw materials. That was the case with flooring giant Mannington®, which in 2010 came out with a new premium tile line made with 25 percent postconsumer content. Mannington said, tile makers using previous manufacturing technology, were only comfortable going to 5 percent postconsumer content. Another example: Half the metal in Crossville®'s lightweight metal tile, Urban Renewal, came from the scrapyard.

Ever wonder whether there's a use for the old tires you see piled up in landfills? While walking the show floor, I found a company, Foam Products, that turns rubber tire crumbs into acoustical underlayment that's made with 30 to 40 percent recycled material; it adds an anti-microbial treatment to make the material resist mold, mildew, and bacteria. Another company, Dal-Tile, uses the glass bottles faithfully recycled in many American kitchens, restaurants, and bars to make two tile lines, Color Scheme and Urban Tones, that contain more than 60 percent recycled content. So, theoretically, pieces of the bottle you recycle in your kitchen could return home in a tile backsplash. All in all, some pretty far-out countertop materials have hit the market in recent years. Companies started with ground-up quartz products that were an immediate hit and then branched out. One countertop maker, Consentino, grinds up salvaged mirrors, windows, bottle glass, porcelain, and residue from industrial furnaces to make its ECO by Consentino® countertops. A full three-quarters of the content comes from industrial and postconsumer recycled waste.

Carpet makers, among the first to incorporate postconsumer waste into their products, keep upping the ante. Carpeting giant Beaulieu®, for instance, guarantees that its Nexterra carpet tile consists of at least 50 percent postconsumer content. Some of that matter may come from job sites. Beaulieu, like many major carpet companies these days, takes pieces left over after installation and recycles them into new carpet. Shaw®, another big carpet company, runs a recycling operation in Augusta, Ga., that converts nylon carpet back to its original material, something called caprolactam, and mixes it with virgin material to make new nylon fiber.

BUILDING PRODUCT COMPANIES ARE NOW much more transparent about the virgin materials used to produce their products. That's partly because they try to stay one step ahead of new building standards by substituting benign ingredients for hazardous ones. This is especially true in the caulking and coatings industry, where manufacturers have been working for two decades to develop products without VOCs—some of which have been linked to a variety of health problems, even cancer—that coat and cover as well as their old lines. The process started with low-VOC paints, caulking, and sealants. The new battleground is no-VOC products; we used a line from Sherwin-

Williams® in our green modular home. Even paints are being made with recycled content. Kelly-Moore™, for instance, offers an eCoat line of interior and exterior paint in 16 colors with 50 percent consumer waste, most of it old paint that's remanufactured for consistency.

Some green standards give points to builders who use products that are produced in an environmentally benign way. Building-product companies have helped by disclosing the energy efficiency of their manufacturing process. They may market the fact that they use scraps from their own factories to make products. Healthier Choice Premium Carpet Cushion says its acoustical underlayment and carpet cushions are made at a "zero-landfill" facility. (It also uses more than 50 percent natural ingredients, including soybean oil.) Bon Ton Designs, one of several companies that issue an "environmental statement," recycles unused clay scraps and seconds into future projects. It sells defective tiles to local artisans at bargain prices. Even the chairs and tables in its offices are secondhand. "Many of these items were headed to landfills before we found them," notes the environmental statement.

Some products with recycled content actually perform better than competitors made with virgin materials. Drywall made with synthetic gypsum, taken from the scrubbers of coal-burning power plants of all places, is a case in point. Coal-burning utilities use limestone or lime to neutralize carbon dioxide emissions. The process produces synthetic gypsum, also known as calcium sulfate, which is significantly purer than gypsum mined from open pits. It produces drywall that's easier to shape and install, and, because of its smooth finish, is easier to decorate and repair as well. For these reasons, and because utilities produce a steady supply of the raw material, most new drywall plants in this country use synthetic gypsum. It's used in more than one-third of gypsum produced in the United States.

The source of lumber is a huge concern when determining a home's carbon footprint because so much is used, about 13,127 feet of lumber boards on average. Laid out end to end, they would extend 2½ miles. It's no wonder that new residential construction accounts for at least one third of the softwood harvested each year in this country. Thirty years ago, forest-products companies would fell trees, mill the wood into lumber and panels, ship materials all over the country, and nobody seemed to pay much attention. Contentious national debates 20 years ago over cutting down old-growth forests changed all that. Consumers demanded to know where the lumber to build homes had come from, whether old-growth trees had been cut down to produce big beams, whether forests had been replanted, and if streams and rivers had been polluted in the process. Debate became especially heated when lumber companies cut down trees on public lands with the blessing of the U.S. Forest Service.

Even before disagreement over forestry practices erupted, manufacturers were making advances to produce engineered lumber made from scraps and small-diameter trees. Many of the structural wood products, from big I-beams that span long distances to studs made by joining small pieces of wood together in "finger joints" with glue, actually perform better than their solid-sawn counterparts. That's because they are engineered and manufactured for strength and stability. (The same can't be said about engineered wood such as particleboard and fiber-based boards specified for indoor use; they may be more prone to humidity-induced warping.) Moreover, long lengths of widely available engineered wood beams, made by gluing together laminates or constructing wood I-beams, have opened up new architectural vistas. They make it possible to span longer runs in homes, open floor plans, and create more dynamic spaces.

Engineered lumber is generally considered a green alternative to solid-sawn lumber, but the calculation is not cut and dried. A big part of the purchase price of lumber, about half in some cases, is tied up in transportation—from the mill or factory to a distributor, to a retailer, and then to the job site. A lot of fossil fuel is burned along the way. It also requires more energy to manufacture engineered lumber than the solid-sawn variety. So, if you live near a sawmill, the greenest alternative may be to use solid-sawn lumber cut from local trees. Also, most engineered lumber is put together with glues that often contain formaldehyde, though it's possible to find some that isn't. Even so, off-gassing from engineered wood, including plywood and oriented strand board, is considered negligible.

If you are going to use solid-sawn lumber, and you want your home to be as green as possible, then you need to be concerned with the harvest practices used to produce it. Two major organizations publish standards that dictate how wood is grown and harvested. FSC lumber—the acronym stands for the Forest Stewardship Council, an international organization—is considered the tougher of the two. Established in 1993, FSC sends teams of foresters, ecologists, and social scientists to inspect FSC-certified forests, which must grow as much timber as they harvest each year. Inspectors make sure that healthy forest conditions for wildlife and a healthy ecosystem are maintained and that rare and endangered species are protected. Accreditors also check the chain of custody to ensure that FSC wood isn't mixed with other wood on its way to the job site. Only about one-quarter of North America's forests carry the FSC certification. The other, far more common standard, the Sustainable Forestry Initiative (SFI), was launched by the U.S. timber industry in 1994. Like the FSC, the SFI promotes wood that comes from sustainably managed forests that protect regional biodiversity, soil erosion, and water quality. And under both standards, certifiers check to see whether an appropriate chain of custody is followed. But the SFI allows companies to make claims about how much of their product comes from certified land, how much contains recycled product, and how much is "noncertified, noncontroversial" forest content. As a general rule, the SFI puts more trust in self-regulation and local laws.

Currently, the U.S. Green Building Council, under its LEED standard, rewards one point for using FSC-certified wood. But after a major lobbying effort by the timber industry, it has floated a proposal that would allow one point for using SFI-certified wood, too. The organization grants an additional point for using wood that was sourced within 500 miles of the building site.

Although green products are coming down in price, and in many cases sell for the same as traditional ones, it still costs a premium to build a green home. That left builders during the housing recession searching for ways to reduce construction costs, yet still build homes that conserve energy and water, produce a clean indoor air environment, and tread as lightly as possible on the planet. The solutions, it turned out, weren't hard to find. Builders discovered that the trail had been blazed years before by government-funded researchers who had identified dozens of wasteful, commonly used construction techniques. They adopted the principles of high-performance home construction, the subject of the next chapter. ❖

CHAPTER SIX

Performance Takes Center Stage

YOU'VE HEARD OF HIGH-PERFORMANCE CARS. Typically built for extreme speed with a sleek futurist design, they cost so much that only the elite can afford them. Well, many of the best builders in the country today build something called a high-performance home, and it tends to be much more attainable, in relative terms. The term *high-performance home*, like "green home," can mean many different things—it could be a very green house, a super-energy-efficient house, or even a net-zero house. The common denominator is that the home went through an engineering analysis of its design, construction, and operation. High performance starts with taking waste out of construction by employing modern building science developed during the last half century. Many of these "radical" methods finally caught on in recent years as builders looked for ways to offset the added cost of green homes.

Despite the groundswell of innovation, it's sad but true that many homes are still built the same way they were 60 years ago, especially when it comes to the building shell. Builders routinely use too much lumber to frame and rough in the home. The biggest issues for notoriously conservative builders are that the home doesn't fall down and that there's enough material on the job site when subcontractors need it—time is money and you don't want to slow down a job. Many builders who've been at it for a long time feel no need to change the way they build. Most home-building and subcontractor businesses are family-owned, with building knowledge passed down from father to son or from master to tradesman. Subcontractors develop their own way of doing things, too. Many people working at frame or trim carpentry companies, including the principals, don't read engineering trade journals. They may not know that span tables for wood products have changed or that new best practices have emerged.

That's a shame because a slew of advanced framing methods have been developed, analyzed, and promoted over the last 40 years, techniques that not only require less wood but also produce a better-performing house. These improvements present a golden opportunity to take the savings from wasteful construction practices and use them to upgrade mechanical, electrical, and fenestration systems that will result in better homes with lower operating costs. Many of these so-called *advanced framing techniques* can be traced back to a 1977 report done by the NAHB Research Foundation for the U.S. Department of Housing and Urban Development (HUD). The study, "Reducing Home Building Costs with OVE (Optimal Value Engineering) Design and Construction," was commissioned by HUD as part of its "Operation Breakthrough" program—an effort aimed at jumpstarting a moribund construction industry through an emphasis on building technology. Interestingly, most recommendations in this report remain viable, and they are still being pushed, with some updating, by government agencies and research organizations.

We employed many of the techniques in our Homelink show home, built in Atlanta in 2002. The goal was to demonstrate how you could frame with less lumber, engineer the HVAC system to do more for less, and use the savings to buy energy-conserving windows, beefed-up insulation, and fresh-air ventilators. Prevailing opinion in building-science circles was that a properly engineered frame would require 5 to 10 percent less lumber and use 30 fewer pieces, which meant the frame could be erected faster and cheaper. To guide the process

The 2002 Homelink show home was built with strictly engineered framing and HVAC systems. The concept was to save on lumber by using modern-day framing techniques and downsize heating and cooling equipment by improving the system for hot and cold air delivery. The savings were used to buy upgraded windows and a heat-recovery ventilator, among other energy-saving features. Builders of high-performance homes employ a similar strategy today.

and develop the construction plan, we enlisted the help of Joe Lstiburek, founder of the Building Science Corporation in Westford, Mass. The fiery, strongly opinionated Lstiburek is widely considered the leading advocate of high-performance housing in America.

The most difficult day on the project may have been when our builder, Morrison Homes, which now goes by the name Taylor Morrison, sat down with its trade partners to go over the framing plan. It called for 2x6 rather than 2x4 studs to frame the home, spaced 24 inches apart rather than the standard 16 inches. Many builders shy away from 2x6s because they cost more. But because they are stronger and can be spaced farther apart, you can actually reduce the board feet of lumber required to build the home. Moreover, the extra space between studs spaced 24 inches apart leaves more room for insulation in the building shell; estimates are that the wall cavity can support 60 percent more insulation. With less lumber, heating and cooling loss through the studs is reduced, and electricians and plumbers have to drill through fewer studs. We used R-19 fiberglass batt insulation in our demonstration, since most builders are accustomed to using batts. However, most high-performance builders today prefer spray insulation because it forms a better seal.

The next step, and perhaps the scariest one for anyone new to these techniques, was employing *in-line framing*. Basically, this involves lining up the house frames so that the first floor supports the second and the second floor holds up the roof—roof framing and trusses are designed to line up with the wall and floor framing. As long as loads are transferred in this fashion, there's no need for a redundant support system for the second story. To give the stacked walls added racking strength, we applied plywood sheer panels—modular units built with 2x4 frames—at designated intervals. We also gave the framers a stack of drawings showing them how to build key details of the home that could save lumber and provide more space for insulation.

The shell was a beautiful sight when we showed up for our customary frame walk. The 2x6 studs, even though there were fewer of them, looked more substantial, creating the perception that the home was built better. With fewer holes drilled by plumbers and electricians, the

The wall framing holds up the roof in the Homelink show home, designed with so-called "in-line" framing to economize on lumber use. With the help of a building scientist, we employed the full panoply of value-engineering techniques, including 2x6 studs, single headers and top plates, and special corners that make it easier to provide more insulation. The tactics result in a cleaner, sturdier frame.

interior walls looked more orderly, too. The corners of the frame, per Lstiburek's instructions, were built with two studs instead of three, a technique that allows insulation to be fitted into the corner wall cavity. We eliminated unnecessary studs around window openings—so-called jack and cripple studs—that weren't load bearing. Most framers install them as a matter of course. We used single instead of the customary double headers over windows, doors, and garage doors. Since the first and second floors lined up, we could use only one instead of two top plates for the walls for load transfer. Many framers think a second top plate is needed to straighten out walls, but that's the job of the floor and roof diaphragms. Taken together, the techniques added up to a big lumber savings.

DESPITE A PROVEN TRACK RECORD, some builders remain skeptical of advanced framing methods. One complaint is that interior walls can be wavy because of the extra space between framing members, which Lstiburek insists is not a problem. To give the walls more sheer strength, some subs may want to specify $\frac{5}{8}$-inch drywall, which is thicker and more expensive than the usual $\frac{1}{2}$-inch variety; it's another safeguard that may not be necessary. Some framers may use finger-jointed studs as a precaution because they are straighter. Trim carpenters may also complain that it's more difficult to hang cabinets when studs are spaced farther apart and there are fewer of them. Putting in wood blocks behind the drywall to accept screws and nails can overcome that problem. One legitimate downside to framing with 2x6s is that most prehung windows and doors are sized to fit into openings left by 2x4s.

When the Homelink home was built, there was heightened concern over "black mold" that was showing up in some supertight homes. Lstiburek developed an ideal response to the warm, moist Atlanta climate, even as he warned that different specifications would be needed in hot, dry climates or cold Northern ones. The guiding principle for this home was to keep rainwater outside and minimize moisture buildup inside. We cloaked the exterior of the frame with 1-inch plastic (EPS) sheathing, joined vertically in shiplap fashion. Each joint had its own flashing—a 6-inch-wide strip of polyethylene foam sheeting placed like Z-flashing over the bottom panel and under the top. The foam sheet was designed to serve as a vapor barrier, preventing humid air from entering the home. Moisture forming on the outside would conveniently drain to the ground. We used latex paint on the interior drywall so that moisture wouldn't build up in wall cavities. The drywall would still act as an air barrier, keeping air-conditioned air in the home on hot summer days.

HVAC systems in new homes often get overspecified because builders depend on subcontractors to size them. The bigger the system, of course, the more the subcontractor gets paid. And builders would rather be safe than sorry—the last thing they want is to be called back because a buyer complains that a room is too hot or too cold. But we wanted our system to be sized just right. So, Morrison Homes asked its HVAC subcontractor to estimate the size (tonnage) of the equipment needed to heat and cool the house. Meanwhile, Lstiburek did his own calculation, based on the improved energy performance of the shell, the energy-conserving windows we had specified, and the series of dampers he wanted to install throughout the house that would distribute heated and cooled air where it was actually needed. Lstiburek's estimate came in at about half of what the HVAC supplier suggested. We compromised on an ultra-efficient, two-speed condensing unit that could adjust to any demand between 2½ and 4 tons.

Lstiburek gave the duct system a thorough overhaul. The biggest problem with ducts in the South is that, when they leak, the air-conditioning system compensates by going into overdrive. To mitigate this problem, Lstiburek simplified and downsized the system, reducing the length of duct runs and keeping them within conditioned spaces. He devised a system of passive airflow through the rooms, which eliminated the need for multiple air-return ducts. The home's tight envelope meant that airflow could be carefully controlled. Air moved passively through grilles in stud cavities and through short ducts in the floors and ceilings between rooms. Remarkably, the home included only one return air duct. Eight electronic dampers in the supply ducts (which cost about $1,500) were programmed to direct heating or air conditioning where it was needed. The system depended on efficiently delivering fresh air through an energy-recovery ventilator instead of relying on leaky walls and windows. The ventilator not only replaced stale air with fresh air in the house but also cleaned it to hold down pollution levels.

WE REVISITED HIGH-PERFORMANCE HOUSING several years later in our virtual reality Home for the New Economy project (see p. 49). Our designer, Marianne Cusato, used a simple rectangular footprint and a modest gabled roof, which would make the home easier, faster, and cheaper to build than a house with lots of bump-outs and roof treatments. A rectangular form also provides the most living space for the buck. Cusato considered the standard 8-foot dimensions of sheet goods, such as plywood and drywall, as she designed the home so that as little lumber and sheet goods as possible would be cut on site. She also limited window selections to a few sizes, operating under the philosophy that it's better to design a strong 6-foot window and trim detail and repeat it consistently than to muddle up the face of the house with 10 competing treatments that create the appearance of a facade in the back lot of a movie studio.

Cusato consulted with a pair of building efficiency experts— builder and author Fernando Pagés Ruiz and building scientist Mark LaLiberte, a leading high-performance housing advocate. The pair immediately recommended that the kitchen and baths be stacked on top of each other, a configuration that permits shorter plumbing runs. They designed cutaways for the virtual rendering that revealed how the home was framed with 2x6-inch studs, providing bigger cavities for insulation, and built with the single top plates and headers that characterized advanced framing techniques. As with the Homelink show home, the lumber savings, coupled with a downsized HVAC system and shorter duct runs, allowed us to budget for better-performing windows and higher-efficiency heating and cooling. The end result is a home that needs less electricity and gas to operate.

USING THE FULL COMPLEMENT of high-performance techniques, building scientists say, can reduce thermal transfer through walls by 16 to 25 percent. But there are other ways to crack this nut. Some builders today, most of them in northern climates, build a double-wall system, with separate interior and exterior walls, which obviates thermal transfer through framing members. Other builders insist on using structural insulated panels. Still others swear by insulated concrete systems, which can take several forms—typically foam is combined with concrete to create the wall. Even formerly esoteric alternative building systems, such as rammed-earth or straw-bale construction, are enjoying a small renaissance. In each case, the idea is to attack thermal transfer between interior and exterior walls.

Alternative building systems should get a boost from the new Energy Star version 3 standards, which require building shells with thermal breaks. The challenge for anyone considering a home built with one of these systems is to balance the construction cost per square foot, along with labor savings, against energy savings and improved durability. Most calculations will show that it's cheaper up front to build with traditional 2x4 wood-framed walls and do a good job insulating them. And builders tend to gravitate toward the least expensive alternative to keep their homes affordable. But nearly every alternative system produces a more energy-efficient and, in some cases, more durable home that will save owners money in the long run. Here's a quick rundown of the most popular alternative systems:

Rammed earth. This is the way most homes are built throughout the world. Builders create walls in part from dirt on the job site, a pretty sustainable practice, to be sure. While rammed-earth construction may be down to earth, it also involves an element of mysticism. The best builders profess an ability to simply feel the dirt on site and know how much water and concrete to add to form a strong wall. Most crews, however, follow a mix schedule based on soil properties. Walls are built by packing layers of moist dirt into sturdy forms and adding concrete. The wall gets its strength from the density of the mix. Walls are usually sealed with an acrylic.

Architects and designers have seized on rammed earth to create some amazing, award-winning homes in recent years. Intriguing patterns can be designed by varying the proportion of fine and coarse material, mineral colors, and even gravel angles. The type of formwork, strata alignment, and compaction technique also influence the finished appearance. But rammed-earth walls don't just look good; they can outperform many other systems on the basis of thermal and acoustic performance. They work marvelously in arid climates with hot days and cold nights, retaining heat during the day and releasing it back into the house at night. The process works in reverse during the day to help cool the home. It's important to build 12-inch-thick walls to get the full thermal lag potential.

Adobe block. This may be the next best thing to rammed earth. Basically, contractors pour a mixture of sand, clay, water, and some kind of organic material (usually either sticks or straw but sometimes manure) into a machine on site that produces blocks used to build walls. Although it takes about 5,000 blocks to build the exterior walls of a 1,500-square-foot home, the typical machine can produce two to 10 blocks per minute. At five per minute, that's 300 per hour, or 3,000 in a 10-hour workday. The blocks are a sustainable alternative to wood, since they are typically made from local materials rather than transported from a lumber mill. Like rammed earth, adobe blocks have thermal and acoustic benefits superior to wood. Plus, bugs don't eat them, and they don't burn.

Steel. Interest in steel framing peaks when lumber prices spike. Steel advocates like to market their product as a more sustainable product than wood, particularly lumber cut from old-growth forests. Many steel studs used today contain recycled steel. But lumber advocates shoot back by pointing out steel's high propensity for thermal transfer. That's why most steel-framing systems employ insulation either on the outside of exterior walls or in between two steel framing members. One common system, with polystyrene foam panels placed between steel-framing members, produces 6½-inch walls with an R-value of 25. Building Sciences Corporation recommends concentrating insulation, at least 2 inches, on the outside of the frame.

Insulated concrete forms (ICFs). This technology can take a variety of forms, so to speak. In one, foam forms are filled with concrete pumped from a truck, then steel reinforcing bars are run through the cells to provide added stability. In another, concrete blocks are filled on site with sprayed polyurethane insulation and steel tension bars. Depending on location, the initial cost of these systems may be higher than stick framing—another term for wood framing—but they typically perform better thermally, resulting in energy savings. The composite systems typically form a wall 6 to 8 inches thick, providing an R-value in the low to high 20s, again better than a typical wood frame.

Straw bales. Yes, we're talking about using baled straw from wheat, oats, barley, rye, and other grains to create walls that are then covered with stucco. You can pick up some real environmental points by using this material because it's waste that farmers may sell to landscape suppliers or use as animal bedding. Straw bales, an ancient building material, were used to build homes on the Plains during the early settlement of this country. They were also common in the Southwest because of their ability to provide thermal mass that keeps homes cool. Straw bales experienced a comeback in the 1990s, when several cities and California passed a straw-bale construction code. There are two basic types of straw-bale construction: post and beam, and structural. The bales support the weight of the roof and provide an R-value in the high 20s.

Structural insulated panels (SIPS). Most builders who stick-frame identify SIPs as the alternative building method with the most promise, though they still aren't that common. SIPs not only provide a thermal break between interior and exterior spaces but also can be installed

Structural insulated panels go up in a Phoenix subdivision. Production builders are enamored with SIPs because they can be installed quickly and provide a thermal barrier between indoor and outdoor spaces. SIPs are often better suited for warmer climates because most panels don't provide much added insulation compared with other alternative building systems.

quickly. SIPs are basically panels with an insulating foam core sandwiched between two structural facings, commonly oriented strand board. The panels are typically taped together to form an airtight seal. As with all alternative building methods, SIPs require some different construction procedures. First, plumbing and electrical runs must go along the inside of the wall. Second, it's difficult to move windows and doors after the frame is built. So, you need to carefully analyze where they should be to begin with. One potential drawback: The typical SIP panel may not have enough insulation to produce a high-performance home in cold climates.

Double-wall systems. Some builders have switched to double-wall systems to improve thermal performance. Typically, they build two walls. The interior wall is often not structural, which means that stud spacing can be wider and smaller lumber may be used. You may lose some interior wall space, and unless the rim joist is detailed correctly, you may encounter problems with thermal heat loss and moisture. One advantage to this system, though, besides superior energy performance, is that it's easier to wire and plumb because of wide-open access prior to installing insulation. That's great when smart home wiring requires placing low-voltage wiring well away from line voltage.

The Sage demonstration project in Eugene, Ore. (see p. 27) employed double walls (only the outside wall was load-bearing) with separate plates, built with staggered 2x4s that sandwiched soy-based spray insulation. The system added to the cost of the project, but it contributed to an energy package that resulted in electric bills in the $40-a-month range. Bill Randall, the project architect, continues to use spray insulation. But instead of just applying open-cell insulation, he now applies a flash coat of more expensive, denser closed-cell insulation under the open-cell insulation to get a higher R-value without a big increase in cost.

You can't just call any builder or architect and ask for a home built with insulated concrete walls or rammed earth. You are better off trying to find one accustomed to working with the material. The good news is that many more builders today have gained experience with those systems as they worked to build better energy-performing homes during the recession. They learned that unless you first build the most energy-efficient building possible, it doesn't make sense to wow people with photovoltaic panels that produce energy. Otherwise, you wind up installing a photovoltaic system that's too big and too expensive. The beauty of high-performance techniques is that if you get the engineering right and you take some other measured steps, you can wind up with a home that produces all the energy it needs. ❖

CHAPTER SEVEN

The Quest for Net Zero

ONE OF THE MOST EXCITING ADVANCES of the last several years has been the rise of cost-efficient net-zero homes that produce as much energy as they consume. For a reporter who started covering home building in the late 1970s, when visions of building self-sufficient homes that could operate free of the oil cartel were rampant, this is a dream come true. Building energy self-sufficient homes has been possible for a long time, of course. But it typically involved a big investment in an alternative energy-efficient building system, along with passive and active solar technologies. Only certain builders—they seem to wear beards and ponytails—knew how to build these homes correctly, and they often built them for themselves or friends in sunny spots in the deep woods. During particularly cloudy spells, as my friend Rick Schwolsky, a solar builder from Vermont, used to say, receiving a fax might prove problematic.

In recent years, net-zero home building has gone mainstream. It has reached the point where even large homebuilders, who may wear coats and ties to work, offer new homes that can function independent of the electrical grid. Builders sell energy independence just as they sell pools or an extra garage bay—it's just another $35,000 option. That's roughly the added cost to convert a super-energy-efficient home with a HERS rating in the low 40s into a net-zero home. But the cost of photovoltaic arrays, the biggest component of that incremental cost, keeps dropping thanks to economies of scale and more production in China. In the meantime, progressive builders have found ways to engineer costs out of their homes to pay for energy upgrades. Today you can find cutting-edge builders who offer net-zero features as a "free" option to induce sales. The movement is only going to gather steam in coming years. The state of California, as is often the case, is ahead of the game; it has mandated that all new homes be net zero by the year 2025.

All of this happened pretty quickly. We built one of the first net-zero show homes with the help of U.S. Department of Energy (DOE) consultants for the International Builders Show back in 2005. To be honest, at 5,300 square feet, our Ultimate Family Home was mostly a lesson in overkill. The home was efficient for its time, but it was too big and too energy inefficient to serve as a model. To power a home of this size required specifying a huge, 8-kilowatt photovoltaic system. We had trouble finding enough room for the panels; they not only covered one side of the roof but also a trellis network in the backyard. We diverted attention from the trellis by building a fantasy backyard for children of all ages, complete with a fake mountain and a pool slide. At roughly $250,000, the photovoltaic system cost enough to build a nice trade-up home in the inexpensive Las Vegas market. Also, the home was net zero in only a theoretical sense because the local utility at the time wasn't required to buy our excess electrical power as it is today. Need-less to say, we learned a great deal on the project. When the home sold for more than the asking price, we were relieved.

Four years later, in 2009, to focus further attention on the net-zero concept, DOE commissioned All American Homes® to build a much more modest Living Zero Home and cart it around to about 16 locations throughout the country. The demonstration project toured middle-size markets such as Louisville, Ky., and Greensboro, N.C., in addition to the big home-building markets of Atlanta and Las Vegas. Built in a factory, the modular home featured a so-called Smart Living System that was both an energy-management system and a home-monitoring tool; it alerted homeowners to things like a water pipe leak. The home included a host of energy-saving features—foam insulation, a tankless hot water heater, and high-performance windows. Major television networks flocked to see it, including *Good Morning America*, the industry's litmus test for whether a project is a public relations success. The project garnered enough attention that it led other builders who had long constructed energy-efficient homes to see if they could get all the way to net zero.

IF YOU LIKE THE IDEA of buying a super-energy-efficient home, you are not alone. Surveys show that many new-home shoppers are willing to roll at least some added costs of energy-efficient equipment into their monthly mortgage. The thing to remember is that spending $5,000 to $10,000 on energy enhancements in the typical new home will only cost an extra $30 to $60 a month, amortized over 30 years. Roughly 40 percent of new-home shoppers in a 2010 survey said they were willing to make that tradeoff. When you think about it, $60 a month is what you pay for cable television or maybe even a tank of gas. But the beauty of a home energy investment is that it pays you back in lower utility bills, forever. The energy features that score highest on consumer surveys also happen to be the least expensive—high-performance (low-emissivity) windows, high-efficiency heating and cooling systems, upgraded insulation, and water-conserving dishwashers. Other options, such as photovoltaic systems and geothermal energy, cost more up front and take longer to pay for themselves.

The question to ask yourself, before you invest in a net-zero home, is how diligent you are about operating your home on a daily basis to reduce electrical, water, and gas consumption. Because if you routinely turn off lights when you leave a room, religiously close the French doors after you go into the backyard, never forget to turn down the temperature on the water heater before you leave town, and use power strips to turn off appliances that otherwise consume phantom power, you might be able to save your way down to net zero or close to it. In that case, you might be better off buying a home that gets you most of the way to net zero, to a HERS rating of, say, 25, then modifying your behavior to go the "final quarter mile," as they say in the trade. Academic studies show that the energy use of two similar families owning nearly identical homes can vary by more than 200 percent.

If you aren't the best at remembering these energy-saving things, or you don't want the hassle of having to do them, then the better alternative is to buy a true net-zero home that does it all for you. Several production builders sell a base home with a HERS rating of 40 or less with a $35,000, 5- to 6-kilowatt photovoltaic system that produces a net-zero home. The photovoltaic system is eligible for federal and sometimes state government subsidies that can make it more cost-effective. A 30 percent federal renewable energy tax credit—which can be applied against the cost of photovoltaic panels, solar water heat, and geothermal heat pumps, among other conservation technology—is available through 2016. If you buy a house that's net zero and then go into overdrive managing your personal energy decisions, you may wind up generating excess power for which the utility will have to pay you, a pretty satisfying situation.

Most net-zero homes, like the one we built with KB Home and Martha Stewart, come with a new generation of energy-management systems that help track energy production and consumption. They typically work through a Web-based system that allows you to control your home from a computer or mobile device. By identifying how you consume energy at home, they can help you adjust your energy usage if your home hasn't produced enough.

For our show home in 2011, KB Home wanted to build a demonstration home that didn't depend on occupant behavior to get to net zero. The home included several fail-safe systems to automatically reduce power consumption that are worth considering in your new home. Simple motion detectors, like the ones commonly used in commercial-building bathrooms, turned lights on and off when you left key rooms. In the bathrooms, motion detectors sent a message to the hot water heater, in this case an on-demand hot water heater, to get ready. Only then does the system pump hot water to showerheads and faucets. Ten to 15 percent of the energy used in hot water systems, according to federal government estimates, is wasted in distribution losses.

Hot water for the home came from a passive solar system on the roof. Water, heated in pipes exposed to the sun, ran to an 80-gallon thermal tank and was then circulated through a loop under the slab. The pipes were carefully sized to minimize distribution runs—each plumbing route off the main loop was limited to less than 10 feet. We thought about ways to conserve water throughout the home. In addition to low-flow faucets and water-conserving toilets, we installed a rainwater collection tank to store runoff from downspouts and redistribute it to the landscaping. We put in a so-called gray-water system—water from the sink and shower was collected, filtered, and redistributed for irrigation. We even installed a system to water the lawn that checks soil moisture levels before it turns on the sprinkler system.

The industry has come up with some ingenious tools for home-owners to monitor energy consumption. For its BrightBuilt demonstration project, a net-zero building in Rockwood, Me., Kaplan Thompson Architects designed a system that operates like a stoplight. LED lights wrapped around the lower perimeter of the building change colors depending on how much power the building has to spare. When the lights turn green, for instance, it's okay to run the dishwasher—your home is producing more energy than it's using. When the lights are yellow, you should use caution. And when the lights are red, you should wait for the home to produce more electricity before you do something like run the dryer. The envelope of the barn building, which could be used as a one- or two-bedroom home, is so efficient, with an R-value of 40, that it doesn't need a furnace. And, with 30 solar panels, you may be able to sell back electricity to the utility grid and erase the "carbon debt" incurred by building the structure.

The BrightBuilt barn raises an important issue: Development, no matter how benign, takes its toll on our natural resources. Even if you bought the greenest home possible, one that achieved the highest LEED rating, it would still be a detrimental event for the environment. Think of the trees sacrificed to make its sheathing, the energy required to produce its concrete, the glues and resins needed to bond its building components. All those have to be produced with natural resources in a process that requires energy. Then there's the gas that subcontractors use to drive to the building site, as well as the power consumed to run saws and nail guns. Selling electricity back to the utility would be one way to achieve carbon neutrality. Another would be to buy enough carbon credits to offset your actions.

WHEN IT COMES TO TACKLING ENERGY USE, it helps to know which systems within the home use the most energy. According to the DOE, the biggest uses of energy in the home are space heating (45 percent), lighting and appliances (12 percent), water heating (18 percent), air conditioning (9 percent), and refrigeration (4 percent). Hot water heating stands out on this list. Simple solar systems—little more than water pipes exposed to the sun and run to a hot water tank—are commonly available that can pay for themselves within a couple years. It's tougher to reduce the amount of energy used by appliances partly because some, such as televisions, CD players, and microwaves, are always on, consuming so-called phantom power that accounts for 6 percent of electricity consumption. A new generation of smart-grid appliances, connected through the Internet to the utility grid and to your energy-management system at home, may help manage electricity consumed by dishwashers and dryers. One day soon your home-monitoring system will not only show you how much energy is being consumed by individual appliances, but it will also suggest when to use them based on the lowest hourly and seasonal charges from utility companies.

But the way a home is built—especially the composition of its frame, roof, and windows, and its orientation to the sun—can have a much bigger impact on its energy performance than the appliances you install. Windows and doors are the weak links. Federal government data show that they account for about 30 percent of the energy wasted in a home, an amount of energy that equals all the oil we get each year through the Alaskan pipeline. An old wooden exterior door may have an R-value of only 2 compared with 5 or 6 for a new insulated steel or fiberglass door. Another big chunk of energy each year is lost through the transfer of heat through wood framing members to the outdoors. That's one reason why so many builders focus on alternative building systems that impede thermal bridging.

Pepper Viner Homes is the only company still building homes in the first section of Civano North Ridge (outside Tucson, Ariz.), where many homes were constructed in the early 2000s to demonstrate alternative construction practices. Signs leading to an adobe model home implore buyers to "Do the Right Thing"—to go beyond Energy Star requirements and buy a solar home with photovoltaic panels. Although

Pepper Viner asks buyers to do the right thing: Buy a solar-powered home that produces as much energy as it consumes. During the housing recession the Tucson builder added upgrades such as photovoltaic panels and solar hot water heaters to its already energy-efficient base homes to produce net-zero homes.

the signs stop short of saying "buy a net-zero home," that's what you could do, for little incremental cost if you played your cards right. Pepper Viner builds a high-performance home that far exceeds Energy Star requirements. With the addition of photovoltaic panels and solar hot water, it can produce as much energy as it consumes.

The process starts with an energy-efficient shell—R-19 walls and R-38 ceilings—wrapped with a vapor barrier to limit air infiltration through wall and window joints but to allow moisture to escape. (Housewrap isn't always the best solution in moist climates.) Low-emissivity windows with thermal breaks in the frames do their best to stop unwanted heat from entering the home during brutal summer months. Pepper Viner not only insulates its attics but also wraps the air-conditioning ducts within them. It insulates the roof deck to prevent the loss of heat or air conditioning through the roof and uses light-colored roof tiles to reflect rather than absorb the sun's rays. We've built conditioned attic space in several demonstration homes. It's always a wonder to go into the attic and find it reasonably cool even on the hottest summer day—which means that you could actually use the attic as storage space and retrieve things on the steamiest summer and coldest winter days. One high-performance San Antonio builder, Imagine Homes, invites visitors to its models to go into the insulated attic on broiling summer days and see for themselves how cool it is.

Pepper Viner builds such a tight building envelope—it saves about half of normal heating and air-conditioning costs—that it can downsize the home's air-conditioning system and use the savings to install a higher-efficiency unit. So in goes an air-conditioning system with a seasonal energy efficiency rating (SEER) of 14 compared with the typical 12. The savings also help pay for a 93-percent-efficient furnace instead of the typical unit that's only 80 percent efficient; so-called high-efficiency furnaces capture waste heat and recycle it. The house winds up being so easy to heat and cool that, to take it to net zero, it requires only a 3-kilowatt photovoltaic system that Pepper Viner provided free during the recession to induce sales.

NET-ZERO HOUSING ISN'T LIMITED TO THE SOUTH, even though more plentiful sunlight there makes it easier to pencil projects. A start-up company in Maryland, Nexus EnergyHomes^SM, is making a big splash with inexpensive "near" net-zero homes in the Washington, D.C., area. The company enjoyed rapid sales during the housing recession at its North Point project in downtown Frederick, Md., an hour's drive north of the District of Columbia. The homes turn the new-home shopping world upside down by including a long list of energy features, including geothermal energy and photovoltaic panels, in the base price of the home. Most builders sell them as upgrades. Nexus EnergyHomes prefers to sell decorator items—stainless-steel appliances and bamboo flooring—as upgrades.

The traditional facade of these Nexus EnergyHomes townhomes in Frederick, Md., belies their high-tech focus. The tightly insulated homes are heated and cooled with geothermal energy. An energy monitoring system, installed on tablet computers tells homeowners whether their home produced enough electricity during the day to run the dishwasher and washing machine at night.

One reason geothermal is included is that, to hold down costs, the company predrilled the wells for this infill community of about 52 townhomes and duplexes before it poured slabs. Geothermal systems, which are also called ground-source heat pumps, work a lot like a refrigerator. They transfer heat from the ground into your home in the same way a refrigerator removes heat from food. During hot months the system reverses to provide cooling, often twice as efficiently as any other air-conditioning system. Geothermal systems take advantage of the earth's constant roughly 55-degree temperature below

Photovoltaic arrays are a standard feature on homes built by Nexus EnergyHomes, which come with energy-saving touches such as LED and fluorescent lights and Energy Star–rated appliances. The builder doesn't guarantee that its homes will produce all the energy they will consume, though; that's up to the owners.

the frost line, which can be anywhere from 3 to 5 feet below the surface. In winter, the ground temperature remains warmer than the air aboveground. The units circulate liquid through underground pipes to warm the liquid. Then it is piped into the house, where the heat is extracted and transferred into the air. In the summer, when the ground is cooler than the air, cold is extracted from the underground liquid to cool the air indoors.

The homes constructed by Nexus EnergyHomes don't require much heating and air conditioning because they are super energy efficient. Walls are constructed with 6½-inch-thick SIPs and filled in with R-24 foam insulation. Simple trussed roofs are insulated with R-40 open-cell foam insulation. Energy consumption of the homes, which range in size from 1,300 to 3,000 square feet, is kept to a minimum through the use of LED and fluorescent lights, Energy Star–rated appliances, and an energy-efficient hot water system, among other carbon-light features. Photovoltaic systems range from 3.6 to 3.8 kilowatts, depending on the size of the house, and should provide all the electricity the homes need, although the builder doesn't guarantee that—thus the slogan "near" net-zero homes. The HERS index drops all the way down to 28 with on-site power generation.

But the killer app, so to speak, is a proprietary energy-management system that can run off a smartphone or a tablet. "When you come home in the evening, the app will tell you how much energy your home has produced," said a capable salesperson, "so you know how much you can use that night." Nexus EnergyHomes doesn't guarantee that homebuyers won't have utility bills, she said, because there's no way to stop them from leaving doors open on hot summer days. Instead, the company tries to influence homeowner behavior with a system that carefully tracks home energy consumption. An energy dashboard with simple graphs shows energy usage in kilowatt hours or dollars by the week, month, and year. It also highlights the total environmental benefit of the net-zero community in terms of the fuel use avoided and trees saved. The system sends you an email or text when an important event occurs within the house—when a window was left open or the air conditioner fails, for example. Buyers receive a tablet computer loaded with the Nexus app and homeowner manuals.

The builder's sales material highlights the price of homes after grants and tax credits for the geothermal and solar systems, since all the homes have them. The "estimated real cost" of owning a 2,400-square-foot townhome, listed in the low $300,000s, is $16,000 less after state grants and federal energy-conservation tax credits. That seems like a pretty affordable price for a super-efficient townhome located within walking distance of historic downtown Frederick, which has become a real hot spot with some great restaurants, boutiques, and nightclubs. Within an hour, you could also be at a concert performance at the Kennedy Center in downtown Washington, D.C.

NET-ZERO HOMES ARE EASIER TO FIND in the sunny Southwest, where photovoltaic systems have more solar power to work with. Palo Duro Homes, which builds in New Mexico and Colorado, offers net-zero adobe homes for a small upgrade, which it can afford to do because its base homes are so efficient. Tom Wade, who owns the company, frames with 2x6 studs, using special techniques that allow him to insulate previously unreachable corners with spray foam and achieve an R-value of 30, when the Energy Star program only calls for R-19. He puts air handlers in a utility room and insulated ducts in a conditioned dropped hallway ceiling. Without ducts in the attic, he can install an uninterrupted blanket of insulation and achieve an R-value of 50, when even 30 is unusual. The net-zero package includes photovoltaic panels, solar hot water, a 15 SEER air-conditioning unit, and a 90-percent-efficient air-source heat pump.

Palo Duro is one of the few production builders to build to the EPA's airPLUS standard. It separates the garage from living areas with an uninterrupted air barrier, mechanically exhausts the garage, and pressurizes the home to keep out unwanted odors and gases. Every three hours, air within the home is evacuated and new air introduced through a three-filter system. Palo Duro guarantees that inside temperatures won't vary between any two spots within the home by more than three degrees.

Some of the biggest production builders in the country now offer net-zero homes. After building a demonstration home with us, KB Home, the fifth-largest homebuilder in the country by number of homes built, debuted a net-zero upgrade package, ZeroHouse 2.0, that it has rolled out throughout the country. What's included in the base price and what's an option varies by market and even community—the company asks potential buyers to call or visit to get the information.

Brookfield Homes recently completed a series of net-zero homes for an Ontario, Calif., community that's significant for its use of mini-split air conditioners, which are common in Asia and catching on in the United States. Mini-splits are a lot like window air conditioners, except

Brookfield Homes was having trouble making the numbers work on a net-zero home until it settled on a mini-split air-conditioning system that doesn't need ducting. Mini-splits, which resemble high-powered window air-conditioning units, are installed in the wall rather than in windows. Brookfield needs to get ahead of the technology curve because the state of California has mandated that all new homes in the state be net-zero by 2025.

they are more powerful, go into the wall, and are operated by a remote. Working with architects at William Hezmalhalch, Brookfield designed a series of small homes with carefully planned window locations, upgraded insulation packages, solar hot water, and photovoltaic panels. The builder was having trouble justifying the added first costs, until it swapped out a traditional HVAC system in favor of mini-split air conditioners that can eliminate the need for ductwork, though you still need a system to ventilate the home. With the assist from mini-splits, the homes wound up costing only about $8,000 (or 4 percent) more than comparably sized homes in the neighborhood.

BECAUSE THE BIGGEST INCREMENTAL COST in all these net-zero projects is the photovoltaic panels, an important consideration is how long it takes these systems to pay for themselves, the so-called payback period. Although photovoltaic costs have dropped dramatically in recent years as China has picked up production, most systems still don't reach a break-even point for 10 to 14 years, even after federal tax incentives. Federal and state tax incentives for photovoltaic installations may make a big difference in paybacks. So does net metering—federal law requires states to buy your excess electricity. Utilities in some states pay a flat retail rate—if the utility charges 18 cents a kilowatt hour, you will be paid 18 cents a kilowatt hour. In other states, utilities pay you based on the time of day that the energy is produced. That's often good for the homeowner because utilities typically pay a higher rate during the day, and photovoltaic systems don't generate electricity at night. Another big variable in a payback analysis is estimating how much electricity will cost in the future, since manufacturers guarantee most photovoltaic systems for 25 to 30 years.

When the Tennessee Valley Authority analyzed system payback periods for Tennessee homeowners in 2011, it found that the financial break-even point ranged from 10 to 20 years, depending on net metering, tax incentives, increases in property values, and the longevity of the photovoltaic system. The utility recommended a 4.0-kilowatt system for Tennessee homes that would produce on average 4,500 kilowatts annually. Most homeowners use between 600 and 1,200-kilowatt hours per month, with an average of 830. A 4.0-kilowatt system in Tennessee would cost between $25,000 and $30,000 before incentives (a $1,000 one-time installation credit from the state and the 30 percent credit from the federal government). Counting incentives drops the price to between $16,500 and $21,000.

Determining the payback period for photovoltaic systems is a complicated equation that may require a spreadsheet. It starts with figuring out how many hours of sun your home will receive each day, using tables published on the Internet. Tennesseans receive about 4.3 hours of sunlight a day, which means that a 4-kilowatt system would produce 17.2 kilowatt hours a day, or 516 per month. Most experts believe you then need to reduce that estimate to account for less-than-optimal solar conditions, so perhaps you take a 20 percent haircut to 412 kilowatt hours per month.

The next step is figuring how much electricity your household would consume. The national average is about 830 kilowatt hours per month, but let's say your house is more energy efficient and you could get it down to 600. In that case, the Tennessee system would cover 69 percent of your electrical needs. If you paid 22 cents per kilowatt hour, that would make your monthly bill about $132 a month. With the photovoltaic system, you'd save $91 a month, or $1,092 a year. The next step—which is where you'd need an expert in Excel—would be to factor in utility rate increases and see what that does to your annual savings. Then you subtract the accumulated savings from the initial cost and figure out how many years it takes before the savings overtake the costs. The crossing point is known as the payback period. In our example, assuming utility costs rise by 4 percent a year, a pretty conservative assumption, it takes 14 years for the photovoltaic system to pay for itself.

Solar hot water systems typically have a faster payback. But if you are building a new home and taking out a 30-year mortgage, you can make money—theoretically at least—right away. That's because your water-heating bills will be cut by 50 to 80 percent. Including a solar hot water system usually adds $13 to $20 to your monthly payments, an amount that's cut by $3 to $5 by the tax deduction for mortgage interest. You save immediately if your fuel costs are more than $15 a month. Not all solar hot water systems are the same. Some preheat incoming water, reducing the amount of Btus that a primary fuel source must generate. Others provide most or all of the heat required during sunny months and rely on a back-up system on cloudy days. The hot water tank may have two coils, one for the solar thermal loop from the solar collector and the other coming from an existing furnace or boiler. Systems could cost as little as $2,500 or more than $8,000 depending on the complexity and installation.

Geothermal systems may cost twice as much to buy and install as a conventional heating and air-conditioning system, though once again rebates and tax credits reduce after-tax costs. You also need a bigger spot to put them in the home since units are larger than regular heating equipment. But again you can save at least 40 to 65 percent—sometimes as much as 75 percent—on your heating bill in the first year, depending on local utility rates. Summer air-conditioning costs can be reduced by as much as two-thirds. The proportion of homes with geothermal systems is relatively small but growing. DOE estimates that as many as 3.5 percent of new homes built in 2009 included such systems. But that's triple the number from 10 years before.

Payback periods are nice to know, but they don't consider the full impact of a decision to purchase a net-zero home. For one, they don't reflect the impact on the environment of reducing the pollution that utilities would otherwise generate to supply electricity to a house. The DOE estimates that every 1,000 kilowatts of electricity generated by photovoltaic panels (your home could easily consume that much in two months) reduces sulfur dioxide emissions by 8 pounds, nitrogen oxides by 5 pounds, and carbon dioxide by 1,400 pounds. Over a 10-year period, that adds up to some very big numbers. Buying a net-zero home may not make complete financial sense, but it makes 100 percent environmental sense. It's a decision—not dissimilar to designing a home in which you can age gracefully—that can create lasting peace of mind. ✤

CHAPTER EIGHT

Universal Design Makes a Lot of Sense

NEARLY 15 YEARS AGO, I had the pleasure of working on a demonstration home with Ron Mace, founder of the Center for Universal Design at North Carolina State University, in Raleigh. At the time, the center was the leading source of information on the emerging practice of universal design. Mace came up for a meeting at our Washington, D.C., office on the train, with the help of a nurse. This was late in his life. In addition to using a wheelchair, he periodically needed oxygen. I had advised the rest of the project team—the builder, the architect, and some key suppliers—about Ron's condition, but they were still startled when he entered the room. They were even more surprised when he started to talk about why the principles of universal design should be included in every home.

The group expected to hear a discourse on handicap access, which is mandated in some public buildings; builders by and large don't want to deal with it in residential construction. But, instead, Mace told the group that it makes no sense to design homes for people with disabilities, except in special cases. Real progress, he said, would come when homes were designed with the needs and limitations of *all* people in mind. What we needed to do was consider the difficulty that older people have seeing and bending over; the need to keep electrical outlets out of the reach of toddlers; the danger that falls in the bath and shower present to everyone; and the shared desire of all people to live safely and conveniently at home. That, in essence, is what universal design is about.

Much of the research on how people use products and navigate spaces, Mace told us, was sponsored by the U.S. military, which during World War II wanted to improve the safety and performance of naval vessels and aircraft. After the war, military-funded research efforts were extended to include commercial spaces. The problem, Mace said, was that much of this data, which was informing decisions such as how high from the floor to put electrical receptacles, was based on the physical abilities of average-size, healthy 18-year-old males who would fly planes and operate submarines. It's no big thing for a muscular soldier to bend over and plug a floor lamp into a socket close to the floor, but older people with bad backs may have trouble doing it. And there's no reason why curious toddlers crawling along the floor should be exposed to the unnecessary risk of putting a finger in a socket.

The kitchen in the LifeStages Home was designed with counters at multiple heights. Lower counters not only facilitate tasks like rolling dough but also are easier to reach for children and people using a wheelchair. The added advantage of the lower counter height is that it can hide dirty dishes and pans when unexpected guests arrive.

In addition to raising the height of electrical sockets, Mace gave us other ideas to ponder in the design of our LifeStages show home; ideas that made good marketing sense. Universal design, he said, needs to be invisible. People walking through the home, which we placed on the floor of the International Builders Show in 1999, should remark on how convenient it would be to roll dough on a lowered countertop in the kitchen or use the extended-arm showerhead in the bathroom—not that it was designed for someone in a wheelchair. We would want visitors to note the stylish, polished-brass lever handle sets that also happened to be easy to use, the inspired task lighting shining brightly on critical workspaces, and the general ease of getting around the home as well as its porches and entryways. It makes sense for anyone designing or building a new home, regardless of how long you intend to live there, to consider Ron's advice. Who knows how old the next owner of your home might be.

TO START, HERE ARE A FEW IMPORTANT FACTS about home safety that can help guide your design decisions. The leading cause of home accidents is falls, usually down stairs or steps but also in showers. It makes sense to change floor colors anytime grades change (which is the reason you sometimes see bright warnings on the floor of commercial buildings). We built our show home on one level but changed floor colors or carpeting from room to room. Showers seem like accidents waiting to happen, especially when joined with bathtubs. Who hasn't lost their bearing and nearly hit their head in the shower? It becomes even more likely as you grow older, as your back weakens and your reactions slow. Using slip-resistant material in the shower and bath, and even on the bathroom floor, is critical to the design of any home.

The next leading cause of injury or death in homes is fire, which is a more difficult hazard to counter. For one thing, most new homes aren't built with sprinklers. Builder interest groups have lobbied hard against sprinklers, which they argue are a needless expense. However, a small number of municipalities require them. Builders will tell you that the bigger risk is ruining your home furnishings if the sprinklers go off inadvertently. Except that most home fires occur in the kitchen, where the threat of water damage isn't as great. Nevertheless, it's easy and not that expensive to install a system in a new home, if you decide on it before construction begins.

As a practical matter, a more immediate danger may be from burns. Thankfully, a new generation of scald-resistant showerheads and faucets mitigates the potential for hot-water burns. In the kitchen, it makes sense to design areas around the microwave and oven where you can immediately place hot pans. Who hasn't picked up a hot bowl from the microwave and wanted to drop it immediately? Raising the height of the oven, or even installing a wall oven, can also help. Who wants to do a deep bend to pull a boiling casserole from an oven near the floor?

A good lighting plan is essential for home safety, especially in the kitchen. Critical work areas, like kitchen countertops where chopping and mixing are done, require extra task lighting. The same goes for office spaces. As the U.S. population ages, eyesight isn't getting any better, that's for sure. Yet in my experience, builders and designers don't pay enough attention to how new homes are lit. They often leave the "lighting plan" up to an electrician whose primary job is to economize on lighting fixtures and may not be thinking about how spaces within the home will actually be used. You should ask to see the lighting plan and go over it with an interior designer who can help select the best layout and devices for different tasks.

For our LifeStages show home, we followed design guidelines outlined by Mace for the U.S. Department of Housing and Urban Development in the 1990s, advice that's still good today. We widened doorways and hallways. We lowered rocker light switches from their usual 48 to 52 inches above the floor to 42 inches. At that height, kids can reach them and turn out the lights when they leave a room. We raised electrical sockets to 18 inches from the ground, which makes it easier to bend over and plug in an appliance. As long as all outlets are at the same height, it doesn't interfere with room design.

Some aspects of universal design help create a more stylish home. The lever handle sets we used on doors and faucets are a case in point; they look more like an upgrade than a nod to those who have trouble turning a doorknob. Lever handles can be a real lifesaver if you are carrying a sleeping child or a bag of groceries and need to open a door or turn on a faucet with a wrist or an elbow. And the wider-than-usual doorways (36 inches) and hallways (48 inches) look like something you'd see in a Palm Springs luxury home. But they also work for someone in a wheelchair or using a walker.

Mary Jo Peterson, a Connecticut designer who has spent most of her professional career spreading the gospel of universal design, guided our work on the kitchen and baths. She recommended, among other things, that we lower the height of the microwave so that a child popping corn after school could reach the bag or someone in a wheelchair could conveniently extricate a meal. Another benefit of lowering the microwave is that a person of normal height can easily look inside and see how the contents of a dish are faring. Peterson suggested that we put a pullout shelf under the microwave where you could immediately put hot plates to cool off. She also specified pullout shelves in lower cabinets to make it easier to access contents deep inside.

Another ergonomic consideration is the height of the dishwasher. Most are designed to open nearly to the floor, but if you raise them a little, they are much easier to load and unpack. There's a similar advantage to having kitchen countertops at different heights. A lower kitchen counter comes in handy if a young child wants to help in the kitchen; it's essential if you want to reach the countertop from a wheelchair. Another of Mary Jo's suggestions was to include two cleanup areas in the kitchen, one accessible to the wheelchair-bound, so that two cooks can work at once. One thing we provided specifically for the disabled was a sink with a pneumatic lift so it could be raised or lowered, depending on who used it. The lift was concealed behind a cabinet panel. We did the same thing with the adjustable-height sink in the master bath.

The coolest space in the LifeStages house was the "roll-through" shower in the master bath, which bridged the master bedroom and bath. Many builders at the time were using concave shower floors without thresholds, so the overall look was familiar. Our shower included a seat where you could conveniently bathe with a pair of handheld faucets. Strategically placed grab bars, attached to backing behind the tile walls, looked as attractive as they were functional.

We accepted the challenge of trying to design a stylish bath that conformed to handicap-access rules. That meant leaving a 5-foot clearance around the toilet so that you could reach it from a wheelchair, a consideration that puts functionality ahead of privacy. We toyed with using a half-wall to create a semiprivate toilet space but couldn't make it work within our square-footage requirements. We left a similar amount of space around the adjustable-height vanity. To an able-bodied person, the bathroom may have looked like it contained wasted space. But to the wheelchair-bound, it would bring a sigh of relief.

One of the most inspired spaces in the house was a sitting room that could be converted into a suite for an in-home caregiver. That's not something everyone needs to think about. But the reality is that many older people don't want to leave home for a dependent-care facility, unless they absolutely have to. Following Mace's advice, we designed the space as a suite with

The LifeStages Home included a "roll-through" shower without a door threshold that worked well for people of all physical abilities. Once inside, detachable showerheads, coupled with overhead sprays and a bench for sitting or storage, made showering easy and enjoyable.

its own bathroom. During the convention, we showed it as a study without a door. But during tours of the home, guides would demonstrate how, with the addition of a door, the room could be easily converted into independent living space. We prewired the room with an intercom system so that the caregiver could "look in on" a client in the master bedroom.

Following universal design precepts, one entry to the house didn't require steps. Steps may create a visually inviting entry, but they are a hassle when you are in a wheelchair, use a walker, or broke your foot playing rugby. They also present an obstacle trying to get a rolling object into a house, whether it's a bicycle, luggage, or a keg of beer. Nobody likes to think about the day when they may be confined to a wheelchair, but many families will eventually have someone in that position. No one should have to move or pay for a big remodel because of impaired mobility. With some foresight, you won't have to.

Single-floor living is another hallmark of universal design. Unless you have an elevator, it's hard for a wheelchair-bound person to make use of a two-story house. Even if you choose a home with a second floor, everything you may eventually need—space for cooking, bathing, and sleeping—should be on the first floor, if possible. Whenever I hear this advice, I think of Franklin Delano Roosevelt's house, actually his mother's house, in Hyde Park, N.Y. After Roosevelt contracted polio, he was forced to use an elevator to get to his bedroom on the second floor. (To increase his upper-body strength, he used pulleys to haul himself up in the elevator.)

The LifeStages house included several interesting lighting features to improve safety and make common tasks easier to perform. Most families, research shows, have at least one person with eye problems. And as we get older, we need more bright light for key tasks such as reading, chopping vegetables, getting dressed, or playing the violin. Also as we age, our depth perception starts to fade, making it harder to see thresholds, stairs, and changes in floor levels. Even people with good eyesight may have trouble navigating the steps to a sunken living room in an unfamiliar home.

If designing another aging-oriented show home today, it would be tempting to incorporate some new hands-free products, particularly if it were an upper-end home. First on the list would be elegant levered handle sets on doors, faucets, and cabinets that can be operated with a palm, fist, or elbow. Most of us have experienced the germ-free convenience of hands-free faucets, soap dispensers, and dryers in airport bathrooms. Residential versions of these products have been available for a while, and prices are starting to become more affordable. I'd use these, along with new hands-free home toilet flushers that retail for about $150. Hands-free operation is starting to invade cabinets as well; there's a new line that opens with the wave of a hand. That feature would be especially nice if you have arthritis or a limited range of motion.

Hands-free light switches are a no-brainer; you can just wave a hand in front of them to turn lights on or off, although lights attached to motion detectors may be an even better option. You can also get heat or occupancy sensors that operate lights and HVAC equipment depending on whether someone is in the room. Even basic home-automation systems could be programmed to open blinds, shades, and curtains at sunrise and close them at sundown. Voice activation is the new frontier in hands-free home operations. Several home-automation systems on the market operate by voice command. And you can buy a voice-activated remote for your television for less than $50. Unfortunately, you couldn't put the Clapper® in my fictitious hands-free concept home; the late-night-television gizmo wouldn't qualify because it requires a clap of the hands. But you could use the new "I've Fallen and I Can't Get Up" product because it responds to voice commands.

ANOTHER UNIVERSAL DESIGN DEMONSTRATION HOME recently made headlines. Once again, the idea was to unobtrusively incorporate accessibility in a way that would be at once functional and aesthetically pleasing. Rosemarie Rossetti of Columbus, Ohio, started the project after she was hit by a falling tree limb while riding a bike and was left paralyzed from the waist down. When she returned from the hospital, she found that her dream home was a nightmare to use. She couldn't get to the second floor or go to the basement, reach food in high cabinets, or easily operate her top-loading washing machine. It took Rossetti nine years to build a 3,500-square-foot demonstration home, the Universal Design Living Laboratory, which was opened to the public in 2012. She raised the degree of difficulty on this project by building the home to a variety of green building standards. She ran into trouble, for instance, when she couldn't find an Energy Star–certified side-by-side refrigerator that met her access needs.

The first thing that a visitor may, or may not, notice about this home is the lack of front stairs. But there's no conspicuous ramp either. Instead, the step-free entrance is designed with a gradually sloping grade, partially hidden from view behind a porte cochère. A good front entry is often the toughest thing to pull off on a home designed to universal specifications. A home without front stairs or a threshold just looks different. We solved the ingress problem on our show home by leaving the front door alone and designing a side door at grade. But it felt like a cop-out.

Otherwise, Rossetti's house, it was gratifying to see, included many of the same features contained in our LifeStages Home. Wide doorways and hallways create spacious interiors. A vertical glass panel beside the front door allows anyone, at any level, to see who is at the door. A side-by-side refrigerator and freezer provide easy access to perishables. Simple cabinet pulls, rocker light switches, and casement windows with low levers are easy to use by people of all abilities. The same goes for the kitchen, designed once again by Mary Jo Peterson, with cabinets at varying heights, full-extension bottom drawers and shelves, a microwave that opens at countertop height, and a cooktop set into a counter with open knee space.

Many products used in universal design have become more commonplace since our demonstration home was built. Low-pile carpeting, which Rossetti made sure to use—when she used any carpeting at all— is one. The spec works better than regular-height carpeting for people with allergies as well. Toilet seats 17 to 19 inches high are another feature that you see much more these days, along with adjustable, hanging closet rods and shelves, and front-loading washers and dryers. Rossetti managed to find most of the products she needed widely available on the market, with a few notable exceptions. She had trouble locating an ironing board that both she and her 6-foot-tall husband could use. A company stepped up and built a highly adjustable one that Rossetti now markets on her website.

THANKS TO THE WORK OF ITS PROPONENTS, universal design is growing in popularity. But it remains unusual to find builders who market universal design, much less build to its specifications. For that reason, I was startled recently to see a marketing brochure for universal design in the sales office of a Southern California community. Inviting shoppers to experience a home "ready to go through life with you," the brochure highlighted the benefits of under-counter knee space, variable-height countertops, lower doorbells, and safety bars in the bath, items that builders would be loathe to feature in decorated models for fear that they remind shoppers of their advancing age. But a second brochure made it clear that few of these features—only the lower doorbells, lever handle sets in the kitchen, under-cabinet task lighting, and antiscald devices on plumbing fixtures—are standard features in a home. Nearly everything else is presented either on a limited basis or as an option. Some accessibility features—such as elevators, a 5-foot turning circle in the bathroom, and a roll-in shower—are not available at all.

Even so, basic design touches that accommodate aging in place are starting to creep into mainstream production housing. Builders are paying more attention to things like allowing natural light to permeate living space, leaving sufficient clear area in the kitchen and bath, and designing specialty work centers in the kitchen. The trend will accelerate in coming years as waves of baby boomers move into old age. Boomers have had a huge influence on new-home design and construction in this country during the last 40 years, arguably precipitating a multifamily boom in the early 1980s, a rush toward comforting traditional designs in the '90s, and the housing boom of the 2000s. Now every seven or eight seconds a boomer turns 65, the age when people accelerate decisions about how and where they will live for the rest of their lives.

It's not clear how this new generation of seniors will want to live. Even experts at the MIT AgeLab, which has been at the forefront of research on this topic, aren't sure. In an address during the housing recession at the Pacific Coast Builders Conference, Dr. Joseph Coughlin rhetorically asked the builders in attendance what new-home features would induce aging boomers to move. "What's the new dream, the new lifestyle for life after 50, 60, or 70?" he asked, noting that life spans in the industrialized world are 30 to 40 years longer than they were 100 years ago. "What's new for the old?" Coughlin went on to answer the question himself. "The fact is we don't know yet."

THE OTHER BIG QUESTION is where aging boomers will want to live. Research by AARP shows that nearly 90 percent of people 65 or older would prefer to stay in their existing home during retirement, or else move to a more accommodating home nearby, so they can be close to their children and grandchildren. During the last decade, a lot of empty-nester housing was built in close-in suburban settings—some attached, some detached—catering to this desire to trade down and stay near a home base. Even so, the 10 percent who want to move—typically to a warmer climate, especially one where property taxes might be lower—continued to fuel a migratory pattern that benefited Sun Belt states such as Florida, Arizona, Nevada, and New Mexico. During the downturn, migration skidded to a halt, along with communities such as Sun City that cater to active adults. Since these moves are often discretionary, many older Americans figured they would wait until they regained some of the home equity they lost on paper. The preretirement housing market was hit early and hard by the recession.

Now that the housing market has recovered, familiar migratory patterns have returned, bringing rising property values to sought-after living locations such as Phoenix, Las Vegas, and Tampa. But it's still not clear whether boomers will follow the lead of previous generations and retire or buy a future retirement home in age-restrictive active-adult communities. These communities typically put the emphasis on community, with shared parks, golf courses, tennis clubs, community centers, and social activities. The biggest of them, like Leisure World in Maryland and Sun City in Phoenix, have concierge services that will help plan every waking hour of your day. The future for these communities is clouded, given the huge up-front costs of the infrastructure. An 18-hole golf course with a clubhouse and facilities costs at least $7 million to develop in most cities.

One compelling school of thought is that, instead of moving to locations where they can play golf and join garden clubs, boomers will gravitate to culturally rich places like Greenwich Village or Santa Monica, Calif. Some research shows that college towns, with their attraction of lectures and culture, may be a big draw. Revitalized suburban centers, like Bethesda, Md., and Scottsdale, Ariz., are another likely destination. Speakers at development conferences often say confidently that boomers will one day sell their large home in the suburbs and buy two—a condo in the city and a home by the beach or lake. Meanwhile, dozens of online publications list cities such as Portland, Ore., Ashland, N.C., and Tucson, Ariz., as the best place to retire based on their cultural activities and climate.

A new social movement, the "Beacon Hill" model, is designed to help seniors stay put. In this living paradigm, which started in Beacon Hill Village, Mass., neighborhood seniors band together to form co-ops to provide in-home services so they don't have to move into assisted-living facilities. Neighbors organize everything from book group transportation services to plays downtown and trips to the doctor. They coordinate to have groceries delivered and emergency medical services provided. More than 100 villages employing the Beacon Hill model are in operation throughout the country, with more than 200 in the works. There's no reason why builders couldn't offer clusters of single-family homes with services that go beyond the typical ones—maintenance and a community center—to include in-home medical care and grocery delivery.

In his speech to builders, MIT's Coughlin said he wasn't sure what boomers will want for housing in their 60s, 70s, and 80s. But when he suggested things that builders might do to draw them out of their current homes, he began by listing some of the tenets of universal design—including more open and navigable floor plans that can work for people who must use wheelchairs or walkers. He recommended building more adaptable homes, ones that could accommodate interior changes—microwaves that must be lowered or dishwashers that need to be raised. His suggestions were hardly revolutionary. If only Ron Mace had been there to hear them. ✧

CHAPTER NINE

Generations Join Under One Roof

YOU MAY HAVE SEEN THE STATISTICS. Or maybe you are one of the data points. The U.S. Census Bureau estimates that as much as 30 percent of the U.S. population is doubling up, a percentage that rose strongly in recent years. During the last economic recession, as people lost jobs and their homes, family members took them in. College-educated children, saddled with debt and unable to find work in an extremely tough job market, came home to live with their parents for as long as psychologically possible. Siblings doubled up after one lost a house to the recession or subprime meltdown. Baby boomers became caregivers for a parent, inviting them to live under the same roof. Meanwhile, a rise in immigration during the last decade boosted demand for multigenerational housing, especially among Asian and Latino families that are more accustomed to these arrangements.

These demographic and economic trends challenged traditional living patterns in this country and could dramatically reshape the new-home market for years to come. For decades, builders have aimed homes at single families, typically providing space for one married couple and their kids. They catered to the American dream to achieve financial independence and earn the right to own the roof over your head. Parents, intent on having their children succeed, pushed their progeny from the nest to build their own lives. In the last several years, many of these patterns broke down due to economic pressure. Millions of Americans lost their homes. Many were forced to move in with brothers, sisters, or parents, until they could get back on their feet.

In most cases, families did what they could to accommodate unexpected guests. They carved living space out of basements, made their children share a room to free up a bedroom, and built out space over the garage. But there are things you can do with a new-home floor plan, prior to construction, to prepare for this contingency so that adults who come to live with you can have their own space. If you plan carefully, you may also be able to rent out the space to provide extra income. Bottom line: Family circumstances can change in a heartbeat, and homes need to be able to keep up. The good news is that even if you never take full advantage of your home's built-in design flexibility, it may ultimately add value to your home when you sell it.

THE BASIC QUESTION IS HOW TO SLICE OUT of the floor plan a second master bedroom (a bedroom with a connected bath). The key is deciding whether it needs to be on the first floor, a luxury in markets where most houses are two stories or more, or whether it could be in the basement, over the garage, or even in a *casita* (a small detached house). An older parent may require a first-floor master suite with some privacy. A boomerang child, on the other hand, should be able to climb stairs. But you may want him or her to be as far away from the family action as possible, making a room over the garage or in the basement the best choice. Detached casitas, which were sold with many new homes in Southern California during the housing boom, are also a nice, although expensive, option because they can be used in the meantime as a home office.

A second master on the first floor is the best solution if a widowed parent may live there one day. Stanley Martin Homes, a builder in the Washington, D.C., suburbs, opened a community of luxury production homes just as the housing market recovered with a plan that included a first-floor master suite targeted at multigenerational buyers; affluent ones in this case, given that the homes start at $684,000. The first-floor bedroom with a private bath sits adjacent to a sunny sitting room just off the front hall foyer. The arrangement, hard to find in expensive housing markets where developers economize on land costs by building multistory homes with small footprints, also works great for houseguests, especially ones who plan to stay for a while. The home features a second master bedroom upstairs.

There are several other ways to prepare for a first-floor master without building one in the beginning. John Wieland Homes in Atlanta, for instance, builds large duplex homes in a close-in suburb with a first-floor office that could easily be converted into a master bedroom. The office is adjacent, across the hallway, from a full bath. The wall separating the office from the hallway could come out, with part of it used to build a closet, to create a first-floor suite. The key to this arrangement is making sure that the bathroom is more than just a powder room; it needs space for a tub or shower. Another common way to design in a second master is to build out storage space over the garage.

The first-floor master suite in this Stanley Martin home, with a sitting room connected to a bedroom with a full bath, is aimed at multigenerational buyers. But the space could also work for a live-in nanny. Owners could eventually move here when they're older and don't want to climb the stairs.

Depending on community restrictions, you may even be able to run a separate set of outside stairs up to the suite. A basement suite works particularly well when you have a walkout basement with a separate entry. A second master—whether it's upstairs, downstairs, or over the garage—is considered a necessity for new-home buyers in markets such as Orlando or Las Vegas, where you can expect visitors for extended periods. Unrelated adults or friends going in together on a home may also prefer this arrangement.

Several years ago, we commissioned some ethnographic research with multigenerational households to see how they were living at home. Market researchers basically set out on foot to interview extended families. They found, to their surprise, that older parents were a more integral part of daily family life than expected. They were cooking dinner, taking grandchildren to soccer games, even going shopping for the family. They didn't want their room to be too far away from the kitchen and family room. At the same time, they valued their privacy. They wanted a place to which they could escape, a place where they could watch TV or read a book when they didn't want to be around their grandchildren (or children) for a while. They also really liked the idea of having private outdoor space where they could sit in the sun or even, God forbid, smoke a cigarette.

Working with architect Carson Looney, we designed a well-received response to these needs—a first-floor suite that was a short walk down a hall from the family room. With windows on two sides, a ton of natural light flooded the room, which was big enough to hold two armchairs for conversation or watching television. We put the TV on a lift in a cabinet at the foot of the bed. We also provided a kitchenette to prepare morning coffee, afternoon tea, or even a small meal. And we made sure that the bathroom was easy to navigate and had both a shower and a sitting tub; grab bars in the shower looked more decorative than functional. Elderly parents could escape to a private, outdoor terrace. This was a nod to a grandfather our researchers encountered who seemed to live in a lawn chair on a small stoop outside his children's house.

The concept of multi-generational living gained momentum during the recession with a national rollout of Next Gen℠ suites by Lennar, one of the biggest builders in America (www.lennarnextgen.com). I say national, but Lennar can only offer these homes where local codes allow. One of those places is the Stetson Valley in Phoenix, an otherwise nondescript suburban tract that I visited recently. The Evolution plan is pretty inspired compared with the other homes for sale in

The Reality House, designed for a multigenerational household, includes a first-floor in-law suite with plenty of room to watch TV, read a book, and relax. A television rises from the cabinet at the foot of the bed.

the neighborhood. As you enter a front entry courtyard, the front door to the main house is straight ahead. A little to the right is the front door to an accessory unit. In its marketing, Lennar makes a big deal of the fact that the suite isn't a detached casita, that it's conveniently attached to the house. An optional door in the den or laundry room of the main house leads to the suite.

The space lives up to its billing as a home within a home—whoever lives here may never need to set foot in the main house. It has a two-walled kitchenette with an oven and cooktop so that it can be used to cook full meals and even entertain guests. An optional third wall creates a seating area that separates the kitchen from the main living space. The "private" living space is big enough to hold a couch, game table, and television. A short hall leads past a laundry nook to a full bath (with a shower *and* a tub) and a bedroom that's as large as the secondary bedrooms in the main house. Walking a little farther down the hall takes you to a private, one-bay garage. Whoever lives there can come and go as they please through the front door or the garage.

The main house has a rather predictable layout: three bedrooms, a den, a laundry, and a dining area. The living areas are ganged along the back of the house, connecting to a covered patio that can also be accessed from the master bedroom. Lennar says that its Next Gen home is not only a "perfect fit" for your needs today, but given demographic trends, it "may be the most desirable home for future generations to purchase from you tomorrow." The builder backs up the assertion with a collection of newspaper articles in the model that documents the multigenerational living trend.

ONE OF THE MOST SOPHISTICATED ATTEMPTS to market to multigenerational buyers in recent years occurred at a subdivision in Orange County, Calif., called the Lampert Ranch, developed by The New Home Company. The builder/developer gave families the option to buy side-by-side homes with joining courtyards and backyards. Another model featured a second front door that leads to an in-law suite, complete with a bathroom and kitchenette. (One hitch: Local government officials wouldn't give the builder approval to run a second gas line to the kitchenette in the in-law suite.) A third model came with a detached casita in the backyard that's big enough for a family room and a bedroom. The space could actually be configured in several different ways, including as two bedrooms. The community sold out well ahead of schedule.

All three of our 2012 show homes, dubbed Generation X, Y, and B because each home targeted a different demographic segment, offered solutions for multigenerational living. The luxurious Gen X house, aimed at a growing affluent family, showcased a high-end solution—a full-fledged apartment, accessible by elevator, designed into a second-story wing of the house. (We had hoped to provide a separate outside entry to the suite, but the city of Orlando, Fla., wouldn't allow it.) The comfortable living room, separated by a half-wall from the bedroom, felt like a Manhattan apartment. The kitchenette was appointed with quartz countertops, an under-counter dishwasher, and high-back chairs. The bathroom included a wall bathtub with a door that opens for easy access along with a low-flow toilet th1lat doubled as a bidet.

The Gen B, or baby-boomer house (see the photo on p. 150), had *two* extra master bedroom suites. We had a ton of fun dreaming up fictitious buyers for this house who would shape its design. A couple from Philadelphia, Vinnie and Flo, we decided, wanted to buy a retirement home before they actually retire. Vinnie was still working as a broker; that's why he had a dedicated office in the house, with a door that opened to the front courtyard, and a safe room hidden behind paneling, where he kept valuables that included autographed baseballs. The couple was really ready to live the good life. Friends from Philly came to visit, sometimes for extended periods. And Vinnie often invited his golfing buddies over to the house for a few belts after a round. But the couple had some very practical concerns as well. Flo's mother was having trouble getting around on her own. Although she was feistily independent, the couple wanted to make sure she could live with them if necessary. Then there was the matter of their boomerang son, Joe, who couldn't seem to stay in a job for long and kept coming home to live with them.

Our architect, Mike Woodley, came up with an ingenious plan flexible enough to accommodate all these needs, even if they were a figment of our collective imagination. A false front door that was more like a gate led to an internal courtyard with separate entrances to Vinnie's office and a bedroom suite that was otherwise independent from the house. The suite was the perfect spot for visiting guests and for Flo's mother, should she move in. Stairs curving to the right led to a second-story tower suite for their son, or a visiting friend, that included a kitchenette and small bathroom. Orlando city officials didn't allow us to run a gas line for a stove to the suite, but we found room for a microwave. There was even space for a small desk.

From the front courtyard, you could look straight through the house to a pool area and the golf course beyond, thanks to sliding glass doors that made up the back wall of the home. We also used the glass doors to connect the formal dining room to the courtyard, creating an ideal

A false front door leads to a wide courtyard in the Gen B show home. Folding patio doors open the dining room to the courtyard, while stairs on the right lead to a second-story guest suite. This second suite, out of sight to the left, provides ideal quarters for a visiting parent. It could also be used as a home office.

party setup. Inside, the emphasis was on informal living; a wide-open floor plan, anchored by a gourmet kitchen and a bar, was conducive to big parties. Everywhere, indoor spaces flowed into outside spaces. We covered the large back patio so that you could enjoy the outdoors but stay out of the sun. We put a swim-up bar along the back of the pool for Vinnie and his golf buddies. After their guests had gone, Vinnie and Flo could sneak from their bedroom to a secluded hot tub.

The multigenerational solution for the Gen Y house was even more ingenious. Again, the city wouldn't allow a detached casita, so Woodley used a covered walkway to connect what was in effect a casita to the rest of the house. The guest suite wasn't big at 11 feet by 12 feet, but it packed a lot of punch; it included enough space for a small kitchenette with a refrigerator and microwave. The bath was tight but functional, for one person at least.

One of my favorite parts of the house was the L-shaped auto court, which merged with a front patio. You could close two gates to create the perfect enclosed hardscape for young kids on Big Wheels®. As the kids grow older, they could transition into more active sports. The driveway was big enough to accommodate two-on-two basketball or soccer. This was actually the perfect play court for kids of all ages. Woodley envisioned that a young couple, fresh from college, could set it up for beer pong before they had kids. Once they had to put the beer pong table away, they could relax on the patio and watch their kids play in the auto court.

(We've always tried to provide a space for active sports in our show homes, partly because my wife and I had two extremely active young boys. The Home of the Future not only had a basketball hoop in the garage, with a ceiling high enough to take a high-arching jumper, but we put special impact-resistant paneling on the back wall so that you could practice your tennis ground strokes. I got this idea from one of my neighbors growing up who converted his garage into a tennis practice court. The garage in our Destinations home in Las Vegas, where extreme heat made it tough to play outside, was designed with a enough space to play half-court basketball.)

The rest of the Gen Y floor plan was just as clever. Most rooms in the house were flexible enough to accommodate a variety of uses. An office near the front door, separated from the main living space by thick sliding panel doors, could easily be used as a bedroom with the addition of an armoire. When no one was home to disturb whoever was working, the barn doors could be kept wide open, providing inspirational views to the backyard and the pool. Two other legitimate bedroom spaces were designed for multiple uses as well. One had a separate door to the front patio, ideal for an out-of-work brother who had come to stay for a while. We showed a third bedroom as an open second family room to watch television, read a book, or do Pilates. But with the addition of a wall, the space could easily be converted to a bedroom.

The coolest part of the house? We installed relatively inexpensive sliding glass doors on tracks along the back wall, something you see in a lot of luxury housing these days but generally not in homes of this size. They completely blurred the boundaries between the indoor and outdoor spaces, making the home feel much larger than it actually was. To cement the illusion, we put a structural pillar holding up a corner of the roof in the shallow end of the pool. The interior tile pattern was carried onto the porch to make the impression seamless.

The weather in Florida was perfect the night we debuted the home for the industry. We sat on the back deck and watched the surprised reaction of builders and architects as they entered the modest starter house, walked down the short vestibule, and confronted a killer view across the dining room to the pool and the outdoors beyond. The eventual owners of the house would probably get the same reaction from their guests. Several of the builders who visited that night remarked that a basic version of the home, which the builder hoped to sell for roughly $250,000, would be perfect for their own son or daughter— exciting *and* affordable. Affordable was the key. ❖

Sliding glass doors made the Gen Y house, at 1,800 square feet, feel much bigger than it looked. The impression was helped by the fact that a post supporting a corner of the home was actually placed in the shallow end of the pool. Four flexible bedrooms, two with separate entry doors, provided numerable possibilities for a young, growing family.

CHAPTER TEN

New Homes Get More Affordable

THE GREAT THING ABOUT NEW HOMES TODAY is that they are more affordable than they were during the housing boom. That's not because of low home prices, however; it's due to cheap mortgage money. In fact, median new-home prices, which fell by 13 percent nationally during the housing bust (much more in some former high-growth markets), now exceed prerecession levels, after big jumps in 2012 and 2013. During 2013, as health came back to housing markets, rates on 30-year fixed-rate mortgages rose, though they remain below housing boom levels. Fixed mortgage rates trended at about 4.40 percent in 2013 compared with a high-water mark of 6.37 percent in 2007. You can buy a lot more house with rates that low.

Let's do the math on a $250,000 new home, with a 10 percent down payment and customary property tax and mortgage insurance charges. That house would cost you about $1,663 a month in 2007 at a 30-year mortgage rate of 6.34 percent. In 2013, paying 4.4 percent for a mortgage, and assuming you put 10 percent down (lenders today may ask for 20 percent), monthly payments come out to only $1,387, a savings of nearly $300 a month, enough to make the payments on a pretty nice car. The difference in monthly payments is much larger if you adjust for actual down-payment requirements in 2007 and 2013. In 2007, it was common to make only a 5 percent down payment. For a $250,000 home at 6.34 percent interest, that meant the monthly payment was more like $1,763.

As tempting as buying a home may seem, the danger today is that prices may fall as interest rates continue to rise. That actually happened to median new home prices during some months in 2013 as lenders lifted mortgage rates. If mortgage rates continue to rise, unless demand for housing remains strong, home prices may fall again. Moreover, demand for housing faces some significant headwinds. First, many homeowners with good credit ratings refinanced their homes for less than 4 percent when rates were low—why would they want to move and take on a potentially higher rate? Second, as mentioned previously, many young adults today are saddled with college loans and low incomes that will make it tough for them to buy a starter house. Finally, 21 percent of homeowners with a mortgage remained underwater in 2013, down from a high-water mark of 31 percent, according to Zillow®, the real-estate listing company. If they wanted to move, these households would have to write the bank a check for their mortgage balance, which isn't the way it's supposed to work. Most households cash in equity in their current home to buy a new one. That's why Zillow states that another 18 percent of homeowners with mortgages, though not underwater, "likely don't have enough equity to move."

The confluence of negative forces creates an undertow that keeps people out of the market. Things would be even worse if many people during the last several years hadn't escaped their negative equity position through a so-called short sale, where they basically take what they can get for their home—even if it's less than the mortgage amount— give it to the bank, and the bank takes a haircut. Banks, not surprisingly, initially frowned on this arrangement, but they came around to accepting it in recent years as a way of cutting their losses. A short sale is often a better financial alternative for the bank than a foreclosure. With no one living in a house, it may fall into disrepair. Then the bank has to go through the costly process of listing and reselling the home, which often takes months.

The problem faced by many households that can and want to buy a new home today is finding the cash to make a down payment—in most cases, a bigger one than was required during the housing boom. To qualify for most privately funded mortgages these days requires putting down 20 percent, unless you have a very high credit rating. That's about $50,000, a big chunk of change in the case of the median-priced home of roughly $250,000. Lenders want to make sure you have plenty of skin in the game; that you won't walk away from the loan if you lose your job or your financial situation otherwise deteriorates. Finding $50,000 isn't easy for people who are still paying off college loans or are stuck in low-paying jobs.

That said, as the housing market improved in 2013, lenders started writing more conventional mortgages with lower down-payment requirements. Households with strong credit ratings and good income may be able to put down as little as 5 to 10 percent, although they will pay a higher interest rate and cover the cost of private mortgage insurance, which may cost an extra $150 a month on a $250,000 home with 5 percent down. These borrowers also must still contend with closing costs, which in 2013 ran about $2,400 on a $200,000 loan, excluding title insurance, title searches, and taxes, according to a survey by Bankrate.

Many new-home buyers have turned to government-insured mortgages in recent years because of lower down-payment requirements—as low as zero in the case of mortgages insured by the Veterans Administration and the U.S. Department of Agriculture. Because few borrowers qualify for these programs—you need to be a veteran or living in a rural area where few new homes are built—most of the action is in mortgages insured by the Federal Housing Administration (FHA), which requires down payments as low as 3.5 percent. Many home-building firms, particularly the largest ones that have their own mortgage-finance subsidiaries, became experts at processing government-insured loans during the recession, despite the sometimes heavy paperwork requirements. Even as the housing market began to improve, one private research firm,

Zellman & Associates, estimated that by late 2012 half of all new-home purchases were financed through government-insured mortgages—31 percent through FHA and the rest through other programs.

There are many explanations why FHA and other government-insured mortgages have become the game of choice. Not only are down-payment requirements lower, but also a family member, friend, or "qualified" organization can gift you the money, as long as you can prove it's truly a gift that you don't have to pay back. (You can even set up a bridal-style registry and have friends and relatives give you down-payment money as a gift.) Moreover, the FHA permits sellers to pay as much as 6 percent of the purchase price to help with closing costs. Builders have been very aggressive about helping buyers with this facet of the sale; it's one reason new-home sales came back faster than existing home sales during the early stages of the housing recovery. The other good thing about an FHA mortgage is that the next buyer of your home, assuming they are creditworthy, can assume the loan at the same rate with the same balance and payment schedule.

Your credit doesn't have to be perfect to get a government-insured mortgage, either. FHA will insure mortgages for people with lower credit scores than conventional lenders require, going as low as 580 on a low-down-payment mortgage, although most of its recent borrowers score in the 600s. (Interestingly, FHA has been approving more borrowers in the higher credit range—often people with college degrees who don't have much cash for a down payment.) If your credit score is in the 500 to 579 range, you may still qualify for an FHA-insured mortgage, although you'll have to make a higher, 10 percent down payment. Even people who have gone through bankruptcy or foreclosure may be able to qualify, if they have reestablished good credit. Typically you must be at least two years out of bankruptcy and three years out of foreclosure. To qualify for an FHA loan, you must also have steady employment and have worked for the same employer for two years.

Government-insured mortgages aren't cheap, though. To compensate for the added risk of low down payments and working with borrowers who have less-than-sterling credit, the government charges a mortgage insurance premium—two of them, actually. The up-front mortgage insurance premium, paid at closing or rolled into the mortgage, equals 1.75 percent of the home loan. It was raised a few years ago to help shore up the program, which was shaken by defaults during the downturn. A second so-called annual premium, which is actually rolled into your monthly mortgage payment, varies depending on your loan-to-value ratio and the length of the loan. FHA charges an annual premium of 1.3 percent on a mortgage of less than $625,000 with less than a 5 percent down payment. So, on a $250,000 mortgage, you would pay $3,750 annually, or an extra $312.50 a month.

Whether they are selling you a government-insured or conventional mortgage, lenders want to make sure that you have enough cash flow to make the payments. They look at two ratios. Once again, there's more leeway on a government-insured mortgage. Your front-end ratio (which is your mortgage payment plus homeownership association fees, property taxes, mortgage insurance, and home insurance) typically needs to equal less than 31 percent of your gross income on a conventional loan. In the case of the FHA, you may be able to get approved with a front-end ratio of as much as 46.99 percent, if you can prove you are a good credit risk. Your back-end ratio (which includes your mortgage plus all your monthly debt, including credit cards, student loans, etc.) needs to be less than 43 percent of your gross income to qualify for a conventional loan. Again, with special approval you may be able to get away with a higher back-end ratio (up to 56.99 percent) on an FHA-insured mortgage.

There are limits to how big of a mortgage FHA will insure, though they are higher than they used to be. The government raised the thresholds during the housing bust when conventional lenders, roiled by the subprime mortgage meltdown, abandoned the market. Limits vary throughout the country, based on median home prices for the market. The threshold is relatively high in San Diego—$697,500, a reflection of the high cost of living. But about 150 miles away in Imperial Valley, Calif., the FHA ceiling is only $325,000.

Given the attractive terms on government-insured mortgages, it's logical to ask why anyone would get a conventional mortgage today, assuming the home they want to buy isn't too expensive. There are several reasons. As long as you can make the 20 percent down payment, which allows you to forgo paying a mortgage insurance premium, conventional mortgages are typically cheaper. Not only can you get a lower mortgage rate, but also you often pay lower closing costs. Mortgage insurance, assuming you have to buy it, may be cheaper on a conventional mortgage, too. And you may be able to negotiate closing costs and accept a gift from the seller to make a down payment on a conventional mortgage, just as you can on an FHA-insured mortgage.

FINANCING A HOME, whether new or existing, is notoriously complicated. Many builders, hoping to create a competitive advantage, took time during the recession to revamp their financing programs, making them easier for buyers to understand. One company sat executives behind one-way glass in a focus-group setting to watch the pain that buyers went through as they were presented with one unfathomable document after another to sign. Some builders created mortgage concierge services to assist with the mortgage process and paperwork, trying to make it as easy to buy a new home as it is to buy a new car. They took full advantage of programs that allow them to assist buyers with closing costs and help buyers identify sources of down-payment assistance. Many took the huge additional step of helping potential buyers with impaired credit improve their scores and qualify for a mortgage.

Understanding how gift programs work is key. Although gift limits vary by type of mortgage, the same process is generally followed. The first step is to produce a gift letter that states the amount of the gift, the address of the property being purchased, and the relationship of the gifter to the giftee. The letter needs to clearly state that the gift is actually a gift, not a loan. The letter should not contain any more information than that; otherwise, it may cause confusion. All parties need to sign and date the letter. You also need to keep a beefed-up paper trail to show that the money was actually gifted. If gifters sell stock as part of the process, for instance, they need to document the sale as well as the transfer of funds from the brokerage account into the account from which the gift is made. The check needs to be in the exact amount of the gift. Keep a photocopy of the check. And deposit the check, in a separate transaction, into the bank account from which your down payment will be paid.

Other sources of down-payment assistance have emerged in recent years. Some cities and counties operate down-payment assistance programs, usually targeting buyers with low or moderate incomes or first-time buyers. Rules vary widely, though you will probably need to put at least some money down, and your home may have to meet certain minimum criteria. You may also be asked to take a homeowner education class. Some local governments provide bonuses for buying a home in a designated economic recovery zone, often neighborhoods hit hard by the housing recession. In fact, restoring these blocks may have motivated creation of the assistance program in the first place. Builders, real estate agents, and mortgage brokers will know about these programs.

Employers may also be a source of financial help. Some universities and local governments make down-payment and other assistance available to employees. Some large companies, and smaller companies that want to recruit the best workers, offer support through employee-relocation assistance programs. You may even be able to negotiate this assistance from a company trying hard to hire you. You could also borrow the money from yourself—from your 401(k)-retirement account—or just pull the money out, depending on the type of account. Another alternative to produce some cash is to sell assets—a second car or heirloom furniture. Otherwise, it's time to start saving—hard. That may mean taking your breakfast and lunch to work, skipping vacations for a year or two, dropping cable television in favor of free Hulu® service and Netflix®, or just purposefully setting money aside. Financial advisors say that putting the money in a separate account helps reinforce the incentive to save, and if the account is online it's harder to pull out the money.

You may be able to get the seller, particularly a builder, to pay part of your closing costs, but don't be fooled—the expense may be rolled into the price of the home. Restrictions on seller help vary based on the type of mortgage. With conventional loans, the seller in most cases can only pay nonrecurring costs; they can't pay items paid in advance like mortgage or hazard insurance. Also, the seller's contribution is limited by how much buyers put down. If the buyer makes a down payment of 10 percent or more, the seller may contribute up to 6 percent of closing costs. If the buyer puts down less than 10 percent, sellers may only contribute up to 3 percent. It's different on government-insured mortgages. Sellers may pay all the closing costs on a VA-insured loan. Same for an FHA loan, only buyers must make at least a 3.5 percent investment in the home, whether through a down payment or closing costs. However, the buyer's funds can come from a family member's gift.

These days, a poor credit rating often stands between a potential buyer and getting the best mortgage deal. Realizing that offering credit-repair services could win over customers, many of the largest builders began programs during the downturn that continue today. Though some builders hired specialists to work with customers, most simply referred them to consultants outside the company. The builder would often pay the fees for a select number of potential buyers. One of my favorite builders, Ivory Homes in Salt Lake City, offers a concierge service—a free consultation with potential buyers to develop an action plan for mortgage qualification. The company then directs customers to credit-repair specialists who help them figure out how to pay off debt, eliminate credit report errors, and negotiate payoff agreements with creditors.

Much of this you could do on your own, if your credit score is a concern. Specialists say errors on credit reports are common; most people have at least one that could be fixed. There are plenty of online resources that can help you understand how the dominant credit-scoring system, FICO, works so you can try to resolve problems yourself. However, you may need expert help to deal with complex issues, such as identifying banks that may approve your loan regardless of your credit history; understanding credit laws and what collection agencies aren't allowed to do; consolidating your debts and negotiating a payment schedule at a lower interest rate; and learning the tricks that credit professionals use to erase negative markings. There may also be ways to include positive items on your credit record.

Homeowners, of course, weren't the only ones who experienced financial hardship during the housing recession—many businesses did, too. For that reason, new homebuyers owe it to themselves to do some careful research before they commit to buying a home from a home-building company. Some are better capitalized, build better homes, and provide better service than others. The problem is that finding reliable information about homebuilders isn't easy. But it's necessary work that can save money and anxiety in the long run. ❖

CHAPTER ELEVEN

Buyers Better Beware

GIVEN THE PRECARIOUS FINANCIAL SHAPE of homebuilders today, consumers need to exercise extreme caution when buying a new home. Purchasing a new home has always been something of a crapshoot because the projects are so complicated, so much can go wrong, and builders are notoriously undercapitalized. It's amazing how little data traditionally have been available about the business practices and financial well-being of home-building companies, considering that they sell the most expensive consumer good most people will buy in a lifetime. Twenty years ago, about the only written source of information was a Better Business Bureau report, if one existed, and even that can be suspect. Virtually the only other reliable form of reconnaissance was to walk the builder's neighborhoods on a weekend when people are out and ask whether they were satisfied with the home and service they received. Those are still two important bases to cover today, especially talking to people who have done business with the builder.

Then along came the Internet and J.D. Power and Associates. These two new sources of information have revolutionized the home-building business, dramatically empowering consumers. The Internet magnified the voices of angry customers so that potential buyers anywhere in the country could hear them. Digitally sophisticated complainants bought

URLs such as crapconstruction.com and used them to influence search engine results and popular opinion. Entire organizations sprouted up, like Homeowners Against Deficient Dwellings, which kept track online of virtually every legal action, newspaper investigation, or customer complaint against homebuilders. The movement gathered serious momentum during the housing bust when legions of builders went out of business, sometimes leaving in their wake unfinished neighborhoods, half-built homes, and broken promises. Some buyers lost all or part of deposits when their builder filed for bankruptcy. A government crackdown on mortgage fraud—steering customers into taking bad deals from captive mortgage providers—took down other builders.

But even before Internet search exposed the industry's dirty laundry, J.D. Power tilted the playing field toward consumers by audaciously publishing homebuilder customer service rankings in the biggest markets. At its height, J.D. Power ranked builders in as many as 34 new-home markets from Sacramento to Orlando. Suddenly, shoppers could compare builders on the basis of service and workmanship, rather than just price per square foot. Unfortunate things happened to some companies when rankings of the best builders were published. Builders that didn't make the list found that customer traffic often stopped in their communities, as potential buyers decided to visit the top vote getters. Some builders taught to the test, emphasizing items covered by the surveys, such as working garage door openers and service calls after three months. Builders with a long history of customer care, routinely servicing and fixing any reasonable problem with their homes, were often vindicated by the survey results. Other builders vociferously objected to the whole exercise, arguing in industry meetings that the surveys, taken at a specific juncture in the home-building process, could never accurately capture the quality of a builder's fluid construction and service. Home building isn't like manufacturing, they insisted. Instead of working within a controlled factory setting with the same workers producing the same part of the manufactured product each day, most builders work outside with an endless variety of subcontractors under varying climate conditions. For that reason, no two homes are close to the same. Yet the surveys would have you believe they were.

In 2010, J.D. Power stopped surveying buyers of new homes, but it wasn't because of builder objections. The recession had taken its toll, and few homes were being built. There wasn't much money to be made, given that J.D. Power sells top performers the right to use its name in marketing material. Nevertheless, old lists are still available online in newspaper archives. If you are interested in working with a large homebuilder, it's worth looking to see if the company's name shows up on J.D. Power's list of the best. Some companies, especially Pulte and Shea Homes, consistently scored better than others, and many builders thought the companies that didn't do well in the rankings deserved their low scores, given their lack of commitment to quality construction and service. One caveat, though: In many years J.D. Power only surveyed buyers of homes built by the largest builders, which eliminated from contention a lot of high-service local firms that built only a handful of homes each year.

SOME STATES MAKE IT EASIER than others to do homework before buying from a builder. The most diligent may have a department of consumer affairs that keeps track of complaints. The state of Maryland, one of the most active, not only tracks customer complaints but also issues standards of business behavior that all licensed builders must follow. This includes the type of warranty coverage that builders must provide. Another potential source of information is your local Better Business Bureau, which may have issued a report on a builder. The Bureau uses data drawn from a variety of sources, including complaints, to assign companies letter grades from A+ to F based on their reliability. Even builders will tell you that these reports may not be the most reliable, since companies must pay to be accredited. Nevertheless, the Bureau sees itself as a "mutually trusted" intermediary to resolve disputes.

Comparing warranties on new homes is another difficult endeavor. It helps when states dictate the level of coverage that builders must offer. Maryland, for instance, requires builders to provide at least a two-year "transferable" structural warranty that, as the name implies, can be passed on to the next owner. New Jersey, Texas, Indiana, and California require builders to issue "express" warranty protection to homebuyers, though they may not specify terms—"it could be written on the back of a napkin," said one warranty salesperson. Otherwise, buyers are covered by sometimes difficult to decipher "implied" warranties that have evolved through case law. Typically, express warranties provide 10-year coverage for structural defects, which is limited to damage to actual "load-bearing" portions of the home. In New Jersey, for example, that includes roof rafters and trusses, ceiling and floor joists, and load-bearing partitions, supporting beams, and columns, as well as basement and foundation walls and footings. Express warranties also usually provide a two-year warranty for internal systems such as wiring, plumbing, and ductwork. This includes supply lines and fittings for gas and water, as well as waste and vent pipes and their fittings. They also include one year of coverage for workmanship issues like drywall cracks, grading away from the foundation, and most building systems, including the home's frame and roof.

These protections became the industry norm during the downturn, even in states that didn't require them. That's because when private mortgage financing dried up, many builders resorted to selling homes with mortgages backed by insurance from the Federal Housing Administration (FHA) and the Veterans Administration (VA). Half of all new homes sold during the recession carried a government-insured mortgage. Those government agencies, in effect, require builders to buy warranties from a third party that provides protection similar to what the states listed above require—one year for workmanship, two years for systems, and 10 years for structural defects. It makes sense to ask for warranty coverage of this kind even if a builder doesn't offer it. You never know if your home will turn out to be a lemon. One company that offers warranty insurance, 2-10 Home Buyers Warranty®, warns that one out of every 200 homes will experience a structural failure, requiring an average of $32,000 in repairs.

The problem, as many buyers have found out the hard way, is that structural warranties may not cover every defect. They provide protection only against the failure of "load-bearing" elements of the house that make the home "unsanitary, unsafe, or otherwise unlivable." Cracked interior walls made of drywall typically don't support the house and wouldn't be considered load bearing. Wood-fiber siding that's been pelted by automatic sprinklers to the point that it's crumbling isn't a structural element. Sagging floor trusses may be considered a structural defect that's covered. But if it turns out the beams themselves were built wrong—the warranty company will send out a civil engineer to check—then the condition isn't covered. Warranty companies report that their biggest source of claims is damage caused by homes settling into the ground, which in turn impacts structural elements. Even when the builder has bored samples to check the earth's compaction, problems sometimes still occur—foundations crack, drywall pops, and windows warp.

If your home doesn't come with an express warranty, the good news is that you are probably covered by an implied state warranty. The bad news is that not only is it difficult to figure out what an implied warranty covers, but to enforce it you may also have to hire a lawyer and go to court. Rooted in common law, implied warranties differ from state to state. There are two main types. An implied "warranty of habitability" guarantees that your new home won't have any major defects that render it uninhabitable. This coverage grew out of the idea that anyone buying a "home" from a builder could reasonably expect to be able to live in it. The other type of implied coverage, a "warranty of skillful construction," stems from the notion that if someone offered to build you a home, you could assume that person was a professional with some skills. As such, that professional has an obligation to fix any problems caused by shoddy construction. The terms of some implied warranties may be better than an express warranty; you want to ensure that an express warranty doesn't supercede them.

Utah was one of the last states to recognize the consumer's implied warranty to a habitable home. But even as it recognized this protection, Utah's Supreme Court noted in 2009 that the implied warranty doesn't require perfection on the part of the builder. "No house is built without defects," it wrote. And an implied warranty doesn't "protect against mere defects in workmanship, minor or procedural violations of the applicable building codes, or defects that are trivial or aesthetic." Nor does it alleviate the buyer's responsibility to perform maintenance, negotiate an express warranty, or inspect the house, the court said.

The reason most warranties provide at least a one-year workmanship guarantee is that it may take at least that long before you can be sure that everything in your home is in working order. You may need a season of heavy spring rains before you can see that water properly drains away from the house and not into the basement. It will probably take at least that long before you know if water leaks through improperly installed windows, doors, or skylights. Conscientious builders often dispatch inspectors to check for workmanship problems within the first year, but you may want to hire your own inspector. Lawyers advise that you keep a list of problems, no matter how minor, as they occur, because they could be symptoms of a larger problem discovered later on. Drywall cracks are a classic example. They could be the result of structural defects.

Many builders today, especially the most customer-service oriented, will fix nearly any workmanship defect within a reasonable time frame. They may even fix a problem that isn't under warranty just to make you happy. Often motivated by more than altruism, they may ask for a recommendation or referrals. Even the most service-oriented builders draw the line, though, at problems that were caused by a buyer's failure to conduct routine maintenance, like changing the air filter on an HVAC system. Other builders may draw a hard line, sticking to the letter of warranty requirements. They may even look for ways to blame the problem on you—perhaps changes you made to the landscaping plan contributed to water intrusion—which is why you need to carefully read your obligations under the express warranty. If you fail to comply with them, you've given the builder an excuse to deny you protection.

The buyer's key obligation is to maintain the home. You need to clean the gutters, drain the hot water heater, touch up caulk or grout, and deal with pests. You also need to maintain adequate ventilation and humidity levels within the home. The builder's warranty may also exclude the deterioration of building materials within expected levels or changes due to natural disasters. Also typically excluded are damages caused by "acts of God," vandals, animals, or airplanes. And remember: Builder warranties don't cover consumer products in the home; those are covered by manufacturer warranties. Most builders will give you manufacturer maintenance material in a binder that also explains your maintenance responsibilities.

Many warranties require that, when you have a problem, you send written notification to the builder or call a hotline. They may require you to act quickly. Lawyers say that sending a letter, which shows you are serious, is a good idea, regardless of what the warranty says. It also pays to keep track in writing of conversations you had with your builder about a problem, including the date problems and conversations occurred. These could be used later in court, if it comes to that. One reason disputes occur is that it's sometimes difficult to determine which party is responsible for a defect like a leaky window. The window could have been made incorrectly, which would mean the manufacturer is at fault. It could have been improperly installed by a subcontractor, a perennial problem that several modern window systems are designed to overcome. Or the building weighing improperly on the window could have caused the problem.

Every few years, a massive product defect problem roils the industry. Even though standards organizations test new products before they are sold to the public, sometimes the testing doesn't unearth a problem that becomes apparent in real-world conditions. This was the case with fire-retardant plywood used on the roofs of townhomes in the 1980s; it disintegrated under high heat. The early generation of high-efficiency furnaces installed in the '90s were susceptible to corrosion from moisture buildup. Some early formulations of hardboard siding in the late '90s decomposed under high-moisture conditions.

The latest mass defect is Chinese drywall imported from 2001 to 2007. Many high-production builders, faced with drywall shortages and higher prices during the housing boom, turned to the overseas variety. The problem was that the Chinese drywall was made with some extraneous materials—sulfur, strontium, and iron. In warm, humid conditions, the drywall would emit sulfur gases that not only smelled bad but corroded copper and other metal surfaces. The emissions posed a threat to air conditioners, electrical wiring, copper plumbing, appliances, and electronics. The situation got so bad that the Consumer Product Safety Commission, which received about 4,000 complaints from residents in 43 states (with more than half from Florida), issued remediation guidance. It recommended that homeowners remove and replace all problem drywall, along with smoke and carbon monoxide alarms, electrical distribution components (including receptacles, switches, and circuit breakers but not necessarily wiring), and fusible-type fire sprinkler heads. Many production builders went ahead and repaired the homes at their own expense, even before a major maker of the tainted drywall, Knauf, had offered to reimburse them.

DESPITE ALL THE NEGATIVE PUBLICITY the new-home industry often receives, some of it for good reason, consumer surveys consistently show that most buyers are largely pleased with their builder and the home-buying experience. Many builders love what they do for a living; they are in it to please the customer. Others, of course, are in it to get rich. The problem, as the Utah Supreme Court wrote, is that virtually every consumer who buys a new home encounters a problem, sometimes a serious one. New homes simply are more complicated and less stable than the new dishwasher or television set that you buy. They are bound to have some problems, especially where two dissimilar materials come together—where windows meet drywall or stone meets glass. Plus, the wood used to build the structure may twist as it dries behind the walls, causing problems with interior walls. Concrete foundations may settle unevenly into loosely compacted soil, causing windows to warp or walls to buckle. Problems can be magnified if the home is built sloppily and hastily. Warranty companies reported a sharp increase in claims on homes built during the boom years when quality control was the least of some builders' concerns.

Other problems may result from poor communication between builders and their customers. As editor of *Builder* magazine, I used to receive about a letter a month from angry customers complaining that their builder didn't do what he said he would. The builder didn't install upgraded insulation that buyers thought they were getting, perhaps because the sales staff never told the construction crew. Or the builder didn't deliver the home on time, despite repeated promises, one of the factors critical to customer satisfaction that J.D. Power used to rate. That's a really bad situation to be in, especially if you've already sold your old home and now you have to find a place to live and store your furniture. Sometimes communication problems were more about attitude than anything else. Construction superintendents, used to dealing gruffly with tradespeople, forgot their manners when talking with homebuyers. Many builders during the last 10 years put their superintendents through customer-service training so that they would act appropriately during drywall walk-throughs and other communications with customers.

Work done by Avid Ratings, the leading firm that conduct buyer satisfaction surveys for homebuilders, shows that lack of communication, more specifically "lack of informative updates," is one of the top five service problems builders face. But the top service problem is the failure to fix problems identified during closing walk-throughs in a timely manner. The problem is magnified when the builder doesn't get to these repairs until after buyers have taken title. Another leading cause of dissatisfaction, related to tardiness in making repairs, is the perception that too many items are on that "punch-out" list. The two other problems in the top five deal with options. Buyers are concerned that options cost too much and don't meet their expectations.

Avid's work highlights the importance of identifying and fixing problems as early as possible. That's one reason most builders insist on doing an inspection walk with the customer before drywall is installed. Builders who are proud of the quality of their work encourage buyers to bring an expert. In addition to making sure that walls, windows, and doors were installed correctly, this walk-through is the best time to move electrical, communication, and plumbing fixtures, if need be. Most home designs include a specified number of outlets in main rooms. But your plans for the use of rooms may change while the home is being built; you may decide to use a secondary bedroom for a home office, which may require a structured wiring outlet. Outlets and switches—their location and number—is one of the top five product-related problems that buyers have with builders.

Walk-throughs can be crucial. We discovered more than our share of construction problems during show-home walks. On one project, to meet a tight deadline, the builder started construction before project details were complete, using an old set of architectural plans. When we visited the home during construction, we found plumbing runs sticking up through the concrete floor where door thresholds were supposed to go. That problem could be fixed inexpensively, but another couldn't be: Trusses had been engineered and built using an earlier design of the house. As a result, the back porch couldn't be built according to the architect's design, which became a source of considerable friction. Frame walks also are an ideal time to check whether the placement of windows has been optimized. We decided to move and enlarge several picture windows in the live-work lofts we built in Atlanta to take better advantage of some great city views. Since the homes were built from a set of plans that could be used throughout the country, the designer hadn't considered the unique views provided by this particular site.

The opposite was true of our HomeLink show home designed the following year on a heavily wooded, downward-sloping lot in suburban Atlanta. Walking the home during framing and after it was finished was a revelation. The architect had considered the view from nearly every room. We didn't have to change a thing. The windows in the master bedroom looked into the tops of trees in the backyard. The view from the bed itself appeared to be framed by picture windows.

THERE'S SOME EVIDENCE THAT CONSTRUCTION quality improved during the last decade, as the Internet and survey firms exposed the industry's weaknesses. J.D. Power surveys done in the mid-2000s, for instance, found that the average new home had 14 defects. That number had fallen to less than 10 by 2009, as builders competed to finish atop published customer-satisfaction lists. Another possible reason for the decline in defects: During the recession, builders—just to get a sale—were forced to work overtime to reduce complaints and better serve the customer. However, the drop in defects appears to be primarily in cosmetic problems such as drywall imperfections, paint problems, and carpet and flooring flaws—items that used to show up at the top of the defect list. The industry apparently sweated this small stuff. By comparison, the most common complaints in 2009 and 2010, the last years of the J.D. Power survey, were landscaping, kitchen-cabinet quality and finish, and heating and air-conditioning issues.

These three big potential problems deserve special attention. It's important not to be swayed by how kitchen cabinets look in the models; you may be looking at an upgrade. Inspect the cabinets that you will actually receive, and learn what they are made of and how they are built. The material used to make the drawers and shelves—whether it's particleboard, plastic, laminate, veneers, or solid wood—makes a big difference. I was reminded of that recently while touring some models with the sales and marketing executive of a large California home-building company. She went straight to a kitchen drawer in a competitor's lavishly designed kitchen, put her hand inside, and cried, "See!"

Sure enough, the drawers were plastic inside, though they looked like a million dollars on the outside. Another indication of quality is the big side panels that end cabinet runs. They can make a whole kitchen look cheesy if done with a cheap veneer.

Landscaping is a perennial problem. It finishes first on Avid's list of top five product problems. The scope of landscape work needs to be in writing. Don't assume that your builder is going to do the work; he typically subcontracts it to a landscaping specialist. You need a written landscaping plan that includes whether you will receive sod or grass seed, the plants you will receive, how big they will be, and where they will go. The problem is that landscaping is often the last thing completed on a new-home project, and in most cases some landscaping must be complete before you can get a certificate of occupancy. If you move in before the work is complete, it may be difficult to get the builder to come back and finish the job, especially if he's relying on a landscape contractor. Then you may have to wait your turn during busy closing months for the landscaper to be available. That's one reason some buyers hire their own firms or do the work themselves.

Heating and air-conditioning systems are another potential headache that can be complicated and expensive to fix. It may feel like hot or cold air isn't distributed evenly through the house. That may be because the system was undersized, zones weren't set up properly, or there are leaks in the house frame or ducts. Even the location of surrounding trees and the position of your home on the lot can contribute to the sensation that some rooms are always hot and others always cold. In the old days, builders would routinely oversize HVAC systems to obviate any potential problems with rooms that might overheat in the summer due to west-facing picture windows or get chilly in the winter because they are located over an uninsulated garage. They figured the added cost of more HVAC tonnage was less expensive than a callback later on. But bigger-than-necessary systems can hide other problems, like leaky ducts. Plus, the savings from right-sizing the HVAC system could be used to buy better-insulating windows that save on utilities.

These days, many builders would prefer to optimize rather than over-specify the HVAC system.

One advantage to buying an Energy Star–rated home is that its HVAC system is inspected during construction. HVAC installers have to follow several checklists that are filled out during system design and installation. Then an Energy Star rater comes in to verify and test the quality of the installation. Energy Star requires that builders test HVAC ducts for leakage, and systems can't be overspecified. Many new homes are built with zoned temperature controls that can not only save money on heating and cooling but also provide more control over temperatures within different rooms. The systems use multiple thermostats and mechanical damper controls to individually heat and cool zones. Dampers installed in the ductwork direct airflow where it's needed. Zoning an HVAC system can save you 20 to 30 percent on energy costs because the system only operates where and when you need it.

Compounding home defect problems, homebuilders who survived the housing bust have downsized dramatically. The first place they cut when business declined was the workforce of laborers and managers who actually built the homes, since there wasn't as much of that work to do. (The building bust hit subcontractors, who perform most of the actual construction work, particularly hard.) The next place builders cut were their staff of customer-care representatives, a class of employee that was only added to most home-building firms in the mid-2000s. These were the people charged with handling defects, often calling on subcontractors to fix the problems. As a result of cutbacks and changes, when home-building activity does return in full force, there won't be as many qualified managers and tradespeople to do the job. The biggest builders, who are in the best position to attract the qualified subcontractors that remain, will be in the driver's seat, along with the best custom builders who do large, high-end projects that attract the best craftsmen who like the artistic and skill challenge. Those jobs also pay the best.

Another pressure already manifesting itself from a pickup in building activity is an increase in material prices. Builders may be unable to pass on material price increases in the form of higher home prices due to competition from the resale home market. As a result, their profit margins may be squeezed, adding pressure to cut corners. The source of the problem is that many building products companies reduced their manufacturing capacity to survive the building bust; they closed or sold factories or converted them to other uses. So there aren't as many plants today that produce, for example, oriented strand board (OSB), a less expensive alternative to plywood sheathing. When demand increases, producers may be forced into the expensive option of resuscitating mothballed plants. Every company associated with home building—from builders, to subcontractors, to suppliers—is looking to recoup losses now that the housing market has strengthened.

ANOTHER PROBLEM IN TODAY'S MARKET is sifting through builder incentives to determine whether you are getting the best deal possible. Thankfully, the most "innovative" offers—the ones that enabled people to buy a home with no money down, even if they couldn't produce a W-2—have been wiped off the financial earth by regulators. But the market is full of varying incentives that make comparisons difficult. One builder, for instance, may offer $20,000 in free incentives such as a finished basement or a sunroom. (The value of free incentives is usually included in a home's appraisal.) Another may include them in the base price of a home that sells for only $10,000 more than the first builder's home. It helps to use a checklist—builders often provide them—to figure out what's included in the base price of a home and how much upgrades cost. Evaluating these kinds of incentives should help you figure out which is the best deal.

It gets more complicated when you have to compare discounts with mortgage inducements. A builder may offer to buy down the interest rate on your mortgage. That may save you much more over the life of the mortgage than $20,000 in design discounts. Another builder may contribute to closing costs, which is a good option if you don't have a lot of cash. It all depends on your financial situation and how long you expect to own the home. You also need to consider how discounts affect the base value of your home, as well as the potential for future appreciation. Remember, homes aren't likely to appreciate as much as they have in the past. And under current federal law, the first $500,000 in capital gains for a married couple ($250,000 for an individual) on the sale of your principal residence is tax-free.

Another thing to keep in mind when you shop for a new home is that appearances can be misleading. Bright lighting and mirrors, liberally applied by model decorators, make rooms look larger. Some builders may even use undersize furniture in their models to make rooms look larger; there's a cottage industry of companies that make tables, chairs, and sofas at 85 percent of their original size. The easiest way to check whether chairs are undersize is to sit in them and see whether they are snug. It's harder to hop in a made-up bed to judge if it's smaller than normal, but you can measure to see if it's closer in size to a queen than a king, or a double than a queen. If you are interested in buying a

Decorated models may divert attention from bigger issues—such as whether there is enough room for dresser and a desk in this child's bedroom.

particular model from a builder, it makes sense to see an undecorated unit. That makes it easier to imagine how your furniture will look in the home.

The size of secondary bedrooms is another important concern. I've seen plenty of children's bedrooms that are so small there's no room for a dresser, a bookshelf, or a desk. You are more likely to encounter this problem in smaller homes for first-time buyers. Most residential designers believe that 10 feet by 12 feet is the minimum size for a secondary bedroom in a suburban tract home, but you may see smaller children's bedrooms in Western markets where builders reason that families spend more time outdoors. Builders usually appeal to trade-up buyers with bigger secondary bedrooms intended for teenage children. In the least expensive starter homes, kids may use a hall bath. But as you move up the new-home ladder, you may see them sharing a Jack-and-Jill bath with entrances from both bedrooms. In high-end production houses, kids often have their own bathrooms.

Another thing to be careful about is what's included as a standard feature in the builder's homes. You may be drawn to a model-home community because the prices seem low, and they may well be—on the base house. But when you show up, you are looking at a beautiful model that contains a raft of upgrades. The best builders will give you a detailed shopping list identifying what's included and what's extra. Unfortunately, these lists rarely include the prices of extras, since they vary by the size of the house. You have to ask for that information. One national builder, Lennar, eliminates all guesswork by marketing homes in which "everything's included." The company, the third-largest builder in the country in 2012, uses its scale to purchase upgrades at a discount. But others, who want to generate as much foot traffic as possible, prefer to publicize the lowest price. Then they attempt to bowl over buyers with granite countertops, hardwood floors, and stainless-steel appliances that cost extra. It's always a good idea to walk a home with standard specifications if you are really interested in buying from a builder. Most have one ready for just this purpose. ❖

CHAPTER TWELVE

Contemporary Design Leaves Its Mark

ONE BRIGHT SIDE OF THE HOUSING RECESSION, if you could possibly overlook the pain and hardship it brought people, was that some builders decided to take a chance on architecture as a way of standing out from older homes. That's one reason why we witnessed a refreshing rise of contemporary design, even in production housing. Contemporary designs, with their strong geometric forms, honest use of materials, and bright colors, may not be everyone's cup of tea—a group of Atlanta builders, gathered to listen to a lecture about innovation around the country, nearly laughed me out of the room when I showed them a picture of the Utah production home shown on the facing page. But during the downturn, many builders embraced the clean aesthetic of contemporary architecture because it can produce savings in building materials as it sets homes apart in the market. Even if only 10 to 15 percent of the population wants a modern home—that's what industry surveys show—it's next to impossible to find an affordable one in the new-home or resale market.

That's always seemed strange, given that contemporary design is commonly used for corporations, office buildings, hospitals, and museums. The contemporary aesthetic is pretty common in new apartment buildings, especially in the big apartment markets of New York City, Los Angeles, and Washington, D.C. If you want to build a con-

Garbett Homes, a relatively new home builder, took a chance on building brightly colored contemporary homes to stand out in the Salt Lake City market. The builder reasoned that buyers drawn to the modern-home aesthetic, marked by strong geometric form and functional design, couldn't find it in resale housing. The homes sold so well that Garbett introduced a similar series of bigger contemporary homes.

temporary custom home, it's relatively easy to find an architect and custom builders who specialize in the style. And several of the upstart modular home-building companies doing business today build almost exclusively in the contemporary style. Yet production builders, until recently, refused to gamble on modern homes, fearing that too few people wanted to buy a home that conspicuously breaks from tradition.

The green house by Garbett Homes is part of a Solaris series that sold out quickly during the recession. It's located in an exciting new Salt Lake City community called Daybreak that blends traditional and contemporary architecture with exciting results. The home appears to be little more than four boxes put together with complementary bright colors. Color is an inexpensive way to create distinctive design. Notice how the doorframes on the green home are painted a complementary blue and the stucco and concrete elements are left a uniform white. There's no useless detail on the house. All the adornment is structural —the brackets, for example, actually hold up the awning and porch.

One cool thing about the Solaris series is that the contemporary look is carried through to the interiors. The model was decorated with $10,000 in furnishings from IKEA®, which explains the platform bed in the master, pendant lighting in the kitchen, and the geometric shapes throughout. The presentation seems much more realistic than the elaborate traditional interior designs of the housing boom. Garbett will even give buyers who want to furnish their home in a similar fashion a list of the products that it used. While prices on the Solaris series started in the low $200s, many buyers spent lavishly on upgrades, so much so that Garbett developed a new line of move-up contemporaries that start in the high $400s. The design program is supported by a strong energy-conservation package. Photovoltaic panels generate electricity, and waste heat from the process is used to provide hot water and heating, so-called cogeneration technology.

A similar story played out in Denver, where Infinity Homes built a series of contemporary LEED-certified homes called Lime that sold two or three times faster than most homes in the market. Infinity built a series of two- and three-bedroom homes with lofts modeled after a show home it built for *HGTV Green Home*. At nearly $500,000 for 2,100 square feet, the homes weren't cheap, but creative touches like limestone siding, black bricks, and a porch roof that riffed on an airplane wing made them irresistible to professionals with small families. It helped that the homes were built with a full menu of green features, including 2x6 walls packed with extra

The interiors of the Lime series by Infinity Homes prove that contemporary interiors long on metal and glass don't have to look cold and uninviting. Interior walls leave plenty of space for expressive art. Infinity gave buyers of these high-performance homes a free iPad® loaded with software to monitor energy consumption.

insulation and copious low-e windows that bathed the modern interiors with light. Infinity made headlines in local newspapers during the recession by throwing in a free iPad to drive the smart-home system.

ONE BENEFIT OF CONTEMPORARY DESIGN, for builders at least, is that interiors can be simplified and costs lowered. Interior molding can be eliminated or smaller profiles used, since, as purists will tell you, they were only used to begin with to hide mistakes. Walls can remain simple and flat, accented with color rather than showy wainscoting, built-in cabinetry, or some other purely decorative treatment. Shea Homes used some of the savings from deleting features from its homes to buy finishes that you don't typically see in a new production home, including frosted-glass doors to separate the toilet compartment from the rest of the master bath, an unusual spec for production housing. Colored pendant lamps hang over functional kitchen islands with room for four to eat comfortably, and sleek, European-style cabinets with flat

Sales literature and an online configurator showed potential buyers how to furnish the big open spaces in Spaces Homes for a variety of uses. Instead of using traditional names for rooms, Shea Homes appealed to younger, hipper buyers by emphasizing the potential use of spaces. The kitchen is labeled "cook" and the island "eat."

Even when neighborhood covenants dictated traditional exteriors, ColRich, a San Diego-area builder, offered contemporary interiors to stand out in the marketplace. The Sol Terra series featured foldaway doors that blend interior and exterior spaces, sleek styling, and open spaces. The strategy worked—ColRich outsold competing nearby neighborhoods.

panels contribute to the modern motif. By putting these items in every home, Shea managed to buy in bulk and secure a competitive price.

In the tradition of contemporary housing, Shea thought about function first, going so far as to drop conventional names for rooms and rename spaces for functions like eat, sleep, and bathe. The kitchen island was designed so that two people can face each other around the counter instead of sitting side-by-side, which is the case with most island designs. The great room was devised with the television in mind, rather than as an afterthought. Television screens need to go where they won't receive glare from windows and where they can be comfortably viewed. Unfortunately, too many family room floor plans orient seating around a fireplace, which often leaves the television screen with no place to go except above the fireplace. Many people don't mind looking up to watch television, but you should see whether you are one of them. Try it for three hours; watch a football game or a movie and see if your neck is stiff the next day.

Even in neighborhoods where covenants require traditional facades, builders are streamlining interiors to appeal to sophisticated buyers. The home shown on the facing page, located in a community called Sol Terra, is one in a series of three-story homes in San Diego by ColRich Homes, a leader in luxury production housing. One of the best-selling projects in California during 2010, Sol Terra earned a big premium from buyers for its interior design. Neighborhood covenants dictated Spanish, Monterey Ranch, and Tuscan exterior styles. But inside, ColRich created a look that the builder calls Metropolitan; it's an elegant finished loft styling that you might see in the pages of *Elle Décor*. There are no exposed ducts, as you often see in true urban loft design, but there's no crown molding or raised-panel doors and cabinets, either. The floor plans are wide open, with delineated living spaces flowing together. As befitting the contemporary design aesthetic, the interiors are highlighted by creative custom touches—an entry hall with vertically oriented tile, an open three-story stairway, and foldaway doors in the family room that open to the outdoors, creating a dynamite party space.

Christopher Homes, a talented builder in Las Vegas, did one of the best jobs of incorporating contemporary architecture in luxury production housing, just before the housing recession began. The company planned a neighborhood of 46 homes in Summerlin on a great golf course near the Red Rock Canyon Conservation Area. The homes are big, ranging from 4,000 to 6,000 square feet. But their design, which optimizes front and rear views, is nothing short of sensational. Features included sky decks, rooftop gardens, terraces, and porches off key rooms. The company put items in all its homes that you'd usually have to build a custom home to get, including disappearing doors, a stainless-steel pivot front entry door, marble or travertine bath tops and surrounds, and commercial-grade appliances.

The interiors, with their creative use of materials, defied the notion that contemporary homes are sterile and uninviting. Concrete interior walls, with telltale marks from their pouring forms still showing, looked like a natural extension of the exteriors. Angled stairways mixed wood flooring with slate that also climbed nearby walls. Walls were specifically left to display art, a hallmark of contemporary design. Ceiling treatments done with unusual wood slats, dark wood beams, and other treatments helped define zones for entertaining, relaxing, and eating within the otherwise open floor plans. As in other communities of single-family contemporary homes, the look was strongly influenced by urban lofts and high-rise condominiums that gained in popularity during the previous decade and continues to tempt buyers today. ✤

Christopher Homes opened a series of striking contemporary models in Las Vegas just as the housing recession began. The designs employed an unusually eclectic palette of materials for production housing, including poured concrete interior walls, slate floors, and stainless-steel pivot doors. Varied ceiling treatments delineated living spaces in the wide-open floor plans.

CHAPTER THIRTEEN

The Rise of In-Town Living

ON A RECENT TRIP SOUTH, I decided to stop in Atlanta and visit a show-home project that we built for the International Builders Show in 2000, if only to make sure it was still there! The series of three live-work townhomes located in the urban fringe Castleberry Hill neighborhood of Atlanta wasn't easy to find. But as I crossed the railroad tracks and reached the general vicinity, familiar landmarks started to appear—the liquor store, a contemporary art gallery, the midrise loft building that was completed about the same time as our project. I turned a corner and spotted the show homes, partially obscured by trees that had greatly matured since I'd been there last (see the photo on p. 186). The relatively peaceful setting belied the turmoil of building these homes in a neighborhood that had seen hardly any new development in a century. The other thing that struck me: The buildings, though relatively new, looked as though they'd been there a long time.

Our live-work project was precariously ahead of its time. We were working without a net. The idea of developing new housing in an urban environment, which magazines loved to cover but few companies were actually doing, was risky enough. But then we added the extra peril of choosing a style of housing—integrated living and work spaces—that hadn't been popular in 60 years or more, though it made perfect sense for this fringe neighborhood. Fortunately, we were working with

The live-work project in Atlanta as it looked when first built. The trees have matured to create an even more pleasing streetscape today.

a great team that was eager to blaze a trail. Beazer Homes, the builder, was led by an English-born CEO, Ian McCarthy, who had built homes all over the world and was no stranger to urban housing. Our architect, Andres Duany, the father of the new urbanist movement had dedicated his career to creating walkable, livable neighborhoods based on historic precedents. It helped that the mayor of Atlanta at the time, Bill Campbell, had praised Duany publicly for his planning acumen.

The first step, a critical one, was finding a suitable lot. We drove innumerable city blocks with Atlanta city officials who were eager to bring national attention to their urban housing market. They took us down downtrodden streets with empty lots that had long ago reverted to the city's ownership, parcels that we could have for a song. Some of the better old neighborhoods of single-family homes were slowly coming back with the help of banks that were required to direct lending to low-income neighborhoods. We visited some slowly emerging mixed-use neighborhoods where urban pioneers—usually artists, gays and lesbians, or people who crave urban culture—had put down stakes. Of all these areas, Castleberry Hill, within walking distance of the Atlanta convention center (if you wanted to take the chance), seemed like the ideal location. Beazer bought a piece of ground across the street from the train tracks. That meant the homes would probably always have a view of the city skyline.

Identifying and securing the site turned out to be the easy part. Before we could build, we needed the blessing of the neighborhood association, which wasn't sure what to make of our desire to build the project in their midst. We also needed the approval of an historic preservation society. The approval process, which took several months and threatened our timeline for the project, resulted in changes to the design of the project. The neighborhood association didn't want the flat roofs that were in the initial design, so we sloped them slightly. The historic commission was concerned that the facade wasn't quite in keeping with the warehouse district, so we modified the overhangs. Also, it wasn't immediately clear whether the townhomes would need to be built to residential or commercial building codes; the three city agencies involved in the project weren't sure either, though they ultimately decided that we needed to build to commercial standards. That meant putting built-up firewalls between the buildings and fire doors between the work and living spaces. Then, when Beazer inquired about construction financing, the bank asked for a list of comparable projects to analyze. We couldn't find any. Luckily, the bank took a chance and provided funding anyway.

To mitigate another significant risk, Beazer took soil samples to check for contaminants before it bought the lots. It's anyone's guess what you'll find when you dig up inner-city dirt where many people, buildings, and sometimes factories have gone before. We had written plenty of stories in *Builder* magazine about great projects that were derailed by the discovery of industrial pollutants that take years to mitigate. Before the EPA went to work, unregulated factories throughout the East and Midwest melted lead and belched smoke that settled in nearby urban neighborhoods. Our live-work project was located within a couple miles of one of the largest brown-field reclamation projects in the country—Atlantic Station. Built on the site of the former Atlantic Steel Mill, the developer had to put down 2 feet of fresh soil to bury contaminants deep in the ground.

Urban builders go through a lot of pain to build projects. It often takes a ton of work—mind-numbing paperwork and a seemingly endless series of meetings—to get urban projects approved. Fresh designs, unique to the city parcel, must typically be commissioned. And developers are never sure whether they will interest enough buyers willing to pay what it takes to cover expenses. But once completed, the projects often sell quickly because there's nothing else like them available. Beazer, which was understandably nervous about the depth of demand for live-work housing, started getting interest in the homes even before construction began. It wound up selling the homes for about 30 percent more than expected to people who pretty closely resembled the target buyers for whom they were designed.

Our designer, Duany, who had spent years combing downtown retail districts in small-town America, had a pretty good idea of who would want these homes. Most people just drive by these buildings; Duany would go inside to see how people had connected work and living areas with circular stairs, or designed back entries that led to two-story townhomes over a real estate office. After he showed us about a dozen basic variations on the live-work theme, we decided to build three that had the most modern-day potential. The first was an "entry-level unit," a simple story-and-a-half loft—perfect for an artist or graphic designer—with workspace below and a small loft bedroom and bath above (photo at left). Next door was a more "traditional" live-work unit—a big,

The Loft, the smallest of our three live-work buildings, was designed for a young graphic artist who could work below and live above in a vaulted bedroom loft. The plan included a fully equipped kitchen with lots of storage space, some of it intended for business storage.

open first-floor space that could house a store or restaurant; the two floors above were a home accessible from within the store and from back stairs. We decorated the building as a real estate office; it ended up being purchased by a fledgling movie production company. The final building in the trio was designed for a lawyer; it featured a simple reception area and office on the front with a living area tucked behind. A lawyer actually did buy it. The single-story home even had a side patio. On my recent visit, I noticed that the current owner had protected the patio with razor wire.

MANY MORE OPTIONS EXIST TODAY for people who want to live in an urban setting, thanks to 20 years of redevelopment efforts. During the 1990s, developers focused primarily on converting old industrial and warehouse buildings into inexpensive loft apartments. Years later, as the supply of restorable older buildings dried up, attention turned to developing new condos and apartments, often with a loft aesthetic. New urban construction took off during the housing boom when developers found that they could charge sales prices high enough to cover development costs. Buildings initially intended to be rental apartments were converted to condominiums with ownership. As a result, many major cities—even unlikely places like Kansas City, Mo., and Tucson, Ariz.—now lay claim to vibrant downtown housing areas. Activity in these urban enclaves cooled during the housing downturn when it became difficult for developers to obtain financing. But the fire didn't go out. In fact, urban construction came back early in the housing recovery.

A happy confluence of economic and demographic factors explains the phenomenon. First, and perhaps foremost, a full 70 percent of American households now do not have school-aged children. That means that the big driver of suburban housing—having your children in good schools—motivates only 30 percent of households. The rest—whether they are singles who like the security of multifamily buildings, baby-boomer couples looking for a more exciting lifestyle, or the huge

Generation Y cohort fresh from college—are free to live wherever they want (and can afford). More and more of them elect to live in the city where they can be close to work, interesting restaurants, sports venues, and cultural events—the good stuff.

The subject of selling a house in the suburbs and moving downtown is a hot topic in my neighborhood. Many of our friends began married life in a downtown apartment and moved to the suburbs when it was time for their kids to go to school. What they find, when they investigate returning to the city now that their nest is empty, is that the move often involves big trade-offs. After living in spacious suburban homes, they are surprised at how little space they get for the money. At the peak of the housing boom, urban developers in Washington, D.C., were getting $500 a square foot for condos, which translates into $500,000 for only 1,000 square feet of living space. And that doesn't include condo fees that add hundreds of dollars a month to expenses. These condos held their value pretty well during the recession; they lost roughly 20 percent but had gained most of it back by 2013.

The urban housing development movement took off in the 2000s after a seminal U.S. Census report showed that many major cities added urban population during the 1990s. Groups that track development issues reported that urban fringe neighborhoods (which initially appealed primarily to single households, gays and lesbians, artists, and other "lifestyle" buyers) were drawing the leading edge of the kid-free baby-boom generation. Urban land that normally would have gone to office or retail development started to make economic sense for condos and high-end rental buildings. Ironically, it turned out that urban populations declined in most major cities during the decade of the 2000s, although it wasn't clear until after the decade was over. By then, new urban housing enclaves had already been established in major cities throughout the country.

Even before the housing market fully recovered, a new generation of urban mid- and high-rise projects began rising from the ground. To hedge their bets, many developers today include a greater mix of smaller units, designed to appeal to entry-level buyers. Developers are wary of how deep demand will be, and they want to attract as many early buyers as possible. Although land prices fell in many urban markets during the housing recession, they didn't decline as much as they did in far-flung suburban markets. Also, the cost to build projects—labor and building materials—didn't come down that much. As a result, the cost of urban development, and the prices and rents developers charge, remains relatively high.

AMONG THE MANY CHALLENGES POSED by infill projects is building a signature structure that's still compatible with the design of the existing neighborhood. A four-unit upscale condo building on Wyoming Avenue in Washington, D.C., designed by Wnuk Spurlock Architecture, is a wonderful example of how that challenge can be met. Wedged into a skinny site between a six-story hotel and a historic Flemish revival mansion, the building is clad in a compatible palette of limestone, brick, and copper. Its sill heights and brick banding are aligned with the mansion next door, preserving the rhythm of the street. Yet the building's geometric form and updated roofline give it a wholly modern expression. Textured limestone designed to look like abstract bays lightens up the massing, as does a clerestory band of glass on the top floor, which steps back from the street to downplay the building height.

The building at 2120 Wyoming Avenue in Washington, D.C., blends with historic architecture even as it makes its own statement. The project, situated between a six-story hotel and a Flemish revival mansion, relates to the massing and color of neighboring buildings with a cleaner, more contemporary style.

Developers often enlist architects who specialize in urban work to do these projects. They need the help of an architect to navigate complicated design standards and requirements. The architect's charge is to include as many homes as possible, typically at a wide range of prices; most urban projects attempt to appeal to a broad range of people of varied means who might be attracted by an urban lifestyle. Also, there's the issue of designing attractive, accessible common spaces within the building, whether that is a shared courtyard, a business center, or a landscaped roof. That's something not every designer can do effectively. It's just one of many factors that raise the degree of difficulty on these projects to a very high level.

We're seeing more grittier, urban projects like the one pictured below in Berkeley, Calif. Acting as both architect and developer, David Trachtenberg bought the former Rose Grocery, a century-old retail

David Trachtenberg's unique Rose Grocery project in Berkeley, Calif., a series of 10 light-filled courtyard homes, sold out quickly. The architect/developer refurbished the facade of the old grocery, converting it to a garage with an upstairs guest studio. A courtyard separates the garage from the brightly lit homes in back.

building that had been abandoned for decades. A neighbor tipped him off that it was available. Trachtenberg kept the old facade with its proud, sculpted false front, pushed out awning windows, and turned the building into a garage. Each of the attached homes has a private courtyard, 10-foot-high ceilings, and abundant natural light. The design and interiors were kept simple to attract a wide variety of buyers, who quickly scarfed up the one-of-a-kind homes.

It's not easy to get in on small urban infill projects such as these. You need to keep close tabs on what's happening within a neighborhood. It helps to know people who already live there who can keep you abreast of pending developments. Local real estate agents may be another good source of information. It makes sense to get on the interest list of the limited numbers of developers who specialize in urban infill work. New media is another important source of leads. Some of the most robust urban markets—Washington, D.C., New York City, Chicago, and Los Angeles in particular—are now covered in intimate detail by bloggers who are often the first to publicize new projects. They will track virtually every new project, competing to be the first to show artist renderings of proposed buildings, then fighting to get inside the buildings and obtain pictures of the interiors.

THE LAST DECADE SAW THE RISE of vibrant urban high-rise markets in major cities throughout the country. Even mid-markets such Omaha, Neb., and Oklahoma City got in on the action. Governments were eager to encourage development on forgotten city blocks where infrastructure—roads and utilities—was already in place. Developers who had previously shied away from doing low-yielding urban residential projects leaped on the bandwagon during the real estate boom when they discovered they could command prices of $300 a square foot or more. Hundreds of successful projects were developed and sold before the credit window dropped like the sword of Damocles.

Many of the projects that didn't make it to the finish line went bankrupt. They were often resold, sometimes more than once, until their value dropped to the point where building owners could afford to offer new units again at market prices. Once these so-called "resets" occurred, some urban high-rise projects took off to become among the best selling in the country during the housing recession. And no wonder. In many cases, the buildings were designed with luxury pool decks and concierge services left over from the housing boom. Now they could be had for a fraction of the previous price. People lined up to buy into resuscitated projects in attractive locations such as San Diego and Miami.

The Spire, a high-rise project in Denver with incredible views of the Rocky Mountains and a now-vibrant downtown area, is a case in point. After prices were reset, it became one of the three best-selling condo projects during 2010. The Spire sits right in the middle of an entertainment district, close to the ballpark, theater, and lots of restaurants. The developer created a luxury resort right on the premises, with a year-round pool deck, a large party space, and a fitness facility. In 2011, you could get into a one-bedroom unit with a parking space included for only $260,000. A two-bedroom, two-bath unit, also with parking, started at $399,000. Three luxury homes on the 30th floor with custom interiors went for about $800,000.

Chicago developed one of the most vibrant downtown housing markets during the last two decades. So many people live downtown now that getting back into the city at 5 p.m. can be a hassle due to the legion of people making reverse commutes. On average, 2,400 homes have been added in the city each year for the last 20 years, according to Appraisal Research, a market tracking firm. Many older buildings in Chicago's warehouse district were converted to lofts early on. Most of the activity now is in new construction, including some iconic high-rise towers along Lake Michigan. The lifestyle benefits are obvious. You can walk to the lake, ride a bike along the park, and shop along the Miracle Mile.

Condo developers in Chicago, Atlanta, Los Angeles, and elsewhere typically offer two kinds of space. Some sell raw square footage that can be configured however you like, though plumbing for bathrooms and kitchens is typically roughed in. You can use your own interior designer, or if you don't have one, the condo developer will make referrals and may even do the work for you. Increasingly, though, developers are selling space that's largely finished. They will install kitchens and baths and may even offer options and upgrades. You may still be given choices for flooring, lighting, and other finishes.

A similar story is playing out in close-in suburban settings. The housing recession favored housing located close to job centers and downtown districts. People who could still afford to buy a home suddenly had access to the most prized neighborhoods, most of them close to town. Projects in far-flung suburbs stopped dead in their tracks, as people voted with their feet, or maybe their cars, to live closer to where they work. The few banks willing to make development loans encouraged builders to develop close-in sites, as opposed to new master-plan communities that would need new roads, utilities, and other amenities. The infrastructure—including shopping, restaurants, and hospitals—is already there for suburban infill projects.

Some of the most creative work done in recent years has been infill condominium projects in suburban and urban centers. One celebrated project is Safari Drive Condominiums in Scottsdale, Ariz., designed by the legendary Seattle architectural firm of Miller Hull, known for its contemporary work with glass, steel, and concrete. Planned for a forgotten triangular city lot, the idea was to create a village-like setting that combines 165 upscale townhomes and flats with some commercial businesses—live-work units and retail—within a dense, walkable environment. The designers organized the project around outdoor courtyards shaped and shaded by buildings that give it human scale. At the center of the project is a circular court shared by cars, pedestrians, and outdoor diners. Walking home, residents pass a rich variety of native landscapes, shopping, and public spaces.

DURING THE HOUSING BOOM, the market for single-family infill homes thrived in many major metro areas. Builders could buy the

The edgy Safari Drive, by Miller Hull, was built on an abandoned triangular lot in busy Scottsdale, Ariz., close to shopping. The architects designed a village on the site, complete with 165 upscale townhomes and flats, live-work units, and retail businesses. Courtyards, including a circular court in the center of the project, provide spots for residents to meet and mingle.

cheapest home on the block, build a new one in its place, and often command a premium for the new home that was well above the median price for the neighborhood. Some of these new homes dwarfed existing ones, leading to cries to curtail Mansionization. Some communities enacted regulations that limited how big these new homes could be relative to the size of other homes in the neighborhood. The in-fill market slowed during the downturn because, with prices dropping, builders and buyers weren't sure what finished homes would be worth.

Now that the market has improved, Craftmark Homes®, a builder in the Washington, D.C., metro market, scours close-in Arlington, Va., and Bethesda, Md., markets for opportunities, checking with government offices to find low appraisals in hot neighborhoods. The builder follows a careful formula: It doesn't want to spend more than one-third of the eventual house price on land. CEO Steve Malm also operates with a self-imposed price ceiling. For instance, he may not want to sell a spec home for more than $2 million in a close-in Arlington neighborhood, so he won't bid more than $667,000 for an existing home to tear down. And he needs to make sure, by checking neighborhood design covenants, that he can build a $2 million home in its place.

Many infill builders prefer that homebuyers purchase the existing home to be demolished and get financing for the entire project. They have taken what they learned project-by-project during the housing boom and converted that knowledge into a business model. Partners in Building®, a suburban infill builder in Houston, is a good example. The firm helps its clients find suitable lots by reviewing land records for below-average appraisals and staying in close contact with real estate agents. It canvases those households to see if any are interested in selling. If it gets a bite, the company advises buyers to make offers with a 30-day study contingency, though in the hottest markets you may not have that luxury. There's a lot of work to do during that month-long period. You need to check with the building department and home-owner associations to find out what you can build on the lot. You need to do a search to make sure you can get a clear title. You might want to take a soil sample. Environmental regulations are something else to look into—part of the lot may not be developable because it might be too close to a stream or water table.

After you are satisfied that you can build the home you want on the site, the next step is to get a construction loan. The first installment typically goes to pay for the land. Then you release the money in installments to pay for construction. In the end, the construction loan gets converted to permanent financing—a mortgage. This is the same process you would follow whether you were building a custom home in the suburbs or redeveloping an inner-city lot. However, given all the things that could go wrong on an urban deal, you might be better off paying an expert to take that risk.

Despite the example we hoped to set, live-work projects are rare because it's difficult to find an appropriate site. The projects seem ideally suited as a bridge between residential neighborhoods and commercial districts. Associations may object to the traffic and noise created by a live-work project in a purely residential neighborhood. On the other hand, live-work owners may not want to live in a purely commercial setting, isolated from other households. Even so, live-work arrangements are making a small and significant comeback. Up to 38 million Americans have home-based businesses, according to the U.S. Census. And a growing number of architects and developers who have completed a successful live-work project are looking for opportunities to do more.

One live-work project located near the beach in Venice, Calif., turned out especially well for the architect, John G. Reed, and his wife, Marisa Solomon-Reed, an interior designer. The couple each formerly traveled 1½ hours a day to work. Now their commute is walking from upstairs bedrooms to a downstairs office, six blocks from the beach. Their new home, designed with material seen throughout the neighborhood—brick, structural steel, and concrete—looks at first glance like the remodel of an industrial warehouse. Big glass expanses reveal a sleek 800-square-foot office at street level. One two-bedroom loft unit above it is finished with unusual bowstring trusses, exposed ducts, and interior brick. A second more contemporary residence behind it, done with steel and glass, is flooded with light from 12-foot-high windows that wrap the living space.

I hunted for another successful live-work project on a recent trip to Los Angeles. Done by MBK, one of the largest builders in the city, 1600 at Artesia Square combined three-story townhomes with live-work space and was selling at an astounding rate of 20 homes a month in the summer of 2012, before the housing recovery took hold in this neck of the woods. I found the project two miles from the interstate, in the close-in suburb of Gardenia, set back behind the kind of nondescript strip retail that you see all along busy L.A. arterial roads. The homes ranged from 1,700 to 2,300 square feet with two-car attached garages and prices that started in the high $400s, pretty affordable for Los Angeles. That bought you into a hip community that included a dog park, a tai-chi garden, and two public outdoor entertaining areas with fireplaces and barbecues. In addition to a private courtyard space, the homes featured stainless-steel appliances, custom paint, and granite countertops, upscale features for Gardenia. Solar panels on each home came with a 20-year prepaid lease, which helped the project earn LEED certification.

The first live-work model I toured featured an attractive glass-and-metal storefront entry and window system. Decorated for a travel agent and selling for $478,190, it included 300 square feet of workspace and enough room for a sitting area, a powder room, and some storage. Going up a side stairway and through a fire door took you to the main living area of the house, which was vaulted with a loft and bedrooms on the third floor. The building even had a built-up flat roof. The presentation, eerily similar to one of our Atlanta live-work homes, brought back fond memories of the project we had done more than a decade before. It provided further evidence of strong, unmet demand for atypical housing projects. ✥

Architect John G Reed and interior designer Marisa Reed designed this live-work building in Venice, California. This iconic building has sparked much curiosity, making it the architect's best form of advertisement. Though new, the main building looks like an industrial warehouse conversion with modern elements giving the illusion that the building evolved over time.

CHAPTER FOURTEEN

Modular Mania Takes Hold

THE HOUSING RECESSION SPARKED a renewed fascination with modular and manufactured housing—so-called factory-built homes. It's easy to understand why people are so enamored of this new breed of housing. *Dwell* magazine has done its part to popularize modular housing in particular as a way for laypeople to access affordable, often contemporary homes designed by big-time architects. Builders have seized on factory-built housing as a way to eliminate on-site labor and construction hassles and maybe make a few extra bucks. Architects like the idea of working directly with factories—so that builders on site can't change their designs to economize—to deliver high design directly to the American public.

Much of the most exciting work in recent years has been done in modular housing, which, as the name implies, is built in modules in a factory and then shipped to a home site where it's assembled. The best modular housing, typically built to local building codes and standards, is nearly indistinguishable from traditional stick-built housing. Manufactured homes are a slightly different animal. They are built nearly in their entirety in a factory under a federal building code and shipped on a wheeled chassis to home sites. A low-slung roofline and rectangular form often give them a distinctive appearance.

The desire to provide high design directly to buyers was part of the impetus behind the series of simple, elegant modular buildings

Lake/Flato Architects designed a series of factory-built modules that can be connected with site-built elements to create a small compound, like this one in the Hill Country of Texas. The Porch House series includes two basic modules—one for sleeping and the other for living. The modules are ingeniously joined by breezeways to create outdoor living spaces.

pictured above. Designed by Lake/Flato Architects and located in the Hill Country of Texas, the project is actually a compound—a series of factory-built modules connected by breezeways built on site. Lake/Flato's Porch House series includes two basic boxes. The living module comprises a simple galley kitchen with sleek contemporary cabinetry and a windowed living area, which in this case affords great views of the Texas Hill Country. A second sleeping module contains little more than bedrooms and baths. But it's the ingenious breezeways that define this project, affordably connecting the modules to create outdoor living spaces—decks and patios—and even garage ports.

DECIDING WHAT TO BUILD COST-EFFECTIVELY in a factory and what to build more affordably on site may be the most important legacy left by factory-built housing during the housing recession. Since a big cost of factory-built housing is transportation, manufacturers find it often makes sense to ship only the parts of the house that need plumbing or intricate design work, then build items like decks, garages, or even simple rooms on site. The rise of hybrid homes is blurring the lines between manufactured and modular housing, since both are combining factory-built and site-built techniques.

Factory-built housing is a media darling. Modular housing in particular receives a disproportionate amount of coverage by consumer-shelter magazines, considering how few modular homes are built and sold each year. Modular construction—even in a good year—accounts for less than 4 percent of the single- and multifamily homes built in the United States, most of it in single-family construction, according to the Annual Builder Practices Survey conducted by the Home Innovation Research Labs. That said, factory-built homes present several distinct advantages. First, materials don't take a pounding from the elements during construction. Second, homes can often be built faster, since construction is separated from the vagaries of nature. Moreover, waste is kept to a minimum—material is cut to tight specifications, under supervision. Modular home manufacturers estimate that their products can be built as much as 30 percent faster than site-built homes.

But there are significant trade-offs to the speed and efficiency of factory construction. To withstand transport, factory-built homes must be sturdier than site-built homes. They often include steel supports that cost money. Some aesthetic downsides linger as well. Most people can identify a manufactured home due to its rectangular form. Although modular-home design is much improved, some homes still look boxy, with telltale seams that give away their form.

I got my first taste of the new work in modular-housing design judging a new-home design competition for *Sunset* magazine in 2005. The magazine had commissioned Michelle Kaufman, who had studied with Frank Gehry, to design a smallish, green modular home that was sitting in the parking lot of the magazine's Palo Alto, Calif., headquarters. Kaufman's Breezehouse design was pretty radical for its time, the McMansion era, considering that it neglected things like vaulted space, a media room, or a six-burner stove. But it would fit right in today.

Kaufman was more interested in how the home responded to sunlight, darkness, and cool summer breezes. She designed two modules, each 16 feet wide and 44 feet long, set 20 feet apart, joined by a thick slate floor that provided thermal heat in the winter. Power came from solar panels on a butterfly-shaped roof. The house opened wide, glass wall panels folding back accordion-style to merge the central living area with a patio and the outdoors.

The home was also expandable, another increasingly common attribute of the new generation of modular homes. The base house included two bedrooms and two baths within a 1,800-square-foot footprint, but you could add a third bedroom by attaching a 248-square-foot module. Also, if a butterfly roof wasn't your cup of tea, you could substitute a flat or slanted breezeway roof. You could also choose among six alternative siding materials, including steel, Kaufman's favorite because it doesn't require maintenance once it achieves its rusty patina. The basic home initially sold for $280,000, excluding land and foundation. Blu Homes, which bought the design, later sold a larger version of the home (pictured here) for as much as $500,000.

In Michelle Kaufman's Breezehouse, two factory-built modules are connected by a site-built breezeway. Glass wall panels open accordion-style to merge the central living area with a patio and the outdoors. Buyers may select among six siding styles. The home is now available from Blu Homes.

MOST MODULAR DEMONSTRATION PROJECTS, like the *Sunset* one, are directed at consumers who want good architecture at a fraction of what it would cost to have an architect design a custom home. But builders are enamored with the concept as well, since it holds out the prospect of quick assembly on the job site and reduced interest-carrying costs. We decided to bring some modular-home excitement to the floor of the International Builders Show in 2009, enlisting the help of LivingHomes, a pioneer in the field. My first meeting with Steve Glenn, CEO of the company, took place in his own modular home, which had been designed by legendary Southern California architect Ray Kappe. Glenn's business goal was to use modular housing as a vehicle to bring architecture, and architects, to a mass audience.

Glenn's urban infill home in Santa Monica was spectacular. When I visited, morning sunlight streamed through large window walls. Glenn explained that three large modules had been lowered in place and

The *Builder* LivingHome, assembled in three and a half days on the floor of the 2009 International Builders Show, demonstrated the appeal of modular housing. Based on a design by KieranTimberlake, the home consisted of four modules joined by a breezeway. Smart panels that held the home's electrical and plumbing components could be snapped in place.

attached to create the 2,560-square-foot house. As he took me on a tour, Glenn pointed out simple spaces like living rooms and closets that didn't make sense to build in a factory and then ship to the home site. There's no reason to pay for "air" in shipping, he said, suggesting that the next frontier would be to pair modular and panellized construction. Glenn wanted to demonstrate another concept as well—smart panels containing the home's main distribution systems that could be snapped together. That sounded like a good idea since we only had five days to put the home together on the show floor.

To design the home, Glenn wanted to use another modular-housing pioneer, the Philadelphia architecture firm KieranTimberlake, which had just won an award for firm of the year from the American Institute of Architects. Specifically, he wanted to do a modular version of the firm's Loblolly House. One critic had gone so far as to dub the home one of the most innovative and important designs of the century. The original home sat on piles in an exclusive location near water. Glenn wanted to find a way to mass-produce it with a different frame and get the cost down to $150 to $200 per square foot so that a wider market could afford it.

LivingHomes operates from a studio on Sepulveda Boulevard in Los Angeles. It doesn't have a factory. Instead, company designers work closely with architects to reproduce their drawings in a way that makes sense to factory craftsmen. The firm works with several factories to build its modules. Factory workers often put them together on home sites as well.

We decided to build the 2,160-square-foot Loblolly house with four modules framed in steel (for transport) and wood (for flexibility) and stacked two-on-two. We also built and shipped a two-story panelized section that could be used for a carport, extra bedroom, or several other purposes. To facilitate a quick build, the plug-and-play home came with a series of smart panels—containing ducting, gas and plumbing systems, and electrical—that attached along the rear wall, where we oriented the parts of the home that consumed the most energy—the kitchen, laundry, bathrooms, and mechanical areas. Built over three months in a factory to the most stringent green specifications, the house arrived at the trade show 95 percent complete.

Concerned that we would barely have enough time to put the home together on the convention floor, we struck a deal with the show's hosts to get our "booth" through the doors and onto the floor first. We figured that we'd need all of five days to assemble the modules, decorate them, turn on the utilities, and, finally, landscape the home and place some displays around it. It would be better if crews could roll the modules from the shipping door to our booth space before too many other vendors set up their booths. Also, we'd need to rent cranes and get them on the floor to stack the units. Only then could specialized crews go to work stitching the modules together and finishing the panelized sections.

We raised the bar for the project by aiming for LEED Platinum, the highest green building standard at the time. That meant using sustainable products everywhere we could. We used a biocomposite wood siding made from resin, sawdust, and laminate. The staggered siding pattern gave the home a geometric feel that hid the seams in the modular panels. Other green features included high-performance windows with frames made from recycled material, tiles made of recycled glass, and blown-in insulation. The home was so tight that we included a system to introduce fresh air. But we also positioned the windows to promote cross breezes, designed overhangs to protect the home from unwanted heat gain, and left space for an active solar system.

Sometimes even the best-laid plans go awry. The first problem we encountered, just as construction was about to begin on the modules, was that the firm we had planned to do the work went out of business. We scrambled to find a substitute and got lucky; the second manufacturer proved so adept at construction that the home was built more quickly than we expected. The modules and panels were ready to go and sitting in a Southern California parking lot weeks before we'd need them in Las Vegas. Eventually, the modules were loaded on several trucks that proceeded caravan-style from the factory. When they tried to clear the mountains between California and Nevada, high winds came up that forced them to sit by the side of the road. The clock was ticking. Exhibitors were already taking their booths onto the show floor.

The weather eventually cleared, and the trucks were able to proceed to Las Vegas. But by the time they arrived at the convention center, only three and a half days were left until show time. We'd lost a day and a half off our assembly schedule. Fortunately, several systems used on the home made the assembly go faster. A stretched-fabric ceiling could be installed quickly—and it hid lines where modules came together. The smart panels came in handy since all we had to do was snap them in place to connect the electrical, plumbing, and HVAC systems. And the 4-by-8-foot siding panels, cut to accommodate windows, could be quickly applied in sections over a moisture-control system.

No one touring the home during the show could tell it had been assembled in such a hurry. Visitors were taken with its space-efficient, flexible floor plan, highlighted by a first-floor bonus room that could be used as a home office, media room, studio, or even a guest suite since it was adjacent to a bathroom. The main living area, which consisted of an open kitchen, dining, and living area, felt spacious by virtue of its visual connection to porches on two sides. After the show, Living-Homes took the home apart, this time according to a more convenient schedule, and eventually reassembled it for a buyer in Santa Monica. The company built and sold about 13 of the homes in short order, and the plan is still available for sale on its website.

WHY DOES FACTORY-BUILT HOUSING ACCOUNT for so little of annual production? When the subject comes up, I'm reminded of the time years ago when I asked a Cincinnati lumber dealer about what looked like a burgeoning trend in modular-home building. He burst my bubble by saying that he didn't think modular would ever get much traction. Why? "Because stick framers need to eat," he said. The Home Innovation Research Labs data show that framers have success-fully protected their share of a shrinking market. Site-built, light-frame construction has accounted for a steady 80 percent of single-family construction for the last seven years. Factories may produce homes faster, but most stick builders can construct a home on site within 100 days, and the fastest have it down to 45 days or less.

The more important trend in the Research Labs data may be the big jump in panelized construction, which nearly doubled its market share from 5.1 percent of single-family construction in 2009 to 9.3 percent in 2010. I've always wondered why builders didn't use more wall panels, prehung millwork, preassembled stair systems, and roof trusses. Now, it seems, they do. If you buy a new home today, it's bound to contain panelized components. Back in the day, carpenters would build stairs on site and maybe integrate railings into chair molds and window details. These days, the stairs are likely to arrive as a package that's lowered in place. The use of roof trusses built in factories is nearly ubiquitous.

Even manufactured, or mobile, homes received a facelift during the housing recession. In 2008, Tennessee-based Clayton Homes introduced a breakthrough model, the i-house, that was nothing less than an attempt to remake the mobile-home industry. The first and most notable departure was the home's butterfly roof that provided a higher ceiling in the main living area; it also happened to collect rainwater for use in the garden or washing the car. Plus, Clayton offered a second flat-roofed module with a bedroom and bath so that buyers could arrange components on site in a variety of ways; seven different ones to be exact. The contemporary impression was enhanced by a galvanized metal roof and corrugated-steel siding.

The base model, with one bedroom, one bath, and 723 square feet of indoor space, starts at about $75,000. But you can add a second 268-square-foot module with a bathroom that takes the home to 991 square feet. That, plus a deck, ups the price to $100,000. So, you're paying $100 to $120 per square foot, which is a lot for a mobile home but not compared with the cost of building a custom home—$200 per square foot and up in many markets. The i-house should appeal to anyone searching for an inexpensive, energy-efficient vacation home.

Clayton Homes made headlines in 2008 with its energy-conserving i-house, a fresh take on manufactured housing. A butterfly roof breaks the rectangular mold. Galvanized metal roofing and corrugated-steel siding provide contemporary appeal. Buyers can use an online tool to configure modules to their liking.

Clayton also offers a stretch version with an additional bedroom. Moreover, you can go online and use a virtual tool to design your home. The system spits out a cost for the home right down to the delivery charge by zip code. The base model is built with 2x6 studs, contains R-21 insulation in the walls and R-30 in the ceiling and floor, and has low-e windows and ceiling fans. Clayton claims that this model is at least 30 percent more energy efficient than traditional homes, with monthly energy costs of less than $70. You can also upgrade to a net-zero option by adding solar panels, a tankless hot water heater, and Energy Star appliances, along with low-flow faucets and bamboo floors.

The funny thing about the home is that, despite its contemporary appearance, you can still make out the trademark rectangular form of a trailer. Inside the box, a bare-bones floor plan with living space in front and a bedroom in the back hasn't evolved much since the old days. One critic even called the second module "a retro-chic nod to the outbuildings commonly found in mobile home parks," noting that the unit provides the "dot" to create the i-shaped footprint for which the i-house is named. Even so, the home has an attention to design that typically isn't found in a factory-built home, including ceramic tile backsplashes, upgraded faucets, and more contemporary lighting fixtures. A deck made from recycled plastic and no-VOC paint enhances its green pedigree. And then there's the added benefit that the home was built in a controlled factory environment. Clayton Homes reports only 2 percent waste in its projects.

The original line proved popular enough that Clayton introduced a second, larger series: i-house 2.0. It features a variety of upgrades and changes, including a second bedroom in the main module, larger and wider hallways, additional interior space, warmer color selections, a defined entryway, and additional covered outdoor space. The more expansive model retains the separation of public and private spaces found in the initial series. But it adds a defined entrance, done with posts that support the butterfly roof in a midcentury modern style. Big windows along the front allow you to see right into the house, providing a feeling of spaciousness that isn't usually associated with a mobile home.

The big challenge for the i-house is where you would put it. The original version is probably too upscale for most trailer parks, and the people who live in trailer parks may not want to pay extra for its green features. The newer, larger version will wind up in places where you might otherwise see custom homes. But the owners of those lots may prefer to work directly with an architect and builder to produce a truly custom home. That leaves the i-house, like many factory-built structures, without a natural home, another big reason why more factory-built housing isn't produced each year, despite its strong appeal. ❖

CHAPTER FIFTEEN

Small Will
Remain Beautiful

I COULDN'T WAIT TO VISIT the State Fair of Texas on a trip to Dallas a few years ago. Sure, I wanted to partake of a large deep-fried mocha ice cream, see the award-winning longhorns, and get my picture taken with Big Tex. But I also wanted to check out the "tiny" house, so deliciously out of place in a state that does everything big. Newspapers have devoted a lot of ink to the curious tiny-house movement, dubiously casting it as the next wave in a small-homes movement. At 172 square feet, Jay Schafer's Tumbleweed House didn't disappoint, except that it was so small that guides had to hurry visitors. It was difficult to imagine spending much time living inside it anyway. There was barely enough space for a built-in bed on one side (changing the sheets would be problematic, and if you slept on the side closest to the wall, you were there for the duration) with a kitchen and bath on the other. A smallish "great room" joined the two zones. That was about it. Even survivalists, I thought, might go a little batty spending any length of time in this home.

The beauty of this tiny home, of course, is that you could take it with you. You could load it on a trailer bed, drive it to points unknown, and sit it almost anywhere you could get some water. The home is powered by solar panels and wind, so finding a connection to the power grid wouldn't be a problem. A tiny house theoretically would be an ideal solution for a guesthouse in a large suburban backyard, although

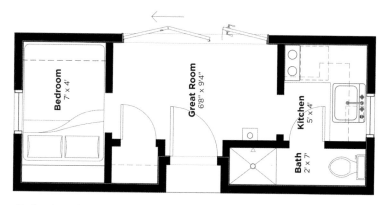

The bare-bones floor plan for the Tumbleweed House takes the small-home movement to an extreme, with a bedroom to one side, a kitchen to the other, and a living area in between. While it would be nice to have a home that you could take with you, it's hard to imagine spending a lot of time cooped up inside this tiny home.

as a practical matter getting approvals would be difficult. Similarly, zoning laws would make it extremely difficult to use a tiny house as suburban infill housing; most ordinances specify minimum home sizes that are much larger than 172 square feet, and neighborhoods probably wouldn't care for the fact that the home could be here one day and gone the next. The best place for this novelty option would be in the country on land that you owned somewhere off the grid, a lifestyle option that's always had strong appeal in this country—thus, the strong foot traffic at the fair.

AMERICAN CONSUMERS ARE FASCINATED with small homes for a variety of reasons, not the least of which is that they are cute, responsible, and attainable. Stories about cottage homes are always among the most popular on real estate websites. Interestingly, the small-home movement took root during the housing boom, when the trend toward overpriced McMansions made new homes seem less obtainable, prompting people to dream about smaller homes that they could actually afford. Then it really took hold during the housing bust as builders, in an attempt to lure wary buyers into the market, introduced a new generation of smaller, less expensive homes. As builders learned, getting government and neighborhood approvals to build small homes is often difficult, especially in subdivisions that have already been platted for bigger homes. The big question now is whether the move toward smaller new homes will lose momentum and maybe even go into reverse as the housing market strengthens. Production builders nearly always follow the path of least public resistance.

I put this question—will builders continue to build small homes?—to a panel of homebuilder CEOs at the Pacific Coast Builders Conference, when the housing market was showing early signs of revival. Knowing that I was up against it—most builders would always prefer to sell bigger homes that produce higher margins, as long as the pace of sales is good—I carefully prefaced the question. Demographic trends support the construction of smaller homes, I argued. The biggest market for the next decade will be aging baby boomers trading down. The Generation Y cohort, moving into their first-time-home-buying years, won't have much money to spend due to low earning power and college debt. In the future, buyers will be wary of buying too much house for fear they won't be able to recoup their investment, now that future appreciation is no longer a slam dunk. More people on margin will be looking to buy only the home they need and nothing more.

The CEOs weren't buying it. One quickly noted that he was already seeing a trend toward buyer demand for more square footage, even in markets that hadn't fully recovered. Value-oriented buyers, he told me, had roared back off the sidelines, looking to pick up five-bedroom, three-garage homes at bargain prices before they rose further. No one comes into the sales office, another executive told the audience, asking to buy a small home; they want to buy the biggest home they can afford. The panelists schooled me for naively ignoring the driving force of new-home sales—American materialism. People in this country aspire to own a big home on a big lot, they said; it's ingrained in our culture. That ambition may have been beaten down during the recession, but it resurfaced as soon as the recovery started.

Nevertheless, the data show that new homes shrunk in size during the early years of the housing recession—for a variety of reasons. One was the availability of government tax incentives for first-time buyers. Builders responded to that carrot by bringing out more starter homes, a logical move given that they were having trouble selling move-up houses anyway. Also, with home values dropping, buyers were reluctant to trade up to a bigger home that might lose even more value. At the nadir of the housing recession, nearly a third of American households with mortgages owed more on their home than it was worth. At that point, industry surveys showed that half of builders changed their design strategy to emphasize smaller-home design.

But as the housing recession continued, and the tax credits expired, new homes began getting larger and more expensive again. This was partly due to the fact that in most metropolitan areas new homes sell for a premium over existing homes; they are generally larger and cost more. One reason new homes are more expensive is the high price of the land they sit on, especially in the Northeast, where land close to population centers is often in short supply. But the size of most new homes also has something to do with the kind of people who want them. A disproportionate percentage of new homebuyers are growing families who want to trade up from smaller, older homes. They want space—space for a second child, a home office, a third car. Most new-home builders will tell you that, despite all the growth in single and empty-nester households, families remain their core buyers.

That said, several factors that contributed to the run-up in new-home size during the boom aren't likely to reappear. Ridiculously easy financing is one. The proliferation of low- to no-doc mortgages and lenient down-payment requirements made it easy for people to buy as much house as they wanted—in fact, it created an incentive to buy as much home as you could afford. Mortgage-interest and property-tax deductions aided and abetted the trend; the more home you bought, the bigger the tax deduction you could take, within a limit, of course. Moreover, with home values rising each year, it seemed to make good financial sense to buy as much home as possible, especially toward the end of the boom when values rose 20 percent annually in some supercharged metro areas. Few buyers foresaw the danger ahead.

Even before the housing bust, interest in smaller homes was sparked by architect Sarah Susanka's book, *The Not So Big House*. After it was published in 1998, Susanka went on a lecture tour, speaking to builder groups, urging them to build better, not bigger, houses. She warned them that the big homes they were constructing were dysfunctional, often telling the story from the first chapter of her book about the woman who cried after trading up to a home with big-volume space. She urged the builders to design smaller homes with more human scale, with flexible activity spaces for reading books, engaging in conversation, or just gazing through windows. Susanka's talks always stimulated discussion, but her advice was widely ignored by builders who privately derided her thinking and kept on building homes with large great rooms and impersonal floor plans.

The irony is that many of these same builders found Susanka's Not-So-Big religion during the downturn, whether they knew it or not. When they sat down to design smaller homes, the first thing to go was over-the-top volume that would be costly to heat and cool. The next big change was to delete rarely used formal rooms in favor of great rooms. Then they had to account for the activities that formerly took place in formal spaces—eating, reading, entertaining, or working. Great rooms were adapted to accommodate these pursuits. A decade after Susanka wrote her first book, her space-planning message had finally struck a chord within the industry.

IT'S AMAZING HOW CREATIVE HOUSES can get when you have to do more with less. One stunning example is Eel's Nest, a narrow three-story townhome in the redeveloping neighborhood of Echo Hill in Los Angeles. The 960-square-foot home, designed by architect Simon Storey of Anonymous Architects for his own use, is further testament to the public's fascination with small homes. At the time I visited, a slideshow of the three-story home was the second most viewed on the *Los Angeles Times'* website. Because it's so narrow, only 15 feet, there's little more than a garage and a front door on the first floor, with stairs that lead up to the main living area. The second floor consists of a simple kitchen with a dining table on one side and a great room with nice views of the surrounding hills on the other. On that day, as on most days, Storey had opened a big pivot door along the back of the house that led to a smallish rear patio where he kept a table and chairs and a charcoal grill.

Up a wonderful set of open stairs, Storey designed two bedrooms off a small hall. The first, used as an architectural office, is equipped with built-in shelving and other storage for his books and drawings. The views from here are even better than the ones downstairs—windows look out on an inspirational, redeveloping urban neighborhood that changes by the minute. A large glass door with views of the backyard makes the one bedroom in the plan feel much larger than it is. When

Simon Storey designed the minimalist Eel's Nest in a transitional L.A. neighborhood for his own use. The home's second floor includes a bare-bones, sunken kitchen, with table space for two, and a big pivot door that opens to a small backyard with a barbecue. An office and bedroom upstairs provide commanding views of the L.A. skyline.

Storey needs further inspiration, he can take stairs to a roof deck with panoramic views of the entire city.

On this same trip, I stayed at an architect friend's beach house on Balboa Island in Orange County, south of Los Angeles. Because space is often at such a premium in these places, floor-plan designs can be quite interesting. The architect managed to squeeze in all the creature comforts you would want into the master bedroom—his-and-her closets, a bathroom with dual vanities. The other second-floor bedroom barely fit a built-in bunk bed, with a queen mattress below and a double above. The third floor got really interesting. Space had been carved out under the eaves for a bed and a bathtub. Neighborhood covenants only permitted two-story homes. But by putting the bedroom under the eaves and limiting the ceiling height to 7 feet, the architect had successfully argued that the space was an attic, not a bedroom. Centuries ago French architects used similar arguments to justify living space behind mansard roofs.

High land prices during the housing boom forced developers to explore some pretty creative small-home solutions. Cluster-home communities, often developed in close-in suburban settings on infill lots, popped up in places like Denver, Southern California, and Phoenix. These developments typically feature shared driveways and parking space. Some early projects were so dense, at 20 units to the acre or more, that there was barely enough room for visitor parking, side yards felt cramped, and privacy was compromised. Architects and planners eventually found that the communities lived much better at 12 to 14 homes to the acre, but even then homes are so close together that privacy concerns are paramount. Some designers and builders figured out how to create "private" courtyards and yards in cluster communities by limiting views from the neighboring home on that side. They also thought through window placements so that neighbors weren't looking into key rooms, one of my pet peeves. When cluster communities first began popping up, it wasn't uncommon to walk up the staircase in one home and look out the windows to see the neighbor's master bathtub.

COTTAGES BURST INTO THE INDUSTRY'S CONSCIOUSNESS during the housing downturn, when small cottage homes popped up in master-plan communities otherwise known for bigger production homes. When Tony Green, the developer of The Pinehills, one of the largest master plans in the Northeast, located in Plymouth, Mass., saw the recession coming, he urged his builders to develop a new series of smaller homes. One builder, the Barefoot Cottage Company, responded by offering cottages on steeply sloped wooded lots that felt like they were in the hills. Second-floor windows look out at the trees, creating the sensation that you are perched in their branches. Barefoot milled eastern white pine, felled to make way for the homes, was used for their floors and millwork. Another builder, MacKenzie Brothers, produced a series of 2,229-square-foot cottages with two first-floor master bedroom suites, perfect if "your partner's snoring keeps you awake." A beaded beamed ceiling, built-in shelves and cabinets, and thick oak flooring contribute to the cottage feel.

Builders at The Pinehills introduced small cottage plans during the recession, some within walking distance of the community's quaint town center. The family room in this home by MacKenzie Brothers includes personal touches such as built-in shelving and cabinets and a stone fireplace surround.

In another section, Green redrew three custom home lots to create space for 16 new cottages within walking distance of The Pinehills' town center, which even has a grocery store. The homes borrow from a palette of materials traditionally used on nearby Nantucket Island— picket fencing, rose-covered trellises, cedar siding, and white trim. But they come equipped with modern features that will help them stand up to the elements, including fiberglass doors, insulated windows, and a special engineered-wood sheathing with a built-in vapor barrier. The builder, the Barefoot Cottage Company again, managed to squeeze two bedrooms and one and a half baths into only 1,200 square feet of living space—and give buyers options.

The two bedrooms are upstairs in the base plan, but half the buyers have added a first-floor master by pushing forward the one-car garage and putting the bedroom behind so that it has a view of the woods. The other basic choice buyers have is whether to put the kitchen and the stairwell in the front or back. Some people have added a bay window to accommodate a nook, but most buyers have learned to live with the space-saving tactic of putting an informal eating area between the kitchen and dining room, an arrangement that grew more common during the recession. Eating on the front porch is an option, too, since it is big enough to accommodate a table and two chairs. The homes all have the same 20- by 28-foot footprint, but every second floor has a slightly different configuration, which provides variety to the roofscape and the community.

At The Pinehills, the developer could respond to the demand for smaller, less expensive homes because mixed-use zoning was permitted when the site was first plotted. When the recession hit, most developers were stuck with large lots plotted for big homes that they couldn't change without local government approval. And that was often hard to get because people who had already bought homes in the community objected to allowing smaller homes that might diminish property values. In recent years, however, a few local governments have actually enacted ordinances to encourage the development of smaller homes, often with shared public spaces.

Small homes at Chico Beach share extensive gardens and a beach waterfront. The homes were designed with large windows and third-story loft towers to make the most of water and garden views. They feature master bedrooms on both the first and second floors so that buyers—mostly singles and empty nesters—can age in place and have guests stay with them.

In Washington state, Linda Pruitt, owner of The Cottage Company, took advantage of Kitsap County's "Cottage Housing" land-use provision to build Chico Beach, a pocket neighborhood of seven small homes grouped around a common green space with a shared Puget Sound beachfront. Pocket neighborhoods aren't as dense as cluster communities and typically have shared green space, maybe even a shared community building. They are a haven for singles and empty-nesters. "There's a whole movement toward 'missing middle' housing typologies (many of them smaller-footprint homes) that were made illegal with the advent of postwar zoning," she said.

The homes at Chico Beach, which range between 1,600 and 1,700 square feet, look like midcentury beachfront retreats, with their low-slung pitched roofs, expansive horizontal windows, and indoor-outdoor covered porches. Though small, they are tricked out inside. Extensive custom built-ins, vaulted wood-panel ceilings, and white-painted cabinets make them feel both elegant and larger. Master suites on the first and second floors provide a lot of flexibility—you could live upstairs today and downstairs later. Built to Energy Star standards, with photovoltaic power and green features, the homes are sited to take full advantage of their location on one acre of prime waterfront property on Puget Sound's Dyes Inlet. Each plan is oriented with large windows to provide a water view from all floors without compromising privacy. Third-floor loft towers, reminiscent of a ranger station tower, provide 360-degree views that encompass Mt. Rainier.

The infill community is located less than a mile from historic Old Town Silverdale. Residents can walk or take a bus to shopping, restaurants, and a YMCA, among other destinations. But there's plenty to do at Chico Beach as well. The homes share a 150-foot beach waterfront, a beachside deck overlook, extensive gardens, a car-charging station, and a commons building for communal gatherings and socializing. A circle hearth and sunbathing gazebo on the open lawn also facilitate community interaction.

Back on the East Coast, in Concord, Mass., Concord Riverwalk is another example of an innovative development of small, high-performance homes (see the photo on p. 222). The community is a pocket neighborhood of 13 "net-zero-possible" homes with on-site solar collection, meaning you have to watch your energy consumption to get to net zero. Residents share a community pavilion, garden, and nature trails. The market-rate cottages, either two- or three-bedroom plans, range from 1,340 to 1,760 square feet. Interestingly, the homes were designed with Sarah Susanka's small-home philosophy in mind. The interiors include inviting spaces where you can relax, read, or socialize while enjoying views of the outdoors. While some rooms are intended to be shared, others are designed as a private retreat. Ceiling heights are varied, interior views are artfully composed, and diagonal views make spaces seem larger than they actually are.

Communities such as Chico Beach and Riverwalk, designed and built during the most trying economic times, managed to give buyers looking for smaller, well-designed homes nearly everything they wanted, including near energy independence. As the housing market recovers, and builders regain the upper hand in sales negotiations, design and building programs for some new communities will inevitably slip. To deliver homes, builders won't have to sweat as many details as they did during the downturn. It will be up to buyers to insist on new homes that do more with less. And that will require a more than cursory knowledge of technical matters that, thankfully, aren't that difficult to understand. ⌖

Concord Riverwalk builds off the pocket neighborhood concept pioneered by celebrated neighborhood designer Ross Chapin. Owners of these small, two-bedroom homes share a garden, nature trails, and a community pavilion (pictured at right). The homes are net-zero possible, meaning that if buyers invest in a power-generating system and watch their energy consumption carefully, they may avoid an electric bill.

CHAPTER SIXTEEN

What to Ask for in a New Home

MUCH OF THIS BOOK HAS DEALT WITH ASPIRATIONAL FEA-TURES in new homes. While it would be nice to have it all, unfortunately most homebuyers end up making trade-offs—a shorter commute for a less-energy-efficient home, or a home with an awkward floor plan for a better school district. For that reason, and because as the housing market improves some builders may take spec levels down a notch, it makes sense to enter the buying process with baseline requirements. At the very least, your home needs to be covered by a warranty with some teeth. It needs to be built well, with proper attention to critical construction details, so that it's durable and water doesn't get inside. It needs to be as energy and water efficient as possible to keep utility costs under control. You need to be sure that the home is properly ventilated, that grading directs water away from the foundation, and that unwanted gases won't seep into the home through the foundation. Details like this used to be secondary considerations when buying a new home. No longer.

A home that meets the EPA's Energy Star guidelines is a good starting point. The program specifies that homes achieve a HERS rating in the low 70s, depending on its size and location (see Chapter 2 for more on HERS ratings). But, more important, it requires third-party inspections that can provide peace of mind, even if you trust your builder.

Independent energy auditors verify during construction, before drywall cloaks wall cavities, that energy details were executed correctly. "Certified" HVAC contractors confirm that the home's mechanical system was sized and installed properly. And before the home receives Energy Star approval, the builder inspects and signs off on key construction details, the ones most prone to leak water. They aren't likely to take this requirement lightly, given the value of having a government "seal of approval" for their homes.

The Energy Star standard, revised in 2012, for the first time requires that homes include thermal wall barriers to repel cold during the winter and heat during the summer. Building envelopes must be either wrapped with a continuous layer of foam insulation or else built with a "high-performance" system—double walls, SIPs, insulated concrete forms (ICFs), or another advanced framing method. Insulation in the wall cavity must be installed without gaps or flaws and with a minimum amount of compression that hampers its performance. Studies have shown that even leaving small gaps between fiberglass insulation and wood framing or compressing insulation can cut its effectiveness in half. Because the compression guidelines are tough to achieve with fiberglass batts, spray insulation, either foam or cellulose, may wind up the default standard for Energy Star homes.

In addition to thermal barriers, wall systems must include air barriers—typically sheathing combined with house wrap, building paper, or rigid board insulation—that block the flow of air between conditioned and unconditioned spaces. Independent energy auditors need to document that builders used an appropriate level of insulation and that it was installed properly. And once the home is complete, auditors return to do a so-called blower door test, creating negative pressure inside the house by pulling air out of the house through a fan. Then they check, often with a smoke pencil, to see if outdoor air leaks in through windows, doors, or unintended openings.

In a major break from the past, "certified" HVAC contractors must now verify that the heating and air-conditioning system is sized and installed properly. As explained in Chapter 11, that means ensuring that leaks are kept to a minimum, air flows properly through the ductwork, and the home is evenly heated and cooled—a major potential source of dissatisfaction with new homes. Supply ducts installed in unconditioned spaces such as attics need to be insulated with R-8 or better duct insulation so air conditioning doesn't literally go through the roof. (The EPA backed away from an earlier proposal to require ducts to be run through conditioned space, which high-performance builders still advocate.) Also, for the first time, the standard sets a minimum requirement for exhausting pollution both close to its source, through kitchen and bath fans, and for the whole building. Whole-building ventilation rates are determined by a formula that considers how many people are likely to live in a home, based on its bedroom count and square footage.

The standard even drills down into how key appliances are ventilated, with the goal of minimizing indoor air pollution. For one thing, it requires sealed combustion furnaces, boilers, water heaters, woodstoves, and fireplaces in mixed and cold climates. Combustion and venting systems in these appliances must be entirely separated from indoor air. Air for combustion must be drawn from outside the home and exhaust gases vented back out through a sealed pipe. The arrangement nearly eliminates the possibility of dangerous pollution backdrafts—when contaminants get sucked back inside the home because indoor air pressure is lower than outside air pressure. Only in the warmest climates may homes include so-called "atmospherically vented" appliances, which depend on temperature and pressure differences to expel exhaust gas and are more susceptible to backdrafts.

Water heaters, air conditioners, and furnaces must be more energy efficient as well, though the requirements depend on where you live. Air-conditioning systems in the South need to be rated at a 14.5 seasonal energy-efficiency ratio (SEER) or better compared with 13 or better SEER in mixed and cold climates. The standard looks for more efficient heating systems in cooler climates—90 percent efficient for gas systems, 85 percent efficient in the case of oil or a boiler. For heating in warmer climates, a unit that's only 80 percent efficient will suffice. A furnace rated at 90 percent typically sends flue gases through a secondary heat exchanger, which captures heat and reuses it, exhausting remaining flue gases through a special tube in the wall. The Consortium of Energy Efficiency reports that a 90-percent-efficient unit will pay for itself in three years, providing roughly $115 in annual energy-cost savings compared with an 80-percent-efficient furnace.

Recommended insulation levels of walls, ceilings, and floors also vary widely by region and home configuration. Energy Star basically follows the requirements of the 2009 International Energy Conservation Code (IECC), which is referenced by many local building codes. In the warmest climates, it calls for R-values of 30 in the ceiling, 13 in a wood-frame wall, and 13 in the floor. Requirements ramp up as you go north, reaching as high as 49 in the ceiling, 21 in a wood-frame wall, and 38 in the floor of homes in the coldest regions. The standard also requires the use of Energy Star–rated appliances and lighting.

Building Science Corporation (BSC), the energy think tank, urges homebuyers to aim higher than the Energy Star requirements. In its baseline criteria for a high-performance home, for instance, the organization recommends buying Energy Star appliances—refrigerators, dishwashers, and clothes dryers—that finish in the top third of the rating scale. It also calls for using windows that exceed Energy Star's prescriptive requirements. The critical variable for windows is their U-value, which gauges heat transfer and how well the window insulates. The lower the U-value, the better the window. A second calculation, solar heat gain coefficient (SHGC), measures how well the window blocks heat from sunlight. The lower the SHGC, the less solar heat the window transmits. BSC believes that windows in warmer climates should have a maximum U-value of 0.40 and maximum SHGC of 0.35. In colder climates, it sets a threshold of 0.35 for U-values and 0.40 for SHGC.

Indoor humidity is another focus of the Energy Star program. High humidity within the home can encourage the growth of mold and attract organisms such as dust mites. The Department of Energy says that humidity levels should be kept to within 30 and 50 percent through proper sizing of air-conditioning systems, prevention of water leaks, and installation of a dehumidifier. Additionally, BSC recommends that indoor humidity be kept in the lower half of the range in colder climates throughout the year and in mixed climates during the winter.

The EPA's voluntary Indoor airPLUS program (see Chapter 5) provides some additional moisture guidance. Even if few builders adopt the full program, they may build to some of its specifications, so it's worth asking about. AirPLUS compliance requires continuous drainage planes behind exterior wall cladding, with a drainage system at the bottom of exterior walls to direct water away, something that BSC also recommends. Concrete walls that extend beneath the foundation must be finished with a damp-proof coating. The program also stipulates that window and door openings be fully flashed so that water doesn't get inside, something that's in the best interest of builders to do anyway.

As far as green building goes, a good starting point would be the industry's own voluntary standard that may be referenced by your local building code. To qualify for the National Green Building Standard (NGBS), builders must meet mandatory provisions in six categories, ranging from energy and water efficiency to lot and site development. The bottom line is that builders must construct homes that are 15 percent more efficient than the 2009 IECC, either by calculating its performance through a computer model or following a prescriptive path. The standard, which received a major upgrade in 2013, requires builders to incorporate a long list of air-sealing and flashing measures. But insulation only has to be installed to a Grade 2 level, meaning that inspectors can be more forgiving about gaps and compression. That makes it easier to use less expensive fiberglass batts. The standard requires whole-house ventilation but only if air changes dip below an airtightness threshold. Certified verifiers must check the builder's work and calculations. Unlike the Energy Star standard though, the green building standard doesn't require blower door tests.

EVEN IF YOUR HOME ISN'T BUILT to a green building standard, it makes sense to look comprehensively at how much water it would use and take steps to reduce consumption. Most builders aren't too concerned with the water use of their homes, with the exception of those working in markets where droughts have sometimes made it difficult to get building permits. They may figure that water conservation isn't worth the risk, since it may impact hot showers, toilet flushing, and lawn watering. Even if reducing water consumption isn't high on your wish list, many local governments in drought-stricken regions are stepping in to require it anyway (see Chapter 5). Regardless, investing in water-conserving features up front is probably a good way to protect the resale value of your home down the road.

Once again, a voluntary government program—the EPA's Water-Sense® program—provides some meaningful guidelines. Following all the recommendations, which few builders do, can cut the average family's $500 annual water bill by $100, or 20 percent. Some provisions overlap with requirements of the NGBS, so commonalities are a good place to look for minimum requirements. Both programs, for instance, require installation of WaterSense toilets, faucets, and showerheads. WaterSense faucets and showerheads don't sell for a big premium over conventional ones, but toilets carrying the label do, and most new homes have at least three. The standards also limit how much of the total landscape can be turf (25 to 50 percent in the NGBS). And both encourage the use of water-saving irrigation systems.

To control water use inside the home, the first place to examine is the bathroom, where the government says you could cut daily water consumption by 36 percent by switching to low-flow toilets, showerheads, and faucets. The next place to look is the clothes washer and dishwasher. A clothes washer that earns an Energy Star designation will theoretically use half the water of a nonrated unit, though whether you regularly do full loads of laundry can have a big impact on water use. The type of clothes washer you choose influences this calculation as well. Front-loading horizontal-axis clothes washers use less water than top-loaded washers, since they tumble clothes in a smaller amount of water, then lift them up and drop them like a dryer. Energy Star dishwashers use 30 percent of the water of conventional units, but they don't have as big an impact on home water use as clothes washers.

Since landscaping is such a water hog—watering the lawn accounts for one-third of our water usage—the key question is how much grass you really need. If you want grass so your kids or dog can play, that's one thing. But if you are an empty-nester household that just wants to occasionally feel cool grass under your feet, that's another. Depending on where you live, you may be able to specify a type of grass that doesn't use that much water—like Bermuda grass in Phoenix, or Zoysia in San Antonio. (Remember, also, that mowing the lawn is not an insignificant source of air pollution—the EPA estimates that gas lawn mowers account for about 5 percent.) Another water-saving tactic is to group plants in the yard by their water usage, which makes it easier to zone them for watering. Delivering water to the base of a plant or in subsoil, rather than spraying foliage, saves water, too.

Another way to reduce water bills: Capture rainfall from gutters and use it to water the lawn. You may be able to install a basic system yourself. You can buy one at retail that includes a 50-gallon barrel fed by your gutters and downspouts. Typically there's a spout at the bottom of the barrel to attach a hose. Bigger systems—you may need a contractor to install these—include underground cisterns, filters, and pumps. They may draw water not only from gutters and downspouts but also from air-conditioning equipment. These would fall into the nice-to-have category, unless you are gunning for a high-level green certificate. So would so-called gray-water systems that collect used water from everything but the toilet and recycle it to refill the toilet and, in some cases, water the lawn. That means running a separate pipe—it's usually purple—to collect the water from bath faucets. You may need a recirculating pump as well.

Builders are still learning about best practices to reduce water consumption. The largest builder in the country, Pulte Homes, is running an experiment with the EPA to test water-efficient construction practices in 20 new Las Vegas homes. It's testing everything from pressure-limiting water-main valves to low-flow toilets and showerheads to satellite-controlled irrigation systems. The idea is to compare consumption of water-smart homes with standard homes built over the previous 10 years. Each home contains a water dashboard that shows how much water the home is consuming, and leak-detection devices. The coolest feature, though, may be an adjustable pressure-reduction valve (PRV) that maintains a maximum water-supply rate of 60 psi, a level of pressure that optimizes the efficiency of the home's fixtures.

Hot water heaters deserve special attention, as they account for roughly 18 percent of the energy used in a home. Going with a high-efficiency conventional water heater is the first choice to consider. But many high-performance homes take it up a notch and include tankless systems that heat water on demand. They are up to 34 percent more energy efficient than conventional storage-tank water heaters for households that use 41 gallons or less of hot water daily, according to federal government statistics. (The savings are about a third of that for households that use a lot of hot water.) Energy Star estimates that the typical family can save $100 per year with an Energy Star–qualified tankless water heater. You can save even more energy if you place tankless water heaters close to fixture outlets, since that reduces the time hot water sits in tubing. It also may be worth exploring a new generation of hybrid hot water heaters, with efficiencies as high as 90 percent. They include a tank to store hot water but only send that water to fixtures when it's needed.

ANOTHER IMPORTANT MINIMUM REQUIREMENT for your new home would be installing structured wiring behind the walls. So-called "smart wiring" not only enables you to route audio, video, and data around the house to specifically configured wall outlets but also prepares your home for other services that you or future owners may want later on. Given the growing popularity of broadband, it's no wonder that a full 70 percent of new homes built in 2012 contained structured wiring, according to the Consumer Electronics Association (CEA). Since it goes behind the walls, structured wiring is much cheaper to install during construction than after your home is complete. Structured wiring may one day be supplanted by wireless technology, but right now it's the ideal way to route high-bandwidth signals.

A chief challenge is to figure out how many outlets you'll need and where you want them. The CEA provides some guidance through a three-tiered tech-home rating system. At the lowest, bronze level, the home is wired to distribute television, video, networking, and communications to "standard" living spaces, including the kitchen, bedroom, family room, and multimedia room. The gold level adds multiroom audio (installed in about one-quarter of new homes in 2012, according to CEA data) to the mix and services more rooms, including the master bedroom, outdoor areas, and dining room. That's a good way to think about an upgraded system, since you'd probably want to pipe music into more rooms than you would television. The platinum level takes it up to full functionality of eight or more rooms, including the home office, and delivers "the ultimate digital experience for the home-owner." Regardless of your current needs, it makes sense to err on the side of caution and put outlets in every room where you think you may one day need service.

The CEA program even specifies what type of wiring and cabling should be installed. The minimum spec today would be so-called RG6 quad cabling for television and radio and Category 6 or Category 5e wiring for telecommunication and broadband. Ten years ago, Category 5 wiring was considered adequate, but some of today's newer network protocols such as Gigabit Ethernet require a minimum of Cat 5e to operate. The CEA program includes installation guidelines as well. Structured wiring goes into the wall cavity at the same time as the electrical wiring, but it's important that the two not cross paths; signal interference (aka electromagnetic radiation) can impede digital transfer rates, compromising the speed and effectiveness of the system.

Installers say that the best time to check the system, to see if its efficiency has been maximized, is after it goes in and before drywall is applied. Ask your builder whether the system will be checked at this juncture.

One reason structured wiring is important is that it's the backbone for many of the high-tech systems and services in new homes today. Even if you don't want an automated lighting or smart-home system immediately—most new homes don't include them—it will make it easier to get them later on. Moreover, new monitoring and management systems are being developed that depend on a broadband network in the home. Nearly half of new homes built in 2012 included monitored home-security systems, which are switching from phone to Internet based. One forecasting group, Parks Associates, predicts that Internet connectivity will expand the percentage of households with professionally monitored services to 30 percent by 2020, and more than half will be Internet based. The group's research also shows that 25 to 30 percent of households with broadband would subscribe to remote monitoring and control services for a variety of purposes—everything from safety and security to energy management. Nearly 50 percent of broadband households like the idea of getting email or text notification of smoke, fire, water, or gas leaks.

ENERGY-MANAGEMENT SYSTEMS ARE THE NEXT big thing. They may not be installed in many homes yet—only 14 percent in 2011, according to CEA—but that proportion will increase because of the potential to save homeowners money on utility bills. Most current energy-management systems do little more than permit you to see how much energy your home is producing and consuming in real time, information that can be accessed over the Internet from a computer or mobile device. Some come with devices that attach to home appliances so you can see how much energy they are consuming as well. The next generation of energy-management systems will share data in real time with utilities so that you can adjust your electrical use depending on how much the utility is charging at certain times of the day. Parks

Associates forecasts that 13 percent of U.S. households will have some type of energy-management network by 2015.

Home health monitoring, another service facilitated by structured wiring, is also likely to grow in popularity, since, as we all know, the population is aging. An estimated 2.2 million households already use some kind of service that enables regular monitoring of chronic health conditions—like diabetes or a heart ailment—without having to visit a clinic on a regular basis. Inexpensive, easy-to-use wireless medical sensors can measure patient data like weight, blood pressure, heart rate, and blood sugar. The big question is how many American consumers will be willing to pay for this convenience. Some evidence suggests that many of them will—especially if it allows them to continue living independently. One survey by PricewaterhouseCoopers, for instance, found that 56 percent of American consumers like the idea of remote health care, and 40 percent of them would pay for it.

Remote health-care systems on the market today can send caregivers a text or phone alert when something goes wrong—grandparents forget to take their medicine or check their glucose levels. Motion detectors can tell you whether your elderly parents are going into their medicine cabinet or have been getting regular exercise. Such services can turn off the stove remotely after an alert arrives on the caregiver's cell phone, or adjust the room temperature if an email alert indicates that it's too low. One system includes a social network so grandchildren can send pictures and messages that can be viewed on a touchscreen. Already, 10 million seniors live alone, and 25 percent of families care for someone outside their home. Seven million Americans are long-distance caregivers, most of them older than 50. More than half of people 65 and older have a cell phone, and 34 percent of them sleep with it. The future, it seems, has arrived. ❖

CHAPTER SEVENTEEN

Future-Proofing Your Home

HOPING TO GAIN A CLEARER VIEW of what the future might bring, in 2008 I visited Microsoft's Home of the Future in Redmond, Wash. The home, which is actually a series of vignettes within an office building, gets a major update every six years and periodic retrofits in between. Given how difficult it is to predict which new home systems will make it, the systems that had been discarded from old homes were as interesting as the new ones introduced. Microsoft had found, for instance, that an iris-scan system at the front door freaked people out; they just didn't like the idea of a machine looking into their eyes after being told never to look at lasers. So retina scans had been swapped out for a palm reader, similar to the one on the Starship Enterprise. Visitors seemed much more comfortable with this technology. Since then, however, airports have started using retina-scan technology for heavy travelers to go through security, and they seem reasonably comfortable with it. Maybe that will be the start of widespread acceptance.

The highlight of each Microsoft home is the kitchen, where the company believes consumers are likely to invest the most money in their homes. During my visit, Jonathan Cluts, who runs the program, explained how you could take food from cabinets and the refrigerator and an automated system would suggest a recipe, project it on the kitchen counter, then offer step-by-step cooking instructions. Dutifully impressed, we moved on to the smart bulletin board. Cluts placed a pizza coupon on the bulletin board and up magically came the restaurant's phone number and menu. You could tap the phone number to call in an order. Cluts pinned a party invitation to the board, and the system asked whether you wanted to attend. Your yes or no response was communicated to an online party invitation service.

While these features appeared to work by magic, they were actually enabled by radio-frequency identification (RFID) technology, which Microsoft was betting would make serious inroads into our daily lives. It hasn't yet, but it may still. Many objects within the house incorporated the low-cost, passive tags—basically chips assembled with an antenna on a label. Chip readers placed inside the refrigerator, on the bulletin board, and inside closets use antennae to locate the chips. RFID technology is already inexpensive and reliable enough to be employed by some big American companies. Walmart® and other large retailers insist that pallets and cases of merchandise shipped to their warehouses come with RFID tags that can be read automatically.

Microsoft made a better, though safer, bet on wireless home controls. At a time when most controls were hard-wired and iPads hadn't hit the market, the home's major systems were run from thin, wireless liquid crystal display (LCD) and organic light-emitting diode (OLED) screens on walls throughout the house. Microsoft officials correctly figured that after prices declined they would become near ubiquitous and allow for all sorts of home-networking opportunities. We used a similar setup in our 2012 show home with KB Home and Martha Stewart. Not only were the wall monitors linked to the home's control system, but you could also manage the home through a smartphone over the Internet. Left on vacation and forgot to turn down the air conditioning? No problem. Do it from a smartphone. Want to see how much power your home's photovoltaic system produced during the day, before you get home, to see whether it would make sense to preheat the hot tub? No problem. The numbers were at your fingertips.

THE LATEST MICROSOFT HOME OF THE FUTURE, rolled out in 2013, features an interactive chef on a huge panel display in the kitchen. The virtual cook employs motion-sensing technology to watch what you are doing and sense where you are in a recipe. If you put a skillet on the stove as you prepare to make a stir-fry recipe that you called up on the computer, "the chef may tell you a wok would probably work better," Cluts explained in a telephone interview. If you grow tired of the chef looking over your shoulder, the big wall display can be used to pull up each family member's calendar, along with messages, appointment reminders, and personal health information. This latest home builds on an earlier health application to provide a visual representation of your entire health history, another area where Microsoft thinks innovation will readily occur. It lists the potential effects of new treat-

A virtual chef in the latest Microsoft Home of the Future uses motion-sensing technology to watch what you are doing and makes suggestions. If you pull up a stir-fry recipe, for instance, and start cooking with a pan, the virtual chef may suggest using a wok instead. The large display can also be used to access health information, family schedules, and the Internet.

ments, helps you find medical experts, and will even track your progress toward better health— you can upload details of a recent workout by placing a smart watch on a smart tray inside the front door. The watch synchs to your personal account, tracking your heart rate, mileage, and how many calories you burned. The same smart tray wirelessly charges smartphones with inductive power.

On my visit in 2008, the most entertaining feature was that you could read a story, *Goodnight Moon* in this case, and the house would follow along, projecting giant illustrations on a screen. Cluts has taken it up a

A grandmother in New Jersey can read a book to her granddaughter in Washington in Microsoft's latest Home of the Future. Scenes from the story appear on a separate screen. Similar technology can be used to visit a store, inspect merchandise, and have it shipped to you.

notch in his most recent iteration. Now a grandmother living in New Jersey (or any other state) can read an interactive story with a grandchild in California over the system. Grandma appears on one screen, and scenes from the story—which can even change, depending on what actions the child takes—appear on another. The same technology can be used to visit other places, like an art gallery or a retail store. You can make a virtual visit, pulling up lifelike 360-degree images on the coffee table, speak with a retail clerk, and browse merchandise just as you would in person. Though you can make a transaction over the Internet, physical goods still have to be shipped through snail mail. (The spread of 3D printing, which allows you to create products with a printerlike device that works in plastic and metal instead of ink, may one day change that.)

The Microsoft Office of the Future, which has been incorporated into the same facility, includes some incredible interactive work tools. It takes whiteboarding to a whole new level. You can take a sketch of something you've been drawing on a tablet computer and swipe it over to a large digital screen that doubles as your work surface. Then you can have that sketch appear on a huge wall screen so that you and a coworker anywhere in the world can work on the sketch simultaneously. In a separate part of the office, content on a "team action wall" can change instantly, depending on the team member who is walking by the wall. A marketing person, for instance, would see a timeline of upcoming marketing decisions, along with tools to guide him or her. Another section of the office includes a pop-up retail space in which a user can place a toy car on a screen to find out more about the toy by touching various areas of the car. The toy can be sent as a gift using the information already on your smartphone.

Cluts works at the concept level in his home of the future, without paying much attention to how someone would create a similar setup in a real home. That said, most of the applications he tests involve hardware and software systems that could easily be retrofitted into a home. What would Cluts do to future-proof a conventional home? "I tell people to put in a lot of conduit because it's cheap to do during construction," he said, referring to plastic tubes through which wires and cables are run. Although he expects wireless connectivity to grow in the future, "some things still need high-speed wire to run effectively." For that reason, Cluts recommends Category 6 structured wiring. Equipped with various adaptors, you could run any signal—from streaming video to high-speed data transfer—through it. "We still wire our cities that way."

The future may be difficult to predict, but there are several good reasons why you would want to build a home today that can accommodate how people will live, say, 10 years from now. The first, of course, is that the way things are going you may still live in the home, and you never know whether your family circumstances will change dramatically. Another is that some incredibly disruptive energy or communication technology may come along and force a major home retrofit—consider what it was like when telephones first arrived on the scene and wire needed to be run, or when natural gas took over from wood-burning fireplaces as a source of home heating, or when the Internet burst on the scene and you had to run telephone wire all over the house. Many of us have lived through an in-home communication revolution during the last 20 years that started with cable television, moved into dial-up modems, transitioned into high-speed communications behind the walls, and blossomed into wireless-networking systems throughout the house. Old systems for security, telephones, television, and much more have become obsolete. Who knows what's next?

WHEN YOU THINK FROM 30,000 FEET about the basic systems of a home, some are more likely to change than others. The structure or foundation of your home will probably never need to be updated, if you build it right the first time. Other components like roofing, siding, and windows may need replacement when they wear out. That's inevitable. You are more likely to change the interiors of a home—remodel a kitchen or bathroom and update cabinets and fixtures. Changing interior wall configurations is always where things get much more expensive. Wouldn't it be nice if you could simply enlarge the kitchen by moving a wall to reduce the size of the dining room, for instance? What if rooms were plug and play, if homes were built like commercial buildings with non-load-bearing interior walls that could be moved easily? That's not farfetched. It's what we hoped to accomplish with the movable walls in our Home of the Future.

New homes have become much more modular in recent years. Even homes with "stick-built" frames are often put together with preassembled wall panels. Most production builders order the roof from a truss company that builds it in a factory, ships it at the appropriate time, and drops it in place with a crane. New homes are commonly built with preassembled stair systems, doors and windows that are delivered in their frames, and boxed fireplace kits. Even so, once everything is set in place, new-home buyers are still stuck with the basic floor-plan configuration that they get. They have little flexibility to reconfigure rooms. It's not like buying a computer, where you can periodically upgrade its memory, install a better operating system, and produce, in effect, a whole new product.

Kent Larson, an architect who works at the MIT Lab, has long dreamed of changing the way new homes are produced and can be modified. He has pioneered "plug-and-play" homes built with a structural frame that could last 200 years or more, outfitted with an endless selection of roofing, siding, interior wall panels, and electronics. Adding a room is a simple matter of moving interior wall modules. When kitchen styles change, you could pull out your old cabinets and pop a new set in their place. Wiring is run behind removable wainscoting or removable ceiling panels, as in commercial buildings, so it's easy to move or upgrade. Larson has even suggested that manufacturers build to an "open source code," standardizing, for instance, how toilets connect to plumbing and light fixtures tie into the electrical system. He started an Open Source Building Alliance with key builders and product manufacturers that, unfortunately, didn't get very far. Manufacturers worried that standardization might stifle innovation, and profitability.

AN INDUSTRY INITIATIVE TO RADICALLY alter new-home technology, the so-called Smart House Project, suffered a similar fate in the late 1980s. The leaders behind this movement (builders, suppliers, and trade associations) wanted to improve the way homes are wired for electricity. One idea was to provide electricity only to outlets that have appliances plugged in or turned on; another was to provide variable power to outlets. Most outlets in American homes, of course, provide 110-volt service, with the occasional 220 volts for heavy appliances. But some consumer appliances such as radios, personal computers, and even power tools may need only 6, 9, 12, or 24 volts. Instead of providing power for peak use, the Smart House concept was to employ a single outlet to supply electricity (and communications) to outlets at different levels, eliminating the need for power adaptors at each appliance.

But the concept was bigger than that. Builders were told in industry meetings that smart homes would automatically control room temperature, humidity, and lighting on a room-by-room basis. Controllers would schedule the operation of heavy-power-consuming appliances such as dishwashers, electric water heaters, and air conditioners to take advantage of off-peak utility pricing. A prototype, built for a homebuilder convention, included several game-changing safety controls, including a controller that would monitor circuits, disconnecting power at the first sign of a short circuit or other failure, and sensors to detect gas and water leaks, smoke, and other abnormal conditions. An electronic controller would shut down the devices and trigger an alarm.

Many of the basic concepts pioneered by the Smart House Project, which was ultimately disbanded, have come to pass, though often through different, less ambitious technology. At roughly the same time the smart home was being developed, ground-fault circuit interrupters that could detect an electrical shock and shut down immediately were becoming commonplace in bathrooms, kitchens, and outside outlets. Rudimentary smart-home systems burst on the scene in the early 1990s that controlled the home's major systems through electrical wires or radio frequency. You could buy them at Radio Shack®. Then, during the mid-'90s, a revolution in home computer use changed everything—builders began to run structured wiring behind the walls to route computers, creating a wiring infrastructure to which other home systems could be tied. More recently, inexpensive wireless protocols, cheaper than Bluetooth®, have been developed to control appliances and systems in the home. Now appliance companies and utilities are preparing for smart-grid technology that will allow homeowners to adjust their electrical use to avoid peak prices, something Smart Home pioneers envisioned in 1985.

SOME ASPECTS OF THE FUTURE are easier to predict than others. For instance, it's pretty likely that electrical, gas, and water prices will keep rising, putting pressure on consumer checkbooks and spawning the development of new resource-conserving products. Wireless controls will grow more sophisticated, infiltrating more home components. More products will think for themselves. Intelligent skylights already on the market are equipped with rain sensors that close before rain enters the house. Smart blinds close automatically when they sense that too much heat is entering the house. Motion detectors know that someone has left the room and turn out the lights. And smart bathroom faucets produce water with the wave of a hand.

Other trends are tougher to decrypt. We put an electric car in the garage of our Home of the Future back in 1997, thinking they would take the world by storm. Although the car drew considerable attention—we put an outlet in the garage to recharge it every night—the cars haven't yet taken off as some futurists expected, despite the availability of huge (up to $7,500) tax credits for buying them and government grant programs to explore better electric-car technology. Electric-car batteries remain expensive, and the cars don't have much range. Even so, equipping the garage for an electric car, which basically involves running a 220-volt outlet to the garage, much like the one for an electric clothes dryer, is worth considering, since it's cheaper when you are building a home from scratch. It's rare that a new apartment building these days doesn't include a charging station for an electric car. Manufacturers recommend that you provide 80 to 100 amps to meet the needs of two cars at 40 amps apiece.

That said, it's funny how things done to prepare a home for the future sometimes wind up looking outdated. Ten years ago, thoughtful builders put deep insets into the walls of family rooms, wall niches, to hold large television sets with tubes. Then along came flat-screen technology that turned the alcoves into anachronisms, or elaborate shelves for potted plants. I still get a hoot out of going into "contemporary" passive solar homes built in the 1970s. They often look the most dated, especially if the big picture windows, worn by weather and blistered by the sun, haven't been replaced. The computer workstations that builders put in upstairs hallway space during the housing boom look nearly as outdated as telephone booths.

Some of the biggest future breakthroughs could be in features for the elderly, now that the massive baby-boom generation is moving through its 60s. Already some people with heart or other serious health problems have smart chips implanted or wear devices that alert doctors and home systems to medical abnormalities. Systems on the market remind you to take pills, get some exercise, or see a doctor. Smart toilets will test your urine and stools, check your weight, and even take your blood pressure—and show the information on a nearby display.

Some of today's home-automation systems can be controlled through voice commands. You can tell your home to turn on the lights, for instance, or lock the doors. One cool thing about the Microsoft Home of the Future is that it can talk back to you. Cluts has given the home-operating system a name, Grace, a nod to computing pioneer Grace Hopper. When he asks Grace what's up, she replies with upcoming appointments and reads your email. She can provide traffic and weather reports. She can even remind you to take your medicine, study for a big upcoming test, or give you the recipe for a mushroom risotto.

You can already do some pretty futuristic things with today's home-automation systems. The question is whether you value the upgrades enough to spend the money. Powerful video cameras can be installed that sense the motion of intruders and stream video to your smartphone, a nice feature to have if you have, say, an art collection. Less expensive systems will monitor your home and text you when someone tries to input a code to open the front door or when the garage door was left open. Several companies now make Wi-Fi-enabled washers and dryers that will tell you via the television or smartphone when a load is done. We're getting texts from nearly every other source—why not the clothes washer?

The next big thing will be new homes with smart metering systems. Parks Associates estimates that 45 percent of U.S. households will have such a system by 2015. The future has already arrived in places like Ottawa, Canada, and Boulder, Colo., where smart meters allow homeowners to react to up-to-the-minute utility pricing and adjust electrical use accordingly. These systems will, just as the smart-home pioneers envisioned, tell you to wait to run the dishwasher or clothes dryer until electricity costs less. Electricity costs the most during peak demand periods, typically from 2 to 7 p.m. in June through September. General Electric® is testing a system in several cities with widgets that allow you to manage different systems—appliances, heating and air conditioning, and even electric-vehicle charging. It hopes to develop systems that one day monitor water and natural gas usage, as well.

The current system of buying electricity leaves a lot to be desired. It's not unlike rolling into a gas station, filling up on gas without knowing how much you put in the tank, and then finding out a month later what you spent. A better model would be to create an energy-use account that enables you to see how much electricity you've used during a specific time period and share that information with the utility so that it can do a better job predicting demand. The privacy of that data, which could conceivably be used to figure out when you are away from home, is a concern. Utilities promise that data will be encrypted, with each household assigned an anonymous number.

Appliance manufacturers, meanwhile, are working on a new generation of wirelessly networked machines. Every year, manufacturers of dishwashers, televisions, and even vacuums roll out exciting prototypes at the Consumer Electronics Show in Las Vegas that can communicate with smartphones, tablets, home-automation systems, and the smart grid. All this new technology, of course, comes with an added price, and it's not clear whether consumers will be willing to pay more for these added conveniences, especially if they take more electricity to operate. At the same time, as more people upgrade to smart refrigerators, prices will fall, creating more demand.

So, let's play this game. How much extra would you pay for a refrigerator that could suggest recipes based on what's inside when you could just open the door and look? You can buy a refrigerator today that keeps track of inventory and allows you to order over the Internet from a grocer. Samsung Electronics markets a refrigerator with an LCD screen and its own apps that allow you to check the weather, browse the Web for recipes, listen to music, and keep tabs on what's inside. The

28-cubic-foot fridge with four doors sells for $2,000. LG Electronics plans to introduce a refrigerator that allows you to scan grocery receipts with a smartphone so that you monitor what's inside. The refrigerator will tell you when fresh food is scheduled to expire. And it, too, will offer recipes based on what's in the refrigerator. Plus, you could access information about your refrigerator's inventory from a smartphone or tablet while you are out shopping.

Consider this: How would you like to get a text alert from your dryer saying that a load is done, as opposed to the simple beep that most now make? A new generation of washers and dryers that you can manage from your phone will give you the option of fluffing shirts for a few more minutes or adding a rinse cycle. I guess that way you don't have to get out of your armchair and miss a critical news report or sporting event. But how hard is it to occasionally check in person on the wash? And you still need to move your clothes from the washer to the dryer, unless you buy one machine that does both. A new breed of air conditioners can be operated from a smartphone so that you could turn on the heat before you come home from work on a cold day. That would be nice. But maybe this could wait until you get home.

Fans of *The Jetsons* cartoons will be relieved to know that one company, LG, makes a smart version of the remote-controlled robotic vacuum. Obsessive-compulsives can watch this one, unlike previous versions, do its work from a smartphone, thanks to a small built-in camera. It can also be activated remotely, which could be pretty handy if you invite friends over for dinner at the last minute and your home is a mess. What's interesting is that many of these same home-control ideas—in particular ordering groceries automatically and controlling home systems from a cell phone—were batted around during the dot.com era of 2000 to 2001 but never got off the ground. What goes around, it seems, eventually comes around.

The cost of connected appliances will fall once the home-products industry works out a common wireless-networking standard. Many connected appliances today use Wi-Fi technology—equal in strength to the wired Ethernet protocol that powers the Internet—that may be overkill for these applications. Several manufacturers and utilities are working with the ZigBee® Alliance to use less expensive, less powerful chips that in many cases function just as well. General Electric has jumped on this bandwagon to develop its smart-grid–enabled appliances and home-metering products that will communicate with utilities.

IT ISN'T POSSIBLE TO GUESS 100 percent correctly on the trends likely to influence new homes over the next 10 years. Even if you knew precisely how homes would evolve, you may not want or need all the new features and gizmos that become commonplace anyway. As long as you take precautions (for example, run conduit behind the walls), you may be able to easily retrofit your home to accommodate many of them. But it's going to be much harder and more expensive to change your floor plan, which is why you want a home that's as flexible as possible. Having a flex room that can serve as an office now but easily be converted to a bedroom later on is a key concern, given the aging of the U.S. population. It's going to make your home much more attractive as a resale later on. And at a minimum, you want a home that's as efficient to heat and cool as possible—lower operating costs will add value to your home. You also want your home to produce the healthiest possible indoor-air environment, which means keeping it free of moisture intrusion.

Many of the topics covered in this book, especially the chapters devoted to what's going on behind the walls, used to be secondary considerations for people buying new homes. In an economy of steadily rising home values, buyers didn't have to worry too much about how well the home was built. What mattered in most cases was living in the best neighborhood possible, with the best schools and a short commute. So, families reached to buy the home of their dreams, with a big, grassy backyard in which to kick a soccer ball, an additional bedroom so each child could have her own, and enough space to spend quality time together as a family. Empty nesters looked to downsize, move to a more comfortable year-round climate, and live a richer lifestyle. And singles sought secure, friendly settings where they could choose to spend time with each other or be alone.

Homes will always mean more to families than the sum of their complicated parts. Jack Bloodgood, who popularized house plans as the building editor of *Better Homes & Gardens* during the 1960s, used to say that the best home is the one that you could come home to with pride every night, one that your children would later drive by and remember fondly as the wonderful place where they grew up. He regularly admonishes his fellow architects for using terms like "units" or even "houses," reminding them that they design "homes" for people, places where precious memories are created. Ultimately, for homebuyers, satisfaction comes from living in a comfortable place, where you can live conveniently and leisurely spend time with friends and family. It comes from living in a secure place, free from the stress of work and break-ins.

But today—after the harsh jolt of a housing recession that left families with homes that may never recover their original value—the bricks and mortar matter, too. Every homebuyer needs to be an educated consumer, sweating details that will hold utility bills to a minimum, provide a comfortable living environment even in old age, and prepare for future changes in technology. Many of these critical details won't cost you extra, but if you don't know enough to ask, you may not receive them. Homes are the biggest, most complicated investment that most people ever make; they require more due diligence than ever before. Home equity is the principal form of wealth for many families, and today many economic and demographic trends may be working against that investment. You owe it to yourself to buy the best home possible, one that will increase in value and insulate you and your family against future financial shocks. ❖

Index

A

Adobe block, 110
Affordability of new homes, 153–61
Air quality, indoor, 84–88
All American Homes, 115
Andersen Windows, 95
Arbor South (the Sage), 27–29
Ashton Woods Homes, 75
Avid ratings, 170–71, 173

B

Barefoot Cottage Company, 218, 219
Bathrooms
  design/space planning, 47, 50, 55–56, 58, 60, 67, 108
  generations under one roof and, 144–45, 146, 147, 149
  green building and, 25, 90, 117–18, 228
  in-town living and, 194–95
  for kids, 55, 58, 177
  master, 46, 47, 55–56, 135, 144–45, 181
  modular unit, 208
  recession lessons, 29, 33
  smaller spaces, 217
  tubs, 25, 33, 58, 132, 217
  universal design and, 134–35, 136, 139
Beaulieu, 97
Bedrooms
  adaptable suite, 50–51
  first-floor, 50, 51, 57, 136, 144–46, 218, 219
  for kids, 25, 55, 57–58, 176, 177
  secondary, size concern, 177
  second-floor, 7, 43, 52–53, 216–17, 220, 221
Bedrooms, master
  first-floor, 43, 57, 144–45, 218, 219, 221
  multigenerational homes and, 144–46, 149
  second entrance to, 67
  second/third, 144–46, 149, 218, 221
  smaller spaces, 217, 218, 219, 221
  space planning, 47, 50, 52, 53, 54–55, 56, 57
  upstairs, 45
BrightBuilt barn, 118–19
Brookfield Homes, 125–26

Builder/quality precautions, 162–77
Building products, green, 94–101
Buying new home. *See also* Space planning
  affordability considerations, 153–61
  appearances, features, and upgrades, 176–77
  builder/quality precautions, 162–77
  getting best deal, 175–76
  what to ask for, 13, 223–33

C

Centex, 38–39
Children
  bathrooms for, 55, 58, 177
  bedrooms for, 25, 55, 57–58, 176, 177
  boomerang, 144
  family-oriented design, 45–46
  homework areas for, 66
  kitchen design and, 134
  outdoor space for, 115, 151
  space planning for, 13, 51–52, 57–58, 59, 60–61
Christopher Homes, 183–84
Clayton Homes, 208–10
ColRich Homes, 182, 183
Contemporary design, 23–25, 178–84
Cost, affordability of new homes, 153–61
Cottages, 218–22
Craftmark Homes, 196

D

David Weekly Homes, 43, 46
Demographic trends, 13–16, 24, 148, 189–90, 247
Demonstration homes, 27–33
Destinations Home, 35–36, 64, 151
Donald A. Gardner Architects, 54, 55
Double-wall systems, 112–13

E

Electronic technology, 62–63, 230–31, 234–47
Energy efficiency. *See* Green homes; Net-zero homes
Energy Star program, 22, 109, 120–21, 174, 223–24, 228–29, 230

Energy-management systems, 70, 90, 115–16, 117, 232–33. *See also* Green homes; Net-zero homes

F

Floor plans
  flexible, 9–10, 49–50
  innovation in, 9–10, 34–36
  limited offering, 42
  open, 99, 150, 184
  optimizing, 56–63
Framing methods, advanced, 103–06
Future, predicting, 7–9. See also Home of the Future references
Future-proofing home, 234–47

G

Garage
  bays needed, 56, 59
  design/location, 33, 147, 151, 219
  electric car outlet, 242
  green building and, 71–72, 86–87, 88, 125, 242
  space over, 56, 67, 144, 145–46
Garbett Homes, 179–80
Generation X, Y, and B homes, 148–52
Geothermal systems, 6, 9, 76, 122–23, 124, 128–29
Green homes, 68–101
  advantages of, 69–71
  clean indoor air and, 84–88
  contemporary design and, 23–25, 178–84
  design analysis, 71–73
  energy efficiency, 74 (*see also* Solar technology)
  features/techniques, 26
  indoor air quality, 84–88
  LEED standard, 23–24, 95–96, 100, 206
  long-term outlook, 23
  marketing challenges, 89
  Meritage models, 19–20
  new building products for, 94–101
  Pardee Homes and, 73–75
  resource efficiency, 70, 75–76, 91–101
  solving problems and, 72
  sustainable lifestyle pitch, 89–90

trend toward, 4, 10, 68–69
water consumption, 70, 75,
    228–30
what to ask for, 227–30

H
HERS ratings, 20, 21–22,
    114–15, 117
High-performance homes,
    102–13
    about: overview of, 102–06
    advanced framing methods,
        103–06
    Home for the New Economy
        project, 108–09
    Homelink show home,
        103–06, 172
    HVAC systems and, 108–09
    reducing thermal transfer, 22,
        109–13
Home for the New Economy
    project, 49–53, 108–09
Home of the Future, 5–7, 8, 151,
    239, 242
Home of the Future (by
    Microsoft), 236–39, 243
Home offices, 45, 52, 53, 58–59,
    66, 144, 145, 149, 151, 198,
    207, 216, 237–38
Homelink show home, 103–06,
    172
Housing design
    all opinions count, 16–17
    boom then downturn, 2–3
    simplifying forms, 26
Humidity, indoor, 87, 168,
    226–27
HVAC systems, 87–88, 103,
    107, 108–09, 121, 126, 137,
    173–74, 224–26

I
Infinity Homes, 180–81
Innovation
    consumer choice and, 39–40
    creativity left on table, 35–36
    custom homes and, 34–35, 37
    demographics impacting,
        13–16
    downside of, 12
    factors/advantages of, 9–12
    factory-built housing and, 35
    forces restricting spread of,
        38–41
    mixed record on, 34–46
    New Urban Challenge
        project, 42–46
    prototype homes and, 37
    public relations challenge,
        34–37
    recession spawning, 3, 9–13,
        41–42

Insulated concrete forms
    (ICFs), 111
Insulation
    alternative building systems
        and, 109–13
    blown-in, 26
    green practices, 68, 72–73, 86
    net-zero quest and, 121, 123,
        125
    new framing methods and,
        104–06
    passive solar and. *See* Solar
        technology
InSync Home, 63
In-town living, 185–99
    blending infill projects with
        neighborhood, 191–93
    expanded options, 189–91
    live-work project (Atlanta),
        171, 185–89
    other infill examples, 193–99
Irvine Company (Ranch),
    29–33

J
J.D. Power surveys, 162–64,
    170, 172
John Wieland Homes, 145

K
KB Home, 89–91, 117–18,
    125, 235
KieranTimberlake, 204, 205
Kitchenettes, 50, 51, 146, 147,
    148–49
Kitchens
    cabinets, 53, 134, 137, 138,
        172–73, 181–82
    combined spaces, 56
    countertops, 64, 132, 133,
        134
    ergonomics, 134
    home safety issues, 133
    innovation reluctance, 38
    lighting, 180
    Microsoft home, 234–35, 236
    New Urban Challenge
        project, 43, 45
    office space in, 66
    plumbing efficiency and,
        90, 108
    second-floor, 216
    smaller spaces, 51, 53
    space allocation, 29, 31, 32
    storage, 64–65
    sustainable lifestyle, 89–90

L
Lake/Flato Architects, 201
LEED standard, 23–24, 95–96,
    100, 206

Lennar, 147–48, 177
Less-is-more trend, 15–16, 47
Levitt, William, and Levittown,
    26, 39–40
LifeStages house, 131, 132, 133,
    135, 136
Live-work project (Atlanta),
    171, 185–89
LivingHomes, 94–95, 96,
    204–07

M
MacKenzie Brothers, 218
Media systems, 62–63
Meritage Homes, 19–20
Microsoft home, 234–39, 243
Miller Hull, 195, 196
Modular homes, 200–210
Mold, 22, 84, 85, 87, 96–97,
    106–07, 226–27
Mortgages, 153–61, 165, 175,
    215
Multigenerational homes, 51–52,
    143–52. *See also* Reality House

N
Net-zero homes, 114–29
    about: overview of, 114–16
    by Brookfield Homes,
        125–26
    considerations for buying,
        116–17
    defined, 20–21
    energy use and, 119–21
    EnergyHome, 122–24
    geothermal systems and,
        122–23, 124, 128–29
    HERS ratings, 20, 21–22,
        114–15, 117
    by KB Home, 117–18, 125
    in northerly regions, 122–24
    by Palo Duro, 125
    payback period, 126–29
    by Pepper Viner Homes,
        120–21
    rise of, 20–21, 114–16
    solar systems and, 114–15,
        117, 118, 119, 120–21, 124,
        125, 126–28, 209
    in the Southwest, 125–26
New Home Company, 148
New Urban Challenge project,
    42–46
Nexus EnergyHome, 122–24

O
Offices. *See* Home offices
Outdoor space, 59, 60–61, 63,
    146, 150, 152, 195, 198, 203

P
Palo Duro, 125